The Genesis and Ethos
of the Market

Luigino Bruni
Professor of Economics, University of Milan-Bicocca

palgrave
macmillan

First published 2012 by
PALGRAVE MACMILLAN

Palgrave Macmillan in the UK is an imprint of Macmillan Publishers Limited,
registered in England, company number 785998, of Houndmills, Basingstoke,
Hampshire RG21 6XS.

Palgrave Macmillan in the US is a division of St Martin's Press LLC,
175 Fifth Avenue, New York, NY 10010.

Palgrave Macmillan is the global academic imprint of the above companies
and has companies and representatives throughout the world.

Palgrave® and Macmillan® are registered trademarks in the United States,
the United Kingdom, Europe and other countries

ISBN: 978–0–230–34845–5

This book is printed on paper suitable for recycling and made from fully
managed and sustained forest sources. Logging, pulping and manufacturing
processes are expected to conform to the environmental regulations of the
country of origin.

A catalogue record for this book is available from the British Library.

A catalog record for this book is available from the Library of Congress.

10 9 8 7 6 5 4 3 2 1
21 20 19 18 17 16 15 14 13 12

Printed and bound in the United States of America

To Giuseppe Maria Zanghì

Contents

Figures

Preface

Political economy or economics is a study of mankind in the ordinary business of life.

Alfred Marshall

This book is a discourse on the market and its ethos. Therefore, it is also an analysis of capitalism. In the last two centuries, the present version of the market economy that can be called capitalism has produced remarkable economic, technological and civil results; but today, in these times of crisis, it seems to have become obsolete. It has played an important role in the transformation of an unequal and hierarchical feudal societies into ones composed of individuals who are more free and equal. Its technological–financial drift has exhausted its innovative and civilizing force because it has betrayed the very nature of the market – that of being a great cooperative enterprise aimed at the mutual advantage of the subjects involved in exchanges and, indirectly, at the common good of society.

As it exists today, therefore, capitalism has lost its underlying basis of civil fraternity. And without fraternity, life – individual and social alike – does not flourish. The crises at the beginning of the third millennium (from terrorism to the environment, from finance to energy) are demonstrating with unusual force that this kind of market economy and market society are exhausting their power for social change and civilization because their achievements in the field of individual freedom are being paid for in the currency of the environment and social relationships. The great task that awaits us is to go beyond *this* market economy without renouncing the civilizational achievements that this economic and social system has delivered in the most recent eras; our task is to discover interpersonal relationships that take us away from the lonely *immunitas* that today dominates our markets and our cities without falling into forms of communitarianism, often illiberal or nostalgic about ancient communities, both of which are remedies worse than the disease they wish to cure.

In the course of its development, the market economy has brought about a change in the nature of human relations. The market has truly become a culture in its own right, an *ethos* that is more than ethics as we intend this expression today, because an *ethos* is a custom or a lifestyle

ix

that surrounds and informs within itself all dimensions of common life (Mancini, 1990). The market gives birth to and fosters its own sense of being human – in particular, as we'll see, it engenders the promise of interpersonal relationships without the *"wound" of the other* (Bruni 2012). It is at this anthropological and relational level that the "ethos of the market", its genesis and its nature must be analysed and evaluated if we are to understand not only economic relationships but also the nature of this, our post-modern society.

In this book, I seek to discover how the nature of the market and the reasons for the appeal it exerts on contemporary humanity have come to be read in relationship to a word that today seems quite distant from economics: *community*. We will see, in fact, that the history of cultures is also the history of the attempts to free individual human beings from the vulnerabilities associated with the presence of another who is equal to oneself and hence always, potentially, a dramatic threat for the individual. It is a grand tale of the roads followed in the attempt to dissolve the paradoxical tension between the invincible desire that drives us toward others in our search for community and the need to free ourselves from the deep and all-consuming ties that every community and personalized face-to-face relationship inescapably creates. The kind of relatedness of web-based social networks can be read as the archetype of the relationships being created in market societies, relationships that weaken the vital but dramatic dimension of the otherness of the body, where the other is not recognized in all its ambivalent reality and vocation, but is used within a unidimensional relationship where one's own ego occupies the centre, ever more narcissistic and therefore incapable of encounter.

Several key words characterizing this *ethos of the market* will punctuate this essay – community, mediation, gift, hierarchy – words uncommon in a treatise on economics, because none of them belongs to today's (nor, perhaps, to yesterday's) vocabulary of economics. Some even more unusual keywords are included in the discourse that we about to enter into – *philia*, virtue, mutual help, which are the principal terms in the second part of this essay. But they will not be the final words, because the conclusion of this book will be entrusted to a word that is even more unusual (although always longed for) in the social sciences: *agape*, the relationship of gratuitousness.

John Stuart Mill, the great nineteenth-century English economist and philosopher, was convinced that over time the market would develop and strengthen people's capacity for cooperation, and therefore their civic virtue. He wrote in his *Principles of Political Economy*: "One of the changes which most infallibly attend the progress of modern society, is an improvement in the business capacities of the general mass of mankind. ... Works of all sorts, impracticable to the savage or the half-civilized, are daily accomplished by civilized nations [...]. The peculiar characteristic, in short, of civilized beings, is the capacity of co-operation" (Mill [1848] 1920, p. 698).

Today, more than a century and a half after Mill wrote these words, looking at cooperation in the market and at the culture it has produced, would Mill still consider the market in the same fashion? In light of his thought, were he to observe a company, a commercial centre and ordinary social and economic life (from air travel to a football league), I believe that he would not have second thoughts, and would see his insights and his predictions confirmed. On the other hand, I would begin to have some doubt about his answer if Mill, or one of the fellow economists or liberal philosophers of his generation (as well as those that have followed), encountered the digital, financial, and techno-logical world of our time. In fact, he would understand immediately that there is an ever increasing fundamental alliance between market and technology, and after brief reflection he would see that the logic of these relationships in a network differs little from that which drives the relationships within a multinational company or in the supermarkets in our cities. He would understand, that is, that the market has not only increased relationships, human contacts, and cooperation, as compared to the pre-modern world; it has also *changed their nature*, becoming a great mediator that more and more makes interpersonal relationships and common life "immune", a change in relation to which ethical judg-ment is complex and ambivalent. Ambivalence is, perhaps, the most characteristic dimension of the ethos of the market, since ambivalence is the characteristic that marks every great human word (which are great *because* of this ambivalence). The great linguist Émile Benveniste (1971, p. 272) reminds us that even the word gift, a word that should look free from any ambivalence, is instead marked by "a curious semantic ambiv-alence", because in many Indo-European languages the concept carried by the verb "to give" can be expressed also by the verb "to take". The market, in fact – we see this above all in the Neapolitan school of civil economy of Genovesi and of Dragonetti – is also a social mechanism that, when working properly, is not in contrast with the authentic gift and can be read also as remuneration for civic virtues.

We can interpret the market from a perspective that seems unusual today but was common in the eighteenth century as well as for J. S. Mill: as a system for rewarding activities that are socially virtuous, but scarce because of insufficient motivation and intrinsic rewards. In fact, in a hypothetical world without markets, where individuals engage in the activities they love or feel as their own vocations – obtaining from them intrinsic rewards – there would be an excess (compared to the levels of social demand) of intrinsically remunerative activities (those of poets, scholars, athletes, etc.) and a lack of activities that might not be rewarding in themselves (those of refuse collectors, porters, miners, and so on). The market offers "extrinsic" rewards for activities that we would not pursue, at least in a quantity considered sufficient by society, were we pursuing them only for the pleasure inherent in the action. Through the price mechanism, the market ensures that remunerated activities are not only the ones that are done because people like to do them, but also those deemed useful by others with whom an exchange is made (and therefore such activities are also rewarded). From this point of view the market is also a mechanism that signals whether the things that people like are of interest also – and above all – to someone else. This allows, therefore, that activities useful for the common good can be pursued freely and with dignity (without collectivist planning or an illiberal hierarchy). It is for this reason that market exchange can also be understood as *one* form of reciprocity and of social bonds, and as a cure for individual and social narcissism.

In this book I claim that there is no opposition, but only complementarity, between the market, civic virtue, gifts, freedom, human cooperation and the common good, as the tradition of Civil economy well knew and still knows. Anyone wanting to direct ethical criticisms toward the market today cannot avoid taking into account its civilizing and social function which, were they lost in search of utopian economies of "gift-exchange", would amount to the loss of centuries of civilization that have allowed the market to grow and develop. Any serious and civil criticism of the ethos of the market and to the "spirit of capitalism" (such as those contained in this book) therefore must at least recognize the market's moral function and direct its critical evaluations in such a way that they do not contradict this dimension of market interactions – as does a certain philosophy of communitarianism today. All of this was and is quite clear to the civil tradition of economics, our point of departure for envisioning the ethos of the market in different ways.

The early chapters (1–5) will demonstrate how and why with modern thinking the market society emerged from the ashes of the medieval sacred community and from the rejection of the major mediators of ancient societies. From the death of the sacred community, beginning for the most part in Greece and in Israel, what was born was not a new community composed of individuals who were finally free and equal. No sooner, in fact, had humankind recognized the possibility – a tragic one – of a community of free and equal individuals that they sought ways to escape it, not facing the tragic, but decisive, enterprise of fraternity. The second part of the book (Chapters 6–10) explores the characteristics that the mediation of the market assumed in the mainstream tradition of Political Economy (the Smithian), comparing it with the Neapolitan tradition of Civil Economy, and by way of a conclusion (Chapter 11) will attempt to open up new courageous possibilities that go beyond Civil Economy.

These pages, then, should be read as part of a research project on "economics, welfare, and human relationships" that I have been carrying on for about a decade, and that has had as its milestones the books *Economics and Happiness* (with Pierluigi Porta, 2005), *Civil Happiness* (2006), *Civil Economy* (with Stefano Zamagni, 2007), *Reciprocity* (2008), a series of papers written together with Robert Sugden (2000, 2008, 2011) and Alessandra Smerilli (2010, 2011), and my book *La ferita dell'altro* ("The other's wound", 2007), published in English as *The Wound and the Blessing* (2012). In the following pages I have sought to draw together passages from what I consider a single conversation that has developed over time, seeking a consistency that I have not always achieved. The inconsistencies that exist, however, can also become the beginnings of new paths of research.

Every essay, then, ought to retain a quality contained in the "gymnastic" meaning of the word: this too is an exercise, an experiment, a leap which always involves an element of risk in those who perform as well as in those who participate in the action (in this case, the readers) because its outcome is always uncertain – a risk that makes the enterprise even more exciting.

Acknowledgements

This work is the result of years of conversations with many people, not all of which were of an intellectual nature. First of all I would like to thank Robert Sugden, who was my PhD supervisor and later became co-author of many papers exploring the ideas that at the core of this book. A special thanks to Alessandra Smerilli, who has been an essential help in the game theoretical part of the book, and, in general, in the maturation of my ideas in a continuous longstanding dialogue and scientific rich collaboration.

I have received fundamental help from the dialogues with many friends and colleagues, including Stefano Bartolini, Giacomo Becattini, Leonardo Becchetti, Nicolò Bellanca, Piero Coda, Luca Crivelli, Benedetto Gui, Gennaro Iorio, Vittorio Pelligra, Pier Luigi Porta, Tommaso Reggiani, Luca Stanca and Stefano Zamagni. Much of what I have written in the following pages I learned from them.

I also thank the various central characters – the poor, workers, entrepreneurs, and citizens – in the many areas of civil and social economy whom I have met and come to know well during these years, particularly those in the Economy of Communion; they have inspired ideas and insights for me, showing me the wound and the blessing hidden in every fully human relationship.

Some of the material presented in this book has been previously published in journals, including *Economics and Philosophy* and the *Journal of History of Economic Thought*. This book is basically a translation (although with some amendments, modifications, and changes that are relevant in some parts, e.g. in Chapter 9 on Dragonetti) of my book *L'Ethos del mercato: Una introduzione ai fondamenti antropologici e relazionali dell'economia* (2010). I would like to thank the Bruno Mondadori-Pierson Economics Editor, Dr Mariarosa Bricchi. Finally, a sincere and deep thank you to Dr Valeria Iacovelli, who has, with passion, quality and competence, translated this not particularly easy book.

1
From the Community-Without-Individuals to Individuals-Without-Community

> His 'no' which he says to life brings a wealth of more tender
> 'yesses' to light as though by magic; and even when he wounds
> himself, this master of destruction, self-destruction – after-
> wards it is the wound itself which forces him to live... .
>
> F. Nietzsche, *On the genealogy of morality*

1. The ambivalent character of the community

Any study of the market and its ethos will inevitably have to confront
the notion of *community* and its inherent contradictions. The ethos of
the market is the main response to the ambivalence of the ethos of the
community.

On the one hand, individuals living in a community are more likely
to establish meaningful relationships and thus to encounter true happiness and humanity; on the other, the community, by its very nature,
poses a threat to individuals liberties and absolute rights, and consequently to individuality itself.

In Sociology – but also in Economic History, Anthropology and
Philosophy – the community has been generally described as the main
protagonist of the ancient, pre-modern, and extra-modern world.
Actually, I claim in this introductory chapter that the very idea of
community was ultimately foreign to the ancient world – at least in its
meaning of *cum-munus* (i.e. reciprocal gift), which we explore below.
It was, paradoxically, only with the birth of individualism, widely
acknowledged as a modern phenomenon, that the community came to
be understood in this new, more tragic and proper sense.

In order to demonstrate this thesis, which is not so common in the literature on community, let us consider as a starting point the following uncontroversial point: whether tribal or archaic,[1] the ancient community was fundamentally *hierarchical* and *illiberal,* and seen as opposed to both an aggregation of free and equal individuals (that we can call society) and a fraternal community.[2] The rise of political economy in the modern era or, from a different point of view, the emergence of modernity out of market economy, marks a time in Western history when we observe the gradual decline of the hierarchical and illiberal community and the parallel affirmation of *the individual without community.*

In this chapter we'll try to make sense of the link between the fall of the ancient *communitas* and the rise of market society. It is in the community and its ambivalent character that we hope to find the key to understanding the reasons that led to this epoch-making transformation.

Drawing on an interesting etymological account, a large part of today's literature traces the origin of the ambivalent quality of the community, the *communitas,* back to the word *munus* (cfr. the Latin *communitas:* from *cum* + *munus*).[3] In this view, the *cummunitas* would mirror the ambivalence of the Latin word *munus,* which denotes simultaneously a

---

[1] According to Polanyi (1977), the tribal community is more ancient (or "primitive") compared to the archaic community. In the first, status alone informs the members' subjective positions; in the latter, status gradually loses its sway in favour of the contract. Strictly speaking, only the tribal society should be termed "sacral" (in the sense I employ here); but many communities referred to as "archaic" by Polanyi (like the Sumerian or Egyptian) are sacral as well.

[2] Here and in the remainder of this work (in particular in the first chapters), I shall not deny that even the ancient "community" or modern so-called "native" societies may be places of genuine love and unconstrained reciprocity; nor do I wish to contend that the kind of sociality they express may only be unjust and hierarchical. In fact, history has consistently showed that tokens of authentic humanity are often found even in those contexts where human rights fail to be acknowledged: the human being is often capable of transcending the boundaries imposed on him by his culture and community. At the same time, ancient (or traditional) culture could hardly be identified with the culture centred on the single individual; rather, it arises from an holistic culture when the centre is the community seen as a whole. Ethnographical and anthropological research has revealed that the small communities of gatherers and hunters of the pre-Neolithic era tended to be more egalitarian and less hierarchical than the pre-historical communities of the Indo-European region (cf. Sahlins 1972).

[3] As illustrated by René Girard with regard to the equally ambivalent term "sacrifice" (1977), when we acknowledge the conceptual ambivalence of a word we are still far from an interpretation of the word's meaning. Only as it informs

gift and an obligation, and of the Old-English *gift* which translates as *poison* in German. This interpretation derives from the groundbreaking *Essai sur le don* written in the early 1920s by the French sociologist and anthropologist Marcel Mauss[4] who studied extensively the ambivalent nature of the gift. His theory of the gift was highly influential throughout the twentieth century. In his studies of archaic societies, Mauss showed that what compels the receiver to reciprocate is the spirit of the object, the *hau*, which is thought to be embedded in the gift. The receiver is thus bound to the giver through the *hau*, which has been passed to him through the gift. He cannot be released from the *hau*'s "poisonous" spell until the gift has been reciprocated in a way deemed suitable by the giver.

For these reasons the ternary process of giving (giving–accepting–giving back), represents a foundational step of the social process of gift-giving and of the intra- and inter-community cycles of gift-exchange.

Gifts affect the inner balance of social relations by generating situations of asymmetry that men – modern-day individuals especially – find hard to endure. An un-reciprocated gift yields disequilibrium and disorder, whereas human societies have a preference for symmetry.[5] We can read in these terms the extraordinary power of the modern market, which is founded upon the symmetrical exchange of equivalents (or values that are perceived as equivalent by the agents).[6]

The topic of the complex grammar of the *munus* (the gift that obligates and pretends restitution) has been explored by a number of distinguished scholars, including the French philosophers Derrida and Marion, and the French sociologists of the M.A.U.S.S. movement (particularly Alain Caillé). In particular, over the past decade the role of

a new inquiry does the notion of conceptual ambivalence become significant in a cultural perspective.

[4] In fact, we could trace it further back – at least as far as Emile Durkheim (Mauss' uncle and mentor) and to his theory of religion with its concepts of the sacred and the profane.

[5] The word 'symmetry' here refers to a situation of equilibrium existing between different communities rather than between their individual members.

[6] Of the three classic (Greek–Christian) forms of love, i.e. *eros*, *philia* and *agape*, the first two tend to preserve a symmetric relational structure without putting social life at risk. On the contrary, *agape* (love moved by gratuitousness) compromises the balance and symmetry of relations, thus endangering entire communities and relationships of status. As a reaction to *agape*'s unsettling force, most communities tend to discourage acts moved by gratuitousness.

the *munus* as the primary source of the community's inner ambivalence has been convincingly emphasized by the Italian philosopher Roberto Esposito. In the following pages we attempt to further articulate the meaning of the ambivalence in the terms *munus* and *communitas*. But let us proceed one step at a time.

Within archaic communities the gift is always perceived as a social event taking place within groups that bear a recognized sacral connotation. In this context, what is "sacred" is the symbolic dimension in which the "total social fact" (in Marcel Mauss (1923–4)'s classic words) of the gift occurs. In other terms, we could say that the sacred works as an intermediary that accompanies and makes possible the very process of the gift in its basic grammar of giving–accepting–reciprocating. Another essential trait of traditional gift circles is that they are built on reciprocity rather than gratuitousness. This point has been highlighted primarily by Karl Polanyi, whose work was key to the anthropology of gift in the twentieth century. In its basic relational structure, the reciprocity of gift is not fundamentally different, in its social function and relational nature, from the phenomenon of economic exchange or barter – a practice that appeared much later than ritual gift-exchange. Through the history of cultures, the difference between gift- and market-exchange can basically be interpreted as a difference *in degree* – in the ways of measuring equivalence, in the acceptable delay between gift and counter-gift, in the types of punishment established – rather than a difference in nature.[7] Thus Polanyi on this point:

> The category of "free gifts" Malinowski found to be altogether exceptional or, rather, anomalous. Charity is neither necessary nor encouraged, and the notion of gift is invariably associated with that of countergift. Consequently, even obviously "free" gifts are usually construed as countergifts for some service rendered by the recipient.
>
> Polanyi 1977, p. 54

Therefore, whereas Smith describes primitive man as inclined by nature to truck and barter (*Wealth of Nations*, p. 25), it can be argued on the basis of the anthropological evidence that the earliest form of exchange between men was not the market nor the barter but the reciprocity

---

[7] Reflecting Malinowski's research on the Pacific Islands, Polanyi's distinction between economic exchange and reciprocity is more accentuated than the one I employ (cfr. Bruni 2008).

of gifts – *munera*. The market or economic exchange emerged long afterwards from the depths of human history as an evolution of gift-exchange. In this context, strangers are not regarded as wholly foreign or different; they are seen at the same time as enemies and guests; as rivals, but also as potential partners in a transaction. In fact, by virtue of their sacral culture, all ancient communities are essentially alike; and this circumstance provides a sort of common ground which makes it possible to connect with each other through a shared symbolic language, to encounter each other, trade or fight.

In the ancient community the political and religious powers are deeply intertwined and no clear separation exists between the religious and political spheres – this is certainly the case for many ancient communities across the Mediterranean, including Rome and Ancient Greece. As noticed by Rudolf Otto and later by Mircea Eliade, the only boundary lies between the sacred and the profane: "For religious man, *space is not homogeneous* [...]. There is a sacred space, and hence a strong, significant space; there are other spaces that are not sacred" (Eliade 1961, p. 20). The sacred community is therefore simultaneously characterized by the absence of a distinction between the political and religious domains, and, as the other side of the same coin, by the existence of an absolute limit between the sacred and the profane that is the main instrument for governing its life in common.

Hence, the contradictory nature of *munus* and *communitas* may be explained as a reflection of the ambivalent nature of the sacred which, as expressed by the Latin word *sacer,* or the Melanesians' *mana*, means simultaneously "holy" and "cursed" (Ries 1982, p. 26). Thus Aldo Schiavone in this passage on Ancient Rome:

> Indeed, the relation between royalty and sacrality [...] well documented, in the case of Rome, by the survival, well into the republican era, of the presence of a singular figure, the *rex sacrorum*, would become a constant in the whole of European history: even Christianity would ultimately rework it in a penetrating and creative way right up to the dawn of the modern age.
>
> Schiavone 2012, p. 66

Each and every aspect of the ancient community (even the profane, from which the sacred is distinct) is imbued with sacredness. Everything is symbol: the religious or magic ritual (a distinction extremely tenuous in, if not absent from, the archaic world) opens a channel to the holy and becomes the language through which this order is conveyed, thus establishing a connection *binding* the members of the community to the deities and with each other (cfr. religion, Lt *religo*: to *bind*). While invisible to men, this order is more real than it may seem: "Space that is sacred – the only real and really existing space" (Eliade 1961, p. 20).

The concept of sacred relates closely to that of *mediation*:[8] every sacred order, every hierophany (i.e. "manifestation of the sacred", to say it with Eliade) requires a system of mediators operating between the community and the deity; inevitably, any possibility of un-mediated contact between the individuals and the deity, or between each other, must be denied, as it emerges in its purity in the traditional caste system. Also Ries (1982, p. 63) underlines the point that the mediator is central to any hierophany. René Girard (1977) in his classic book claims that sacrifice has often described as an act of "mediation" between a sacrificer and a "deity". In fact, sacrifice could be interpreted as ultimately representing a means, an *instrumental* device enabling the mediator (priest, shaman) to establish a link between the community and the deity within the sacred space. In this perspective, we can argue along with Durkheim that the sacred serves a fundamental social function.

Sacral communities are necessarily hierarchical: status is ranked and classified as "high" and "low", "pure" and "impure" in response to each individual's supposed closeness to the deity and to its order as reflected in history (i.e. priests are typically at the top of the hierarchy; artisans, peasants and slaves at the bottom).[9]

The human community is ordered according to this wholly sacred framework, in which every element gains its meaning from the supreme purpose of preserving the community. Individual members have no autonomy: they are subjected to the sacred community and may even be sacrificed for the sake of a higher good of the community (or one

---

[8] On the social role of mediation cf. Morineau (2010).

[9] It is significant that the Indo-European religions that later evolved into the great monotheistic doctrines, and into Hinduism and Buddhism, tend to share an essential feature: the so-called "theology of the three functions" (Ries 1982). Divinity presents itself across three hierarchical orders of deities: thus, for instance, in the Indian Vedic religion, among the Hittites, in the Iran of Zarathustra. *Deva* is the Indo-European word for "deity" and also refers to the sun. Each of the three orders of deities is relevant to social life: to each is attributed a social function, which eventually comes to be identified with a class in a rigid hierarchical ranking. Analogously, in Italy the Iguvine Tablets carry the names of Juu/Mart/Vofiono, later transliterated in Jupiter/Mars/Quirinus in ancient Rome, where peasants (Quirinus) were at the low end of the hierarchy, the priests (Jupiter) at the top end, and the warriors (Mars) in the middle – a triadic order present in several Indo-European cultures and religions.

that is perceived as such by the members and, most importantly, by their chiefs). In an environment that is naturally hostile and character-ized by the extreme scarcity of resources, the community's survival and growth inevitably become the highest goods. Mechanisms of individual incentives are discouraged through the provision of various types of social bonds and sanctions, thus enhancing solidarity within the community. Figures like the *pater familias,* the Roman pontifex, Moses in Israel, the Egyptian pharaoh, the Medieval ruler differ in many ways but, from our point of view, they are also very much alike in that they guarantee, by virtue of a sacral hierarchical authority and mediation, the order of the community as a whole.

In the following section we shall further explore the meaning of the hierarchy in ancient communities.

2. Hierarchy

Hierarchy could be described as an instrument for the exercise of authority. In fact, the *Oxford English Dictionary* defines hierarchy as "a ranking system ordered according to status or authority".

A former student of Mauss, French anthropologist Louis Dumont dedicated much of his research to the study of hierarchical socie-ties (focusing on traditional Indian societies in particular) and to their comparison with modern-day egalitarian societies. He describes hierarchy as "a ladder of *command* in which the lower rungs are encom-passed in the higher ones in regular succession" (Dumont 1980, p. 65). This term and its concept are derived from the religious domain. Hindu castes in India, as well as the pre-conciliar Catholic church, are paradig-matic examples of the essential traits of hierarchical systems.[10]

---

[10] In fact, the history of hierarchical culture in Medieval Europe is complex and still partly unexplored. What we know is that the system of hierarchical relations commonly known as "feudalism" emerged from the encounter of several cultures. Amongst these is certainly the Christian culture, which in the wake of the then prevailing Neoplatonic and gnostic influences and despite the decidedly horizontal structure and fraternal ethos imparted by its Founder, came to fully embrace the notion of hierarchical society. And, in addition, there are the Aryan or Indo-European cultures which, through the German popula-tions, brought to Europe the Indian notion of caste hierarchy. In other terms, the culture of hierarchy became considerably more widespread in Europe in the Middle Age than it had been in the Greek-Christian culture during the early centuries of the first millennium. And this occurred in spite of Christianity. We shall return to this subject later in this work.

Pre-conciliar Catholic ecclesiology and, by way of its influence, all European culture have been strongly affected by the hierarchy theories of Pseudo-Dionysius the Areopagite. Inspired, in turn, by the Neoplatonic works of Plotinus, in the fifth century AD Pseudo-Dionysius[11] composed a theological treatise built upon the concept of ecclesiastical hierarchy as mirror of the celestial order.[12] In this view, the attainment of spiritual goods in the human world becomes possible through the mediation of the ecclesiastical hierarchy that in turn receives them through mediation of the celestial hierarchy.[13]

Such a highly hierarchized structuration of the world entails the need for constant intermediation between the various orders; as a result, lower ranks may never have contact with higher ranks, except through the intervention of a mediator belonging to an even higher order. The lowest ranks (laymen, for example) may only approach God through the mediation of the highest rank (the priests). According to Dumont, hierarchical societies[14] are holistic (the existence of the group precedes that of its single members), whereas egalitarian societies are individualistic (groups have value only inasmuch as they are chosen or created freely by individuals). The individual comes into existence only as he steps out of the caste network, thus becoming a *sannyasin* (the ascetic). Outside the caste structure, the individual won't find a community of individuals but solitude, i.e. a *non-community*.

---

[11] Much more could be said about the role of Neoplatonism and Esotericism in the Western reception of the theory of hierarchy.

[12] In *De coelesti hierarchia*, Pseudo-Dionysius defines hierarchy as "a certain perfectly holy Order in the likeness of the First Divine Beauty, ministering the sacred mystery of its own illuminations in hierarchical order and wisdom, being in due measure conformed to its own Principle" (III, 2). In the world of Angels, such mediation is regulated through the celestial hierarchy, which is composed of three orders further divided in three sub-hierarchies (Seraphim, Cherubim, Thrones – Dominions, Virtues, Powers – Principalities, Archangels, Angels). Every order in the celestial hierarchy serves a particular purpose in the transmission of the divine power, by way of the double descending and ascending mode dictated by the Thearchy itself (that's how he defines the Trinity).

[13] Pseudo-Dionysius places the Bishop at the top of the human hierarchy. The Bishop is enlightened by the angels and transfers this enlightenment to the *fedeli* through the mediation of presbyters and deacons during the celebration of the sacramental mysteries. From this point of view then there is a strong link between hierarchy and liturgy (and relating rituals of initiation), which becomes the instrument for transmitting "spiritual goods" from the highest to the lowest ranks.

[14] Dumont (1980) sees the caste society as the archetype of the hierarchical society.

For Dumont, three elements characterize hierarchical societies. Though theoretically distinguishable, they are deeply interwoven in real societies:

1. The society is ordered in ranks – be they castes, groups or classes;
2. Detailed rules are laid out in order to enforce the boundaries between different ranks;
3. There is a rigid division of labour and, as a result, a high degree of interdependence between ranks.[15]

Such tension between separation and interdependence permeates every aspect of the Indian world and possibly of any ancient or traditional culture. Another important aspect, again observed by Dumont, is that the three elements above can all be traced back to the radical distinction between pure and impure on which the entire traditional Indian culture is built. A higher degree of purity corresponds to a higher position in the hierarchy. But how have we to interpret the meaning of the dichotomy between pure and impure in the context of the caste culture and of other traditional ancient cultures (Jewish, Greek, etc.) showing similarities in the notion of impurity?

The dichotomy between purity and impurity is ultimately instrumental in managing the fear generated by the risk of contamination. The very word "caste", introduced by the Portuguese in the sixteenth century, means "un-mixed". Not dissimilar is the other fundamental separation between sacred and profane, which, combined with religions' role of administrations of the sacred, inevitably dictates their highly hierarchical structure.

The caste system counts numerous variations (from the five fundamental Indian castes to the multitudes of sub-castes defined by occupation, function, etc.), but one element remains constant, i.e. the two polar classes, *Brahmins* and *untouched* (*pariah*), the highest and lowest caste by which all others are delimited.

---

[15] In the Roman society, for instance, where all three elements were present, a greater emphasis was placed on the functional division of labour than on the other two elements. In all traditional societies we tend to find the metaphor of society as a body (as in the apology of Menenio Agrippa in Rome; or the image of the Church as the body of Christ contained in the letters of Pauline-tradition; or still in the various representations of a people as a collective person, also present in Israel). The third element (i.e. division of work and interdependence) can exist even in the absence of the other two, as in the market ideology where the economy is seen as a highly interdependent and individualistic reality.

Again according to Dumont, purity and its opposite, i.e. contamination, constitute the real foundation of the hierarchy, of separation and division of labour, because the very idea of superiority, of someone being "superior", may only exist when someone else, "the inferior", keeps contamination away from the superiors by carrying out tasks that are considered impure but essential to a society. The pure is defenceless and vulnerable before the impure.[16] The risk of contamination thus poses a threat to the existence of the caste system itself and to the social order it informs.

The hierarchy is thus bound to the notion of *immunitas* (immunity) through a profound logical and historical connection that is also reflected in the twofold etymology highlighted by Esposito (2009): *immunitas* as "absence of *munus*" and privilege over those who are exposed to the contamination (of the *communitas*).

3. *Nomina sunt numina*

We shall take one more step. Ancient structures of reciprocity show yet another fundamental trait: the exchange of gift and counter-gift is not meant for the single individual but for the whole community (the clan, tribe, village, patriarchal family, etc.). In the exchange, each community sends its own representative to encounter the other community's representative – not as individuals, but as the communities' "corporate" personalities.

We may attempt to refine the meaning of the community's ambivalence by taking into account the following two points:

a) by understanding the *communitas* as a "community of communities" can we fully appreciate the nature of the mutual processes of gift-exchange in which the various local communities (family, clan, tribe...) take part for the purpose of establishing and consolidating intra-communitarian relations and agreements. However, within each community (*ad intram*) the *munus* is seen by the subjects as "duty" to their community. This entails (see *b*) what is perhaps a non-trivial implication, though not sufficiently emphasized in the discussions in the literature.

---

[16] Even in Judaism, and more generally in religions of Indo-European derivation, the contraposition pure and impure lies at the core of the cult and of the social hierarchy. See further Ries (1982).

b) The ambivalence of the *munus*–gift and obligation–can and should be read in terms of its intra- and inter-community dimensions. The inter-community circle of gift shows the twofold nature of the *munus*; but in the context of intra-community relations only the obligation component of gift exists, generally in a servant-to-master hierarchical dynamics. The members of the community (wives, children, slaves, servants…) are "expropriated" because there is nothing they can call their own, except for the obligation they have towards the community: "The community isn't a mode of being, much less a 'making' of the individual subject. It isn't the subject's expansion or multiplication but its exposure to what interrupts the closing and turns it inside out…The common 'rose' of its being 'no subject'" (Esposito 2009[1998], p. 7). The reciprocity that Polanyi, among others, describes is a relation between communities (as Sumner Maine [1861] fittingly remarked in his theory of ancient societies), rather than within a single community. The community is a sort of no man's land.

For instance, consider the case of ancient Rome: the *patres familias* of the Roman community were tied by relations of reciprocity based on equality, but within each single family the governing principle was certainly not reciprocity but hierarchy (Schiavone 2012). The father had the right to sacrifice his children's lives, even once adult (at least in principle). A similar situation existed in ancient Greece: while the democracy of the *polis* was indeed an experience of *philia* – of reciprocity between citizens (i.e. males, adults, free, not artisans or peasants, etc.) – the experience of the *oikos* was dictated by status, gender and hierarchy. We could continue with analogous examples from other cultures of the ancient world (and well into the Modern Age).

There is obviously a radical difference between ancient and non-ancient communities. In other words there is a radical difference between the community *before* and *after* the birth of the individual or, in the words of Benjamin Constant, between the "liberty of Ancients" and "the liberty of Moderns". Roberto Esposito's compelling analysis of the *communitas*, for example – from which I have taken the passage quoted above (in a position where it sounds deliberately ambiguous) – is completely centred on the ambivalence of the modern community, that is as a community of individuals where the community "is not perceived as painless by the *subject who experiences it. It is the most extreme of possibilities*, but also the most dangerous of threats" (*ibid.*, p. xviii, my italics).

Before the birth of the individual, the community is not "the most extreme of possibilities" simply because the subject-individual doesn't choose anything, does not experience (or create) any possibility; and because in the ancient community there is basically no individual, or at least the individual cannot be "seen" in that culture.

4. Community without individuals

The sacred community would continue to exist through the entire Middle Ages, gradually developing a range of new attributes. The emblematic incipit to Gurevic's classic work on the rise of individualism in Medieval Europe reads:

> One of the drawings illustrating the Garden of Delights ("Hortus deliciarum) of Abbess Herrad von Landsberg (late twelfth century), depicts nuns from her convent at Hohenburg and includes a portrait of the author. There are more than sixty portraits in all, but what cannot fail to attract the beholder's attention is the almost exact similarity of all the subjects: not only are their poses and attire identical, but their faces and expressions resemble one another to an astonishing degree. Where it does prove possible to find minor deviations, they are only definitely of secondary importance and in no way can they be seen as reflecting any endeavor on the artist's part to bring out individual features. The Abbess herself is distinct from the other figures only insofar as she is depicted standing and holding a large scroll. ... They are all 'Brides of Christ' stripped of age or individuality.
>
> (1995, p. 1)

Analogous pictorial scenes can be found in various pre-Renaissance paintings, for instance the frescoes of Giusto de' Menabuoi located in the Baptistry of Padua's Cathedral and dating from around 1376. There, little emphasis is placed on the individual characteristics of the Blessed, while the figure of Christ *pantocrator* dominates the scene.

As a matter of fact, one of the symptoms of the birth of individualism at the beginning of the Modern era is the season of individual portraits – depicting nobles as well as ordinary citizens or villagers (as in the works of Caravaggio). A clearer definition of the community as *community of individuals* arrived with Hobbes and later with Kant, to whom we owe the concept of 'sociable unsociability' – which sees man as caught between the desire and fear of the tragic experience of life with others (always given as possibility, not necessity). As we shall see, the emergence of the individual from the sacral community has been a process which originated in Greece and Israel before crucially evolving in Christianity and in the ethics of the Medieval merchant and citizen; and, eventually, it became transformed into the ethics of the market – the point of arrival and solution to the inner tensions of the *communitas*, which is thus reconciled in a subject who no longer entertains any communitarian relations and is unbound from the tight laces of status.

In pre-modern culture, the *communitas* is dominated by status, which is accompanied by a condition of subjection for the vast majority and of domination for few. Individuals are the direct result of their position or role within the community. They have no absolute right over the community, but only duties and obligations to serve the common good. There can be no room for individuality since *the community is the only in-dividuum*. The relations that such non-individuals share with each other (or with the community and its representatives) are neither chosen, nor equal; through the sacral hierarchy the relevant roles and masks (*persona, prosopon*) are forced upon the individual. The three great foundational principles of modernity – i.e. liberty, equality, fraternity – are the great absent in the *ancient régime*. For this reason they have been subsequently proposed as the great project but also the radical utopia of a humanism concerned with the newly-born individual longing to become adult.

H. Sumner Maine's theory of primitive societies centred upon the concept of "patriarchal family" is still compelling. Thus reads one of the passages of *Ancient Law*:

> society in primitive times was not what it is assumed to be at present, a collection of *individuals*. In fact, and in the view of the men who composed it, it was an *aggregation of families*. The contrast may be most forcibly expressed by saying that the unit of an ancient society was the Family, of a modern society the "Individual."
>
> 1875[1861], p. 121

Family was the 'basic unit' from which *gens*, tribes and society originated as in a system of concentric circles. This theory is essentially in line with Aristotle's Politics and later with Aquinas' political theory, and not entirely original (similarities can also be found in the works of

Vico and Montesquieu). Maine combines this theory, known as "patri-archal theory", with the more famous "law of progress":

> The movement of the progressive societies has been uniform in one respect. Through its course it has been distinguished by the gradual dissolution of family dependency and the growth of individual obligation in its place. The Individual is steadily substituted for the Family, as the unit of which civil laws take account. [...] Nor is it difficult to see what is the tie between man and man which replaces by degrees those forms of reciprocity in rights and deities which have their origin in the Family. It is Contract. Starting, as from one terminus of history, from a condition of society in which all the relations of Persons are summed up in the relations of Family, we seem to have steadily moved towards a phase of social order in which all these relations arise from the free agreement of Individuals.
>
> Ibid. p. 163

And he concludes with the celebrated argument: "the movement of the progressive societies has hitherto been a movement *from Status to Contract*" (ibid., p. 165).

Few other theories have shown such a prophetic nature, considering that Maine's "law of progress" has managed to predict many subsequent trends in law, society, economics, and politics. While definitely imbued with the culture of its times and with Darwinism and the prevailing climate of optimism of the Victorian era (think of J.S. Mill's contemporary works on the co-operative future of market economy mentioned above), Maine's theory was able to capture the most radical trend dominating the one-and-a-half centuries following the publication of Ancient Law: the decline of the family and the hierarchical community, and the proliferation, in their place, of the culture of freely-negotiated contracts.

Tönnies (1887), Weber (1922), and more recently Karl Polanyi (1977) have re-examined and further developed Maine's fundamental idea, although – especially in the case of Tönnies – the community is not theorized as a place of un-chosen relations regulated by power (status) but is seen as a sort of "paradise lost", a place of warm human relations that the anonymous society of the contract tends to destroy. In any case, the status–contract dualism and the law of progress have been taken as starting points for twentieth-century studies investigating the fall of the community – a fall which, according to some authors, would lead to a better world, while for others it would be a prelude to the decay of human relations because – to say it with Thomas Carlyle (1898) – the "cash nexus" would become the new social bond of the "dismal science".

The advocates of individualism will undoubtedly find that the ancient community cannot represent a satisfactory conclusion, since in the sacred community there is no place for the individual. The category and the human experience of individuality are indeed products of modernity; more specifically, they are the products of a cultural process in the Greek-Jewish-Christian traditions – Socrates, the prophets, and Jesus Christ are amongst the first individuals, or more properly persons, to emerge from the ancient sacred community. In the following pages we also suggest that the notion of community (the *cum-munus*, with its simultaneous reference to gift, not just to obligation) also arrives with modernity; although someone might find this claim rather bizarre, if not incorrect, we shall present both theoretical and empirical reasons to demonstrate that where individuals are not free and equal there can only be the sacral community; this – while tragic – is not an encounter of individuals but a hierarchical aggregate of un-chosen status and non-individuals.

We shall show that the discovery of the essence of the *cum-munus* and of its tragedy belongs to the modern and Western man (heir of the humanism of the Greek, Jewish, and Christian traditions) who is able to see a "you" as well as an "I" (no authentic experience of otherness can ignore the experience of oneself). However – and this is the theoretical knot of the present work – the discovery of the other, equal and free, prompts above all the fear of potential wounds the other can cause, and hence reveals the possibility of death associated with this new relational paradigm (also highlighted by Hobbes and in more recent times by Elias Canetti); as a result, instead of opening to the age of fraternity, man introduces new intermediaries; these are no longer openly sacral but basically serve the same functions as the mediators did in the sacred community, and they partly inherit their symbolic code, as with the State-Leviathan and the "Invisible Hand" of the market.

In order for the ambivalence of the *munus* to become manifest, the individual must arise from the *communitas* in an anthropological and sociological perspective. This is why it is necessary to begin from Israel and Ancient Greece, where this emergence of the subject from the sacral community first occurred and in a powerful way, providing us today with the necessary categories to interpret similar dynamics in different cultural contexts. In Israel, the frailty of common life is accompanied by the departure from the sacral community in order to enter the Alliance;

in Greece the fragility of the *koinonia is* linked to the rise of the *polis* and founded on *philia*.

We shall see as well that the Alliance with JHWH (Yahweh) as well as the *philia* of the *polis* were both conceived as a remedy against the fragility of the *communitas* that those experiences of freedom had brought about.

2
The Dawn of the Tragic Community in Greece and Israel

> Cain said to his brother Abel, 'Let us go out'; and while they were in the open country, Cain set on his brother Abel and killed him.
>
> Yahweh asked Cain, 'Where is your brother Abel?' 'I do not know,' he replied. 'Am I my brother's guardian?'
>
> *Genesis*, 4

1. The original reciprocity

In our search for the advent of the culture of the individuals from the sacral ancient community, let us start very far back in western history, by looking first at the Bible – possibly the greatest existing code of western culture.

In the Bible's humanism, life in common bears the signs of pain inscribed within its flesh. Such is the humanistic, anthropological message of the Bible, which, mostly through some of the great symbols and myths contained in *Genesis*, portrays the other as a "blessing" (without him or her, life may never be authentically humane or happy). At the same time the other is also someone who "hurts" me (as in the tale of Jacob's struggle with the angel, *Genesis* 32, 23–30): a wound and a blessing that may not be separated in any authentic human encounter.

The beautiful myth of Adam and Eve in the Garden of Eden in the early chapters of *Genesis* embodies the ambivalent tension inherent in the inter-human relation: the other (in this case, the woman) is for Adam the only being with whom he is not alone, and hence happy. Only the woman, the other, his peer, the Hebraic *ezer kenegdo* (*Genesis* 2, 20), makes it possible for Adam to be completely happy. Full happiness may not be achieved through the sole relationship with nature, nor through the sole relationship with God (Adam used to walk together with God in the Garden, but his happiness was not full). Even the relation with the cosmos is seen in *Genesis* in the context of an Alliance between God and man–woman, in which the act of *keeping* plays a central role. The verb that the author of *Genesis* uses to convey what we translate as "keeping" is *shamar* (*Genesis* 2, 15). Man (*adam*) is placed by God in the Garden of Eden with the duty, or vocation, to cultivate and keep the land (*adamah*) – a semantic combination whose richness is virtually impossible to render outside the Hebrew language.[1]

So, for instance, the vocation to human labour is a call to a relationship of care and guardianship towards the land. A relationship of reciprocity, even: the land donates her gifts, and man keeps and looks after the land. Human labour too is seen as an experience of reciprocity and is expressive of the foundational reciprocity between the *adam* and God, and of the reciprocity between man and woman. *Genesis*'s anthropological approach strikes the contemporary reader for its human stature and for the way it sees the woman, both in the older account (Eve as Adam's rib: *Genesis* 2, 21–22) as well as in the more recent one describing the simultaneous creation of man and woman (*Genesis* 1, 27). The main theme, unprecedented and surprising (given the cultural climate in which the text was written) is the fundamental reciprocity between man and woman:

> God said, 'Let us make man in our own image, in the likeness of ourselves, and let them be masters of the fish of the sea, the birds of heaven, the cattle, all the wild animals and all the creatures that creep along the ground.' God created man in the image of himself, in the image of God he created him, male and female he created them.
>
> *Genesis* 1, 26–27

The Bible's structure and the Semitic technique of parallelism (see verse 27)[2] are revealing of the anthropological conception in *Genesis*: man's image of God may be seen in the relation between man

---

[1] The profound nexus between land and man also arises in the Latin language: "humus" and "homo".

[2] The word "image" occurs in the first few lines of verse 27, but from the third line onwards this word disappears to be replaced by "male–female". This parallelism tells us that God's image is fully visible in human relationality: cf. Ravasi (1999), where some of the issues I am discussing here are presented also from the artistic point of view.

and woman, in the human ability to share a relation of reciprocity with another. Furthermore, the very terms *ish* and *isha* (*Genesis* 2, 24–25) – a semantic message still present in the English *man* and *woman* – indicate a relationship in which one's name (the profound essence) necessarily recalls the name of the other. In the same biblical account, however, such reciprocity is situated in the context of a broken relationship, of sin. Reciprocity between man and woman, the only place where the *adam* may find himself completely, his happiness, is also the place where sin will destroy a project of love. And as soon as one of these relations of reciprocity is broken, all other relations start to fall apart. Thus, the rupture between Adam and God immediately leads to the rupture of the interpersonal relation ("the woman whom you put with me, she gave me some fruit from the tree" *Genesis* 3, 12), of the relation with the animals ("the serpent tempted me…"), with nature and with labour: the two are expelled from Eden, giving birth will no longer be as simple for the woman as it is for animals, and labour will become painful.[3]

The relation between man and woman is itself crossed by a tragic tension between reciprocal attraction and the tendency to dominate one another. Here, the author describes the then prevailing historical condition (i.e. the domination of man over woman) as a result of the "fallout" from the original communitarian condition based on reciprocity and equality (*ezer kenegdo*). This tale is significant: man's domination over woman, or over animals, is not the natural condition or vocation of human relations (neither could it be a condition in which any being dominates others: in the Bible the man–woman relationship always stands as the paradigm of all human relations); nor is it a condition in which working is painful.[4] Instead, it is the expression of

---

[3] 'To the woman God said: "I shall give you intense pain in childbearing, you will give birth to your children in pain. Your yearning will be for your husband, and he will dominate you. To Adam he said: "Because you listened to the voice of your wife and ate from the tree of which I had forbidden you to eat, Accursed be the soil because of you! Painfully will you get your food from it as long as you live. It will yield you brambles and thistles, as you eat the produce of the land. By the sweat of your face will you earn your food, until you return to the ground, as you were taken from it. For dust you are and to dust you shall return'" (*Genesis* 3, 16–19). Cf. Wenham (1998).

[4] The painful quality of labour is not directly related to labour's inner nature: when Adam used to work in Eden, labour was an experience of happiness, reciprocity and blessing. As the relations (with God, with the other) fall apart, labour suddenly stops being a blessing and turns into a curse.

a pathological situation, a disease, a sin, that caused the original design of *good* reciprocity to change.[5]

2. Wounded fraternity

Once outside the Garden of Eden, Cain murders Abel. In answering God's question "Where is Abel, your brother?", Cain will reply: "Am I my brother's keeper?" (*Genesis* 4, 9). In this sentence we find the same verb *shamar*, to "keep" or to "care", used by the author of *Genesis* only a few verses earlier to describe the relation of reciprocity shared with the land: to Adam is given the land in order to care and keep it: "God took the man and settled him in the garden of Eden to cultivate and take care of it" (*Genesis* 2, 15).[6] The Bible's message here is clear: as the relationship with the other being falls apart, the relationship with nature is also lost: if I cannot care for my brother, I cannot keep the land either; I cannot cultivate it nor experience it as a blessing. As soon as Cain stops being his brother's "keeper" he becomes his murderer: without keeping, there is murder, and no intermediate state of mutual indifference may exist. Outside the alliance of reciprocity is not the indifference of the contract, but conflict (think of one of the first tales about contracts[7] in the Bible: the purchase of Esau's birthright by Jacob, in exchange for a portion of lentils[8]).

In this light, Cain's story becomes emblematic: he is the fratricide, who later becomes the founder of the first city (Enoch). But Cain's story is not without precedent: similar myths surround the foundation of Rome and other ancient cities (particularly in the East).

---

[5] A similar idea was also present in Greece and in Rome with reference to slavery: it existed and was recognized by civil law, not by nature.

[6] Another interesting version of Cain and Abel's myth is narrated in the Koran: the twins talk before the killing and Abel says to Cain: "If you extend your hand to kill me, I am not extending my hand to kill you" (*The Sacred Koran*, al- Ma'idah: Sura 5, 28).

[7] The first commercial contract in the Bible is between Abraham and the Hittites for the purchase of Sarah's burial ground (*Genesis*, 26). Another reason why this story is interesting is that it offers an example of the art of negotiation that characterized the ancient eastern world (traces of which may still be found in today's eastern markets).

[8] *Genesis'* humanism shows a certain nontrivial similarity between contract and deception: both are "tools" which allow transferring one brother's status to another.

An echo of the conflict between Cain and Abel may be heard, perhaps less violently but no less tragically, in the relation between Jacob and Esau – and we should not forget that Cain's lineage will end with Lamek and his terrible song of war.[9]

What kind of message may we then derive from the fraternal conflicts narrated in *Genesis* between Cain and Abel, Jacob and Esau, Joseph and his brothers?[10] Of course many interpretations are possible, from many different angles. From our viewpoint (the viewpoint of the ambivalent *communitas*), brothers fight for power (in the form of the Father's blessing, of the birthright) in order to become fathers themselves. They do not murder the father,[11] nor do they fight him, but they challenge their peers and rivals (their brothers).

These tales are important because they are among the earliest signs of the rise of individuality from inside the *communitas*: they do not describe only "fathers", or Kings; nor do they tell only of vertical and hierarchical relations (liturgy, command, etc.). We read of brothers who fight to achieve a certain status (birthright) and who are *not* equal (not in the modern sense) despite being brothers: here, fraternity (like generally any fraternal relation in the ancient world) is separate from equality.

The story (beginning outside Eden) starts not with the gift, but with broken fraternal relations willing to kill in order to achieve a certain status. The story of brotherhood thus commences with a refusal, with a *no*, with death and conflict. The decay of human relationality (from the original condition of man–woman reciprocity) culminates in the tale of Noah and the deluge, which also marks the beginning of the Torah (Law), while also representing one of the solutions to the ambivalence of the *communitas*, as we shall see in the next chapter.

---

[9] Jacob buys his birthright from Esau, taking advantage of Esau's weakness in a moment of hunger (25). Later in *Genesis* (27) a second trick is described in which Jacob obtains the blessing from his old and nearly blind father Isaac after disguising himself in Esau's clothes. Fraternal conflict also characterizes the relations between the sons of Jacob (who sell their brother Joseph to the camel caravan travelling to Egypt (37)). Such conflicts mark the entire "cycle of Joseph" in *Genesis*.

[10] This is different from the man–woman rivalry of earlier chapters (in which there is no struggle for power). The rivalry between brothers extends to sisters as well: for instance think of the rivalry between Leah and Rachel (both wives of Jacob, also in *Genesis*).

[11] The killing of the father is typical of the Greek world. In Freud's *Totem and Taboo* (1913), of no historical foundation, sons often kill their fathers to have their women and their place.

As Leo Strauss interestingly remarks:

> *After* the expulsion from the Garden of *Eden*, God did not punish men...Nor did he establish human judges. God as it were experimented, for the instruction of mankind, with mankind living in freedom from law. This *experiment*, just as the *experiment* with men remaining like innocent children [Adam and Eve], ended in failure. Fallen or awake, man needs restraint, must live under law.
>
> Strauss 1967, p. 14

We shall stop here. According to the humanistic view offered by the Bible – or actually by *Genesis*, even though the book of *Genesis* is foundational for all Jewish anthropology[12] – life in common does not coincide with the *communitas*: there is no reciprocal gift. A mutual relation of equality (between man and woman and between brothers, both fundamental archetypes of all other communitarian relations in the ancient world), and hence the *communitas*, never materializes; it remains a mere possibility, unaccomplished and denied, marked by death and associated with the expulsion from Eden and with the rupture of a harmonious original design. As we compare the Jewish and Greek cultures, we are immediately presented with one initial question that goes back to the beginning of the Greek philosophers' discourse about the good life: why do the Greeks see in the city and in civil life the place of good life (as we shall see) and happiness (*eudaimonia*), while for the Jews the city tends to be associated with murder[13] and with Sodom and Gomorrah,[14] and the good life tends to be associated with the country?

The chronological datum is important: the stories of *Genesis* trace back to traditions that are older than the Greek *polis* and its philosophy. But perhaps there is something more to it. Greek philosophy depicts

---

[12] Of course, the Bible's anthropology is far more complex than the anthropological approach contained in the book of *Genesis* (and, on the other side, the latter is far more complex than our simplified account). Other emblematic figures who may help to better understand the Bible's concept of community include Moses and the prophets, all of whom are characterized as great personalities who receive and follow a certain vocation, a call. The prophet (think of the greatest, like Isaiah or Jeremiah) follows an inner voice, which typically leads him outside the city and the *communitas*, to be persecuted and often killed.

[13] And not just for them: think, for instance, of the myth of the foundation of Rome.

[14] Not even few just individuals were found by God among those citizens and God decided to destroy the cities: *Genesis* 18.

man as the political animal and citizen, without any separation between person and citizen. The *polis* is the place of friendship (it is founded on *philia*), it is the place of horizontal relations and reciprocity.

There is also a second point of diversity. While the conflict between brothers occupies the centre of the political scene in Jewish culture, in the Greek world the strongest archetype is the murder of the father (Uranus and Chronos, Chronos and Zeus, Zeus and the Titans, King Oedipus, etc.). What might be the explanation?

The anthropologist Giulio Chiodi proposed an interesting one:

> The term for "brother" in Indo-European languages occurs mainly as part of expressions that indicate the son of the same father (frater, broader, bruder). By contrast, the Greek work for "brother", *adelphos*, contains the word "*delphys*" which means uterus, or maternal womb. It recalls, therefore, a remote matriarchal origin in which brothers are children of the same mother, not of the same father. The attenuation of brotherly conflicts in Greek mythology may then be explained by their being children of the same mother. The mother is a reconciling force and sons born to the same mother have no reason to desire to violently take her place. The father, on the other hand, exerts an authority which, we might say, tends to be projected into action and is therefore open to conflicts. Hence the sons of the same father are, for this very reason, constitutionally prone to compete with each other.
>
> Chiodi 2006, p. 7

In both cultures life in common continues to be associated with death (the death of brothers in the Jewish world; of fathers in the Greek world). But in both cultures we observe as well the emergence of new subjects, typically sons, who give up the status they have been assigned by the *communitas*' sacred order and break that order to establish a new one.

In this respect, the sale of Esau's birthright to Jacob represents an especially interesting tale (*Genesis,* 25): it is (as far as I can tell) the first case in the history of cultures in which the "contract" is not only opposed to "status" – to say it with Sumner Maine – but the former even becomes a tool for the latter: birthright, which establishes the brothers' respective status in terms of future authority, is given away through a contract (lentils in exchange for birthright). Indeed, we are still within the sacred world,[15] but this episode reveals the beginning of something

---

[15] As a form of guarantee, Esau demands an oath from Jacob, instead of recurring to an external judge.

new: the use of the contract – the great protagonist of the society of individuals, as we are about to see – to disrupt the sacred and unchosen order by status. In both the biblical and the Greek myths, a few individuals suddenly gain the centre of the scene, through violence and deception. But something new arises: it is the dawn of the history of individuals.

3. Happiness and fortune in Greece

The tragic nature of life in common is a central issue in Greek philosophy and in Aristotle's ethics in particular. The *Nicomachean Ethics* (NE) contains the intuition of the paradox at the heart of the entire western world: the "good life", the happy life, is at the same time civil and then vulnerable. Aristotle reminds us, in the ninth chapter of the *Nicomachean Ethics* (1169b) that "the happy man needs friends" and hence we may not be happy alone.

In this cultural and anthropological view, happiness may not be achieved in solitude or by escaping civil life and the relationship with the other. On this point, Aristotle's ethics represents a truly new step compared to other positions in Greek philosophy. Thus Charles Taylor on this point:

> Aristotle manages to combine in his 'good life' two of the activities which were most commonly adduced by later ethical traditions as outranking ordinary life: theoretical contemplation and the participation as a citizen in the polity. These were not unanimously favored. Plato looked with a jaundiced eye on the second (at least in its normal form of competing for office). And the Stoic challenged both.
>
> Taylor 1989, p. 212

For Aristotle happiness requires social relationships, i.e. friendship and reciprocity, and because friendship and reciprocity are always in some way related to freedom and may not be completely or unilaterally controlled by one person only, our happiness dramatically depends on the answers of others – on whether, to what extent and how others share our love, friendship and reciprocity. In other terms, if happiness requires friendship, which in turn always entails reciprocity (in its various forms), then the happy life has a necessarily ambivalent nature: the other person is for me joy and sorrow, the only possibility of true happiness, but also someone on whom my unhappiness depends.

On the other hand, if in order to avoid such vulnerability and the likely chance of suffering I retire in solitude and contemplation, away from others (the great Platonic and Neoplatonic alternative), life cannot fully flourish.

For this reason, in the Aristotelian tradition even more than in Aristotle's own thought (as we'll see), the happy life is associated with tragedy. Thus the contemporary philosopher Martha Nussbaum on the topic of interpersonal relations: "these components of the good life are going to be minimally self-sufficient. And they will be vulnerable in an especially deep and dangerous way" (Nussbaum (1996)[1986], p. 344).

But let us take a closer look at this important tension within Greek culture, which centres upon the great word *eudaimonia*. Greece has been the first place in the West where a systematic philosophical inquiry about good life and happiness ever took place, and within this inquiry we can also trace the theme of *communitas*.

After the age of the Greek myths, in which the theme of happiness was already significantly present, with the rise of philosophy *eudaimonia* assumed a central role in all Greek culture.[16]

It is only if we consider the evolution this ancient word has seen over thousands of years, and not without difficulties, that we may today translate the Greek word *eudaimonia* as happiness. *Eudaimonia* "is always desirable in itself and never for the sake of something else ... for this we choose always for self and never for the sake of something else" (NE I, 7, 1097a). Happiness then "is the best, noblest, and most pleasant thing in the world" (ibid., I, 8, 1099a).[17] It is the "highest of all goods achievable by action" (ibid., I, 4, 1095a).

---

[16] Socrates and, later, Plato and Aristotle, as well as many ancient philosophical schools (like Stoicism or Epicureanism), produced several theories of *eudaimonia*. Such theories shared certain fundamental insights: a) the pursuit of *eudaimonia* is the ultimate end of agency, it is the greatest good, self-sufficient and autonomous, from which nothing else is missing; b) there exists an indissoluble link between happiness and the practice of virtues; c) virtue bears its fruit, i.e. happiness, only if sought in non-instrumental ways (with intrinsic motivations, we shall say). Different schools, however, had different views on the relation between active and contemplative life, and hence about the role of sociality and civil virtues with regard to the good life.

[17] Writes Alberto Peretti at the entry "eudaimonia" from the *Italian Dictionary of Civil Economy*: "[...]*eudaimonia* is *autárkes*, self-sufficient ... ." The term *autárkeia* might be misleading. Aristotle does not in the least wish to argue that happiness may be achieved by oneself, in autarchy and isolation. Aristotle claims man has a political nature and happiness is a social, relational fact, which stems from the encounter of one individual with others. Rather, since *autárkes* is one of the

All other goods (including wealth and honour) are only means to achieve happiness or fruits of happiness. Happiness then is never a means but always an end; it is the only end that, by nature, can never be instrumental. For this very reason (non-instrumentality) *eudaimonia* is defined as the "ultimate end", for there is no other goal beside it which is not already included in *eudaimonia*.[18] Hence the argument that neither wealth nor any other goods may constitute happiness; they are only means, although important in certain circumstances in order to be happy, to lead a good life.

The *Nicomachean Ethics* contains the first systematic theory of *eudaimonia* in relation to virtue, thus making of the Aristotelian ethics of virtues an irreplaceable reference for any later theory of happiness in the western world. While the reflection on the connection between happiness and *philia* was not new to the Greek world, in the *Nicomachean Ethics* Aristotle "invents" a new theory of happiness that is deeply related to *philia*.

4. Eudaimonia and philia

According to Aristotle, *eudaimonia* is not a static reality, but rather a sort of movement or activity, whose essential characteristic is to occur only when its pursuit is not instrumental to something else: it is a "prize of virtue" (NE I, 9, 1099b, p. 104). It is good life, human flourishing; Aristotle identifies being happy with "living well and doing well" (I, 4, 1095a, p. 87).

---

formal constituents of the eudaimonic condition, he characterizes *eudaimonia* as a state of autonomy, of self-completeness. The eudaimonic condition puts man in a condition of fullness. In virtue of its being perfect and self-sufficient (*téleion kai aútarkes*) (NE 1097b 20), *eudaimonia* is then something that suffices by itself to make life pleasurable, complete and perfect in itself". (2009, pp. 2–3)

[18] If "beyond" *eudaimonia* something else existed, *eudaimonia* would be different: it would be a reality including something else to come. This is also the reason that the Greek notion of happiness (and Aristotelian ethics in particular) was never fully integrated within the Christian humanism: in Christianity joy may be fully attained only in the afterlife; in life we may experience an earthly happiness which is never complete (hence we never live in *eudaimonia*). Perhaps this could also be the reason that Christianity preferred other words to happiness: joy, delight, bliss. In the New Testament Christianity remains adherent to the Jewish notion of "blessing", so that the most frequent term is *"makarios"* (blessed) which occurs frequently, for instance, in the Sermon on the Mount (the Beatitudes). Another term more rarely employed is the locution *"eu ghenetai"*, which means "to be well" (cf. Mt 5:1–11; Lc 6;20–23; Gc 1:25; Ef 6:3).

Therefore "in Aristotle happiness is strictly connected with virtues, intended not in a moralistic sense, but as action, activity". The ancient root of 'areté' is 'ar', which gives origin to both 'virtue' and 'art'. Virtue is therefore to be understood in the same sense as we would call an acrobat "virtuous", that is, being capable of excellence (Natoli 2003). The English Utilitarian philosopher H. Sidgwick stated in his *Methods of Ethics* that "even the English term Happiness is not free from [...] ambiguity". And he adds: "It seems, indeed, to be commonly used in Bentham's way as convertible with Pleasure" (1901, p. 92). In a footnote he also reminds us that "the fact that, after all, we have no better rendering for *eudaimonia* than 'Happiness' or 'Felicity' has caused no little misunderstanding of his [of Aristotle's] system" (ibid., footnote 2).[19]

Happiness is therefore the indirect (non-instrumental) result of a virtuous life. The term *eudaimonia* originally meant (in the pre-philosophic age) "good demon" (*eu daimon*), thus indicating that *eudaimonia* may only be attained by those who have on their side a good demon, that is, a good fortune.

The word *daimon*, whose etymological origin remains uncertain (perhaps from the verb *daiomai*, "to distribute", it might indicate "he who distributes destiny") is a term whose meaning remains largely obscure and certainly ambiguous. In the great Homeric poems, as in Greek tragedies, it designates a divine power, which differs from the gods, i.e. from the *theos;* it is a force that is external to man and may rather be assimilated to destiny, fate, or fortune as it cannot be controlled by the subject. This view of the *daimon* remained virtually unchanged until Socrates and Plato, when it underwent a semantic turn. The *daimon* was so important in Socrates' philosophy that Socrates' very mission was to listen to the *daimon* guiding him from within. It was also partly due to his special and unprecedented relationship with the *daimon* that

---

[19] *Eudaimonia* then is not a search for pleasure, since only "men of the most vulgar type, seem (not without some ground) to identify the good, or happiness, with pleasure" (NE, 1095b). Pleasure can only be a sign that the action is good, that it is virtuous; pleasure is the sign of the value of an activity, not his goal: "virtuous actions are such, so that these are pleasant [...] in their own nature" (NE, 1099a). This is the reason that the neo-Aristotelian philosophers in the American–English world prefer to render *eudaimonia* not as happiness, but as human flourishing, for in ordinary language nowadays happiness may also designate a temporary euphoria, unconcerned contentedness, a pleasant feeling, or pleasure *tout court*. Elisabeth Anscombe (1958) was the first to translate *eudaimonia* as "human flourishing".

Socrates was accused of atheism: he did not follow traditional gods – "external", made of stone, but the voice of God (the *daimon*) talking to him from within. This change in the notion of *daimon* has an impact on Greek post-Socratic philosophy, which would consequently modify its notion of the word *eudaimonia*, no longer related to fate, fortune, or to the will of distant gods, but now seen as the full development of one's own vocation, as the attainment of excellence, as the liberation of one's *"genius"* (as it was called by the Latins and as it is still called in the western world with reference to artists or people "of genius").

With Socrates, the word *eudaimonia* acquires new meanings, and the idea starts to emerge that man's choices may lead him to happiness, as a process of individual growth, listening and obeying one's inner *daimon* (Natoli 2003; Nussbaum 1996, 2005). Above all, the great idea starts to arise that it is possible to emancipate the good life from fortune through the practice of virtues and this will be one of the pillars of the Greek philosophic thought. The virtuous man can no longer be attacked and defeated by fortune: such great anthropological promise inaugurates the remarkable season of Socrates' philosophy, soon followed by Plato's and Aristotle's – and arriving through them to western philosophy.[20]

In spite of Greek philosophy's attempt to separate *eudaimonia* from luck, happiness and fortune were and are, as a matter of fact, two over-lapping concepts. This initial meaning has been maintained in several modern Anglo-American languages: in German *glück* means both happiness and fortune, *"happiness"* comes from "to happen".

Such ambivalence has not disappeared and the entire research project about the measurement of happiness is subject to this semantic ambiguity.[21] A different etymology marks the Latin word *felicitas*, from the

---

[20] Greek philosophy (among others) will indicate the practice of virtues as the way for the liberation of one's own *daimon*, in order to prevent it from remaining trapped in the cages of our passions. In Christianity, the doctrine of the *daimon* follows an ambiguous evolutionary path, partly due to the encounter between the Greek and the Jewish cultural universes. On one side, it becomes a sort of devil, the Demon, a worldly presence (not inside man) which divides (*dia-ballo*), separates and leads to unhappiness when its temptations and voices are seconded. At the same time, traces of the Greek *daimon* may be found in the angels, as well as in the Person of the Holy Spirit, whose inner voice guides and gives direction to human actions.

[21] The questionnaires used for empirical research often distinguish between "happiness" and "life satisfaction", with the purpose to capture through the latter the more "eudaimonic" dimension of well-being: as far as I know, such twofold distinction is not employed in methodological and theoretical works.

prefix *fe*, which recalls the terms *fecundus, femina, ferax*; it recalls the concept of fecundity, and hence the cultivation of humanity: in the Latin culture *infelix* designates the sterile tree, which gives no fruit – an idea of happiness which is therefore closer to the idea of the cultivation of virtues rather than to the mythical idea of "fortune".

5. Happiness and others

A remarkable evolution has then characterized the word *eudaimonia* in the passage from *mytos* to *logos*, reflecting also the evolution of the concept of *daimon*. It is through the analysis of *philia* that the Aristotelian theory of *eudaimonia* may be fully appreciated. Aristotle defines happiness as "a virtuous activity of the soul [hence not external]" (NE, 1099b). The core idea in the Aristotelian reading of happiness concerns its *civil* or political nature:

> Surely it is strange, too, to make the supremely happy man a solitary; for no one would choose the whole world on condition of being alone, since man is a political creature and one whose nature is to live with others. Therefore even the happy man lives with others.... Therefore the happy man needs friends.
>
> NE, IX, 9, 1169b

And later: "What it is that we say political science aims at and what is the highest of all goods achievable by action.... Both the general run of men and people of superior refinement say that it is happiness" (NE, I, 4, 1095a). Happiness is the end of politics, because it "spends most of its pains on making the citizens to be of a certain character, good and capable of noble acts" (NE, I, IX, 1099b). Political life[22] is then the only place in which it is possible to experience happiness fully: "It is natural, then, that we call neither ox nor horse nor any other of the animals happy; for none of them is capable of sharing in such activity" (ibid.). For happiness "there is required, as we said, not only complete virtue but also a complete life" (ibid.). Moreover, like we already said, only the free man may be happy (slaves, like animals, cannot "flourish" as human beings). The political nature of the happy life is extremely significant for what we are about to say.

---

[22] It should be noted that Aristotle, like the entire tradition of classical thought, makes no distinction between civil and political society, a distinction which shall emerge with the modern thought.

Friendship, which is a virtue for Aristotle and is therefore more important than wealth, being also part of *eudaimonia*, is also in some sense an end (while wealth is always a means):

> For without friends no one would choose to live, though he had all other goods; even rich men and those in possession of office and of dominating power are thought to need friends most of all; for what is the use of such prosperity without the opportunity of benefi-icence, which is exercised chiefly and in its most laudable form towards friends? Or how can prosperity be guarded and preserved without friends? The greater it is, the more exposed is it to risk. And in poverty and in other misfortunes men think friends are the only refuge.
>
> NE, VIII, 1, 1155a, p. 339[23]

This is another central point required to understand the significance of Aristotle's ethics with reference to our inquiry. Like Socrates and Aristotle, Plato aimed at making happiness independent from good fortune, by suggesting that the wise man should detach himself from external circumstances. Among such external factors, Plato – as well as Epicurus, Plotinus, and many other authors in ancient times – used to include also relations with others, so that individual happiness would not have to depend on the free responses of others and so that happiness could be self-sufficient, the perfect good independent of anything else. Aristotle, instead, argues for an essentially relational and social nature of *eudaimonia*, and for the need to have friends at all times in life, because even the perfect man, who contemplates good for its own sake, always needs friends, for there is no good life alone:

> Now by self-sufficient we do not mean that which is sufficient for a man by himself, for one who lives a solitary life, but also for parents,

---

[23] Even trade and exchange, as highlighted by K. Polanyi (1957), follows from the requirement of *philia*, i.e., that the good will among the members persist. For without it, the *community* itself would cease. The just price, then, derives from the demands of *philia* as expressed in the reciprocity which is of the essence of all human community. And thus the entire original (and in many ways surprising) theory of chrematistics (the art of commercial exchange), which is extremely critical and problematic, may be explained with reference to *philia* as foundation of the polis: if the exchange and the pursuit of money distract human beings from virtue, the commercial bond "puzzles" the social bonds of friendship, thus turning the search of happiness into an uncivil pursuit.

children, wife, and in general for his friends and fellow citizens, since man is born for citizenship [*anthropos estì zòon politikòn*].

NE, I, 7, 1097b

Thus he writes in the *Eudemian Ethics:* "we consider a *friend* to be one of the greatest goods, and friendlessness and *solitude* a very *terrible* thing" (VII, 1234b). Civil commitment, or political life, has an intrinsic value, which is necessary for human life to flourish. *Eudaimonia* must be self-sufficient (it cannot depend on "fortune"); at the same time, some essential components of the good life have to do with others: having a civil life, friends, loving and being loved, are all essential for the happy life. And this is where, as effectively noted by Martha Nussbaum (1996[1986]), the Aristotelian theory of life in common becomes exposed – or might become exposed, as we shall see – to paradox. Raphael's painting, the "School of Athens", is a splendid icon that allows to present the two souls of Greek philosophy: by raising a finger towards the sky, Plato indicates the contemplation of beauty in itself; while Aristotle, embracing his *Nicomachean Ethics*, points to the earth with his open hand (perhaps to recall the multiplicity that is always associated with the *civitas*).

At this point it is possible to grasp the paradoxical and anti-nomic nature that Martha Nussbaum above all others perceives in Aristotle's moral philosophy, in which a substantial role is played by the so-called "relational goods" (Gui and Sugden 2005), an expression which Nussbaum herself helped to create and spread within the scientific community in the 1980s. In Aristotle's work, relational goods are friendship (by virtue), mutual love and political commitment – activities which, in view of their being made of relations, may only be enjoyed in reciprocity:

> Mutual activity, feeling, and awareness are such a deep part of what love and friendship are that Aristotle is unwilling to say that there is anything worthy of the name of love or friendship left ... But if this is so [...] then these components of the good life are going to be minimally self-sufficient. And they will be vulnerable in an especially deep and dangerous way.
>
> Nussbaum [1986][1986], p. 344

By stating the important role of relational goods for the happy life ("the happy man needs friends") Aristotle paradoxically makes happiness *fragile*, because he leaves it exposed to the *power of fortune*. But, as we shall see in the next chapter, Aristotle also possesses an antidote against this possible paradox.

One first antidote to the frailty of life in common, somehow the most radical, had already been indicated by Plato. The centre of his metaphysical and ethical system is the individual (male, free, adult, not overly poor, and citizen) and his path *to the attainment of truth*. The relationship with the other, *philia* is above all a means used by the philosopher, in his younger years, to achieve perfection. Plato's typical form of love is not *philia* (which is more Aristotelian), but *eros*, which is a form of love that remains self-centred. In the wake of Socrates' humanistic project, Plato discovers, and with Socrates somehow "invents", the individual and invites him to self-realization through philosophy, that allows everyone to free one's *daimon* (think of Socrates', and Plato's, saying "know yourself").

In line with the Greek idea of *eudaimonia* as perfect good and self-sufficient, Plato invites the individual to be independent of others and not be subjected to reciprocity. The project of his humanism is fully coherent: just like man ought not to depend on material goods in order to avoid being vulnerable to fortune, in the same way, he should not expose himself to relations with another, which, not unlike material goods, would expose him to the fragility of reciprocity. The relation with others renders one dependent, fragile and vulnerable: the Platonic solution to the frailty of the *communitas* is then radical, as it indicates the renunciation of relationality itself as a solution to the frailty of the good life. The Platonic solution, therefore, does not address the ambivalence of the *communitas*, but is rather a negation of the *communitas* (this is why we mention it here and not in the next chapter). It is, however, a solution of surprising philosophical coherence, even though it opens up a radical question: could the good life, flourished, realized, not be *civil*? May we realize our potential without exposing ourselves to the ambivalence of a relation of *philia* with another?

There is not much that we need to add in order to appreciate the influence that the Neoplatonic doctrine exerted in the Middle Ages, at least until the Renaissance, on the concept of good life. Monasticism, which we will consider briefly in the next chapter, is also (but clearly not simply) the fruit of the encounter between Neoplatonism and Christianity, with a specific note: prayer, the relation with God as an escape from other men and women, is a form of relation perceived without frailty – a concept already present, to some extent, also in Plato.

In the next chapter we shall address some of the solutions that have been proposed to avoid the radical vulnerability of the good life, including those offered by Aristotle himself and by the biblical tradition. Later on, in the central part of this essay, we shall focus on the solution offered by market economy, which lies at the centre of the western trajectory, of its ethos and its paradoxes.

3
Solutions to the Ambivalent Quality of Life in Common

> Unable to strengthen justice, they have justified might; so that the just and the strong should unite, and there should be peace, which is the sovereign good.
>
> Blaise Pascal, *Pensées*

1. *Communitas* as *immunitas*

In the previous chapter we have seen how the tragic character of life in common was first recognized in Greece and Israel. We are still far from the tragic dimension of the modern age, which we will discuss later, and yet we can already discern the prodromes that much later will evolve into modern humanism. In this chapter I wish to outline some of the solutions or, as we shall see, some of the escape routes that have been proposed in response to the fragility of the *communitas*. These solutions have in common what Esposito and others have called *immunitas*, albeit none of them mention that the main place of *immunitas* is actually the market, the economic space – which is what I try to demonstrate in the final part of this essay.

The argument of this chapter, which is one key point of this work, may be formulated by way of an antinomy: the most radical solution to the ambivalence of the *communitas* is the *communitas* itself.

As the community exchanges, trades, or fights with other communities, the basic relational structure of pre-modern societies necessitates the intervention of a mediator (typically sacred) in all intra- and inter-communitarian relations. Inside the community the hierarchy operates and orders the various relationships, as I have tried to illustrate in the following figure.

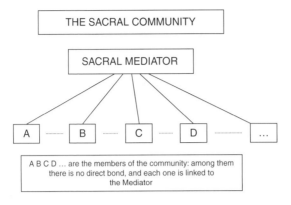

Figure 3.1   The sacral community

We have seen that in the ancient sacred community there is as yet
no binding agreement between its single members, but each of them
is hierarchically subordinated to the head of the community (king,
father, shaman...) according to status (i.e. not according to contract,
nor to agreement). For as long as human cultures have adopted structures that reflect this scheme I have called the "sacred", horizontal
relationality has never presented itself as a problem, for the simple
reason that the subjects of the problem, i.e. individuals, did not yet
exist. Relations between members were mediated in the space of the
sacred and in the space of the authority (hypostases of the community), thus preventing the autonomous emergence of horizontal
relations.[1] We argue, in line with Esposito, that the ancient *communitas*
is founded upon *nothing*, meaning that there are no horizontal bonds
(notice the dotted lines in Figure 3.1). Let us consider Weber's definition of community: "A social relationship will be called "communal"
if and so far as the orientation of social action... is based on a subjective feeling of the parties, whether affective or traditional, that they
belong together" (1978[1968] p. 40).

In the ancient community there is no "subjective feeling of the
parties that they belong together", because, quite simply, *there are
no individual parties, no individuals*. Esposito's remarks about the

---

[1] Clearly, free and equal relations of friendship have always existed in the
ancient world (think of Socrates and of Job in the Bible): my claim is rather that
this type of relation cannot be taken as representing the culture of the ancient
world.

community as a "nothing-in-common",[2] then, certainly apply to the ancient community even though the *munus* is not ambivalent between gift and obligation: *it is solely obligation*, not gift. The latter would require a kind of freedom that is foreign to the ancient world. It is only the modern observer who perceives the "nothing-in-common" of the ancient community, whereas the ancients could not even conceive the cultural possibility of a *communitas* of individuals. In the modern community, on the other hand, such a "nothing" (caused by reciprocity being under constant threat) is quite different from the "nothing" of the ancient *communitas*. The tragic quality of fraternity (intended as the foundational paradigm of free and vulnerable relations between equals) needs the appearance, on the horizon of mankind, of this new event that is the rise of the individual, who carries along his new radical equality with other individuals and his freedom. This process occurred differently in different cultures and if we had the means, we would certainly find it, albeit with different characteristics, in the great Chinese, Indian, African, American, and Celtic cultures, and so on.

From the archaic community up to the modern age, and still today in several non-western cultures, the sacred community *becomes the archetype of immunitas*: a radical *immunitas*, unchosen yet very real. The *communitas* and its hierarchical hypostases come between individuals, giving rise to the most radical immunity, that is, man's immunity towards himself: unlike the community hypostases, man is subject to no *munus* other than his unilateral duty towards the *communitas*.[3] Despite being the archetype of every ancient community, in real communities this relational dynamic rarely takes such a pure configuration. So, for instance, we may not grasp the modern age in the great contractarian tradition unless we start by looking at this mediating community that modern man, on his way to becoming an individual, sees as the most

---

[2] Thus Esposito: "communitas is the totality of persons united not by a "property" but precisely by an obligation or a debit; not by an "addition" [plus] but by a "subtraction" [minus]: by a lack, a limit that is configured as an onus, or even as a defective modality for him who is "affected", unlike for him who is instead "exempt" or "exempted" (2009, p. 6). In fact, I wish to add, in an Aristotelian fashion, that he who is "exempt" in the pre-modern world can only be a "god" or a "beast", since in ancient cultures belonging to a *communitas* is a need, not a choice: this is the difference between the ancient *communitas* and the modern community.

[3] About the King's rights and obligations, see for instance the books of Deuteronomy (17, 24–20) and of Samuel (8).

radical obstacle to the affirmation of the great modern principles: equality, freedom, and most importantly, fraternity.[4]

The various solutions we outline in the next few pages are also somehow different declinations of the great solution that is the *communitas* archetypical of pre-modern society, which are essential to understanding Hobbes and pre-modern political science as well as the birth of modern political economy.

It is necessary, however, to add an important *caveat*. We must remember that the concept of *immunitas* bears also a great positive meaning that makes modernity a 'point of no return' for anyone who believes in a free society of free individuals, living with dignity and autonomy. Immunity is also one of the dimensions of a good society, for the reason that the archaic society, the ancient community, did not guarantee every citizen's immunity in terms of rights and freedoms (but only of some, in fact very few, among the male, adult, wealthy citizens, and preferably non-workers).[5] *Immunitas* also means protection from the abuses of those who do not respect the dignity of others. Here too "only" and "without" are important words: there is no good life, both individual and civil, *without* immunity; there is no good life that has *only* immunity as the new ethos, the ethos of modernity and of the market. If the fearful thought that the other might "hurt" me (as someone who is free and other than myself) turns into a system of total and generalized protection from every relationship – if it leads to the sterilization of every affective relational component from public life (where several immunities are important and even essential) to private life – then the ethos of immunity typically leads to poor patterns of life that, in the long run, may even cross the limit of what is human.

2. *Jus* and law

2.1 The Covenant

A certain analogy exists between the juridical solution to the ambivalence of life in common (considered in the next paragraph) and some

---

[4] We shall not forget that the modern individual finds a radical conflict between fraternity (not just freedom and equality) and community. It is in fact worth noticing that fraternity too was considered by the founders of the modern society as a new principle for the new world, because the "old" fraternity, based on blood and natural affiliation, was one of the enemies of the later conception, that older fraternity usually being coupled with inequality and serfdom.

[5] I am grateful to Martha Nussbaum for this important remark.

aspects of the Law in the Jewish tradition.[6] With the people of Israel, God establishes a Covenant, a pact, in which each party enters a commitment to give and take. The Covenant may be considered also (but not exclusively) an answer to the ambivalent nature of life in common.[7]

The book that deals most closely with the content of the Covenant is Deuteronomy, which revolves around the figure of Moses as mediator in the Covenant between the people and JHWH.[8] Israel had previously established covenants with several foreign powers (Egypt, Babylonia, Assyria), but these had brought only famines and humiliations. The opportunity to subscribe a covenant was always offered by the dominating power, but never on a level of equality: these presented Israel with its only hope of survival (as opposed to complete devastation and/or slavery) after suffering the domination of a foreign power and the destruction of its cities.[9]

---

[6] Here we merely skim this theme, which would otherwise deserve more extensive consideration.

[7] Historically, the Covenant starts to settle in the conscience of Israel as a category starting especially from the exodus to Egypt, as with Moses Israel starts to assume the identity of a people (rather than a group of tribes). The traditions and myths that had been handed down and tell about the patriarchs start now to be read in the framework of the Covenant between the people and JHWH, the only God. The theme of Israel's monotheism, one of the fundamental traits of its religion as opposed to other cults from the Mesopotamian area, is still today at the heart of many controversies. One increasingly accepted argument, already mentioned by Freud (1977) in his essays about Moses and monotheism, traces back the cult of a single God to the Egyptian period, an argument further sustained today by Moses' almost certain Egyptian origins (he had an Egyptian name and had not been circumcised).

[8] Deuteronomy is a Book whose finding is ascribed by Jewish history (Book of Kings) to King Josiah (640–609 B.C.), who recovered it during the reconstruction of Solomon's Temple. We cannot exclude that the recovering of the book inside the Temple might be a political–literary artifice by the author of Kings (or by Josiah, and hence historical) aimed at giving a more ancient and solemn foundation to King Josiah's religious reformation. The "recovered" book described in Kings is Deuteronomy (or at least its central part, focused on the Law, chapters 12–26). In fact the refurbishment of Solomon's Temple by Josiah is itself a sign of that religious reformation (a response to the decadence of the worship of JHWH in the reign of Josiah's father and grandfather). Based on the recovered ancient text of the Covenant (which contains a sort of "second" law), Josiah initiates a religious reformation of Israel by fighting idolatry (the cult of Baal, for instance) and renewing the ancient Covenant with the one God, and placing it at the origin of the history and identity of Jewish people.

[9] The alliance offered by the great powers at the time was in fact a vassalage agreement: the people who had lost the war, or who recognized their inferiority

As the superpower Assyria loosened its grip, Josiah, in the attempt to gather back together several different tribes no longer tied by bonds of blood or clan, tried to re-launch the identity of Israel by proposing a new Covenant.[10] In order for this new covenant to be effective, however, it was necessary (in accordance with the principles of middle-eastern culture) that it be *more ancient* than the ones offered by the neighbouring powers: the covenant with JHWH, the relationship at the origin of the history of the patriarchs Abraham, Isaac and Jacob – Israel was this new, yet ancient, alliance, with deeper roots.

For this reason, the Covenant[11] between God and Israel has the same structure used in the pacts between nations or even in vassalage agreements. Through king Josiah, Israel chooses a (new) covenant with JHWH, still a Lord, not equal in power, but loving, loyal, and forgiving (yet also punishing) – a Lord who makes a new "promise", like he had done with Abraham before. The pact is asymmetrical (the offer, for example, came from God), but it keeps some symmetry, because each part commits to give and take. *The fruit of the covenant* will be the Law, the Torah.

The Covenant is described in the Bible through the term *berît*, which literally means to "slash" (cutting through in the middle – of slaughtered animals, for instance, like Abraham in *Genesis*, 15, 9). Not only is the pact binding for God, but also for Abraham and his descendants: they will have to commit to be loyal to God. The Covenant is very similar to a commercial/political contract, but it is certainly not the same: there is no equivalence of exchanged goods, no symmetry between the parties, no external enforcement, which instead are left to the parties themselves; and finally the Covenant entails the possibility of forgiving and starting over, unlike the contract. Even though,

---

if confronted with the threat of a foreign attack, had the chance to submit to becoming a vassal, committing to the payment of a (very high) tribute and to accept the customs and religion of the winning power. In the middle-eastern world, vassalage hence stood mid-way between slavery and a commercial contract.

[10] As shown by several biblical texts (e.g. Book of Kings, Book of Jeremiah, and others), the Covenant with JHWH is also a pact between the various tribes of Israel. The Law has two dimensions: a vertical one, more foundational and radical; but also a horizontal one, via which the tribes find in the Law a bond that unites them in a moment of crisis and of re-launch (or even creation) of Israel's unity as one people.

[11] This is especially true of the alliance with Moses. The first covenant, with Abraham, had a different structure (this is the covenant emphasized by Paul, in his Letter to the Romans, as the more original one). That first covenant did not present the synallagmatic structure of the later covenant with Moses.

as we have seen, the Bible adopts the image of the political-economic vassalage, the Covenant is not limited to this: so, for instance, among the images illustrating the Covenant we even find the metaphor of marriage (cf. Hosea).[12]

Moses' story and character may be read as the great story of the development of the Covenant – a much richer relationship than the laws and commandments that make up Deuteronomy, for instance: the Law is essentially a reciprocal relation of love between God and Israel. The great gift of God to his people as a result of the Covenant is the Law, the Torah, which, if obeyed, shall allow Israel to become a great people, but also – and this is the point – to overcome its inner conflicts. The Torah is also a response to Cain's fratricidal act and to other fratricidal fights in Genesis, culminating in Lamek the murderer, whose song of revenge echoes old and broken relations: "I have killed a man for wounding me, a young man for injuring me. If Cain is avenged seven times, then Lamek seventy-seven times" (*Genesis* 4, 23–24).

Men, sons of Cain, lived outside Eden in a condition very similar to Hobbes' "state of nature", a condition of *bellum omnium contra omnes*. The Law, donated to the people of Israel as the fruit of the Covenant with God, has a similar function[13] to Hobbes' Leviathan: i.e. to allow

---

[12] Moreover, the prophets, and Jeremiah in particular, will remember that the Covenant with God stands on a different level compared to other political alliances; to the point that Jeremiah will do everything in his power to persuade Israel of the impossibility of resisting Babylonia, and hence of the need to surrender and accept a vassalage agreement: the Covenant with JWHW lies on a different level and is not affected directly by any political events or other vassalage agreements known at that time in middle-eastern culture. On this point Jeremiah's argument differs from the one championed by Isaiah (also in view of the new historical and geopolitical context) who, less than a century earlier, asked that Israel not surrender to the Assyrians. The prophets will interpret the entire story of the relationship between God and the chosen people as an alliance that is more than a contract between states, and for this reason they will claim, on one side, submission to the Alliance and to the Law of the King; and on the other side the uniqueness of Israel in comparison to any other people. They will read the Covenant as a love story that began previously in Eden, then became more evident with Noah and later with Abraham, as described in Chapter 15 of Genesis (i.e. the alliance established through the offer of slaughtered animals traversed by God), and in the tradition described in Chapter 17 (1–8).

[13] Jewish Law is obviously more than this, i.e. this is not its only function: the Law is much more: it is also a matter of love, of caring for the poor and the orphan, it is forgiveness and Jubilee and still much more. The institution of the Jubilee, for instance, is an extraordinary invention that consists in giving each

life in common to be good and peaceful, a life that men lost as a consequence of sin, as part of the history they built for themselves. After Cain a new sociality becomes necessary, which ought to be possible, good and worthy of the Covenant: the Law has arrived to make this possible.

It is no surprise, then, that Hobbes decided to found his own political theory upon a strong analogy between the Covenant of God with Israel (via the mediation of Abraham and later of Moses) and the modern State, founded upon the social contract with the Leviathan's mediation. And it is certainly not a coincidence that Hobbes, both in *De cive* and in the *Leviathan*, dedicates considerable attention to the story of Israel and Christianity as a pact, an alliance, between God and the people of the Covenant. Even the image of the Leviathan, a horrible monster similar to a large crocodile, was borrowed from the Bible (Book of Job).

The Law, therefore, is also *a remedy to the failure of the first community* outside Eden, a Mediator who should allow life in common to be good and peaceful. At the same time, Jewish Law is unique, and therefore similar yet different compared to any other law or juridical systems that may share some of the Torah's characteristics.

2.2 *Jus as immunitas*

Thus writes Aldo Schiavone on the topic of law in the opening pages of *The Invention of Law in the West*:

> Law is a social and mental form that has invaded modernity, quickly becoming an essential component of our lives – and it is a form invented by the ancient Romans
>
> 2012, p. 3

We have mentioned before that the contract was conceived in the modern age in opposition to status. In fact, it also represents the evolution of another ancient category, namely the Covenant or Pact. In the ancient community the primary form of pact was not the contract between individuals (who, as said, did not yet exist) but the Covenant, which is a holistic–communitarian concept. The contract[14] is an evolution of

---

person at least one second chance over a lifetime. In this paragraph I wish to suggest that in the experience of the Law there is also one attempt to respond to the ambivalence of life in common.

[14] Intended, in the modern sense, as exchange of equivalent values, as the tie that keeps together individuals who are radically untied, the new "bond of society" of subjects who have been freed from the sacred, who need law (the

the Covenant, which was originally a *pact* between communities; it was hardly ever founded on the exchange of equivalent values or on values independent of status. People (the community hypostases) are what matters in an alliance, while things are only means By contrast, things lie at the core of the contract and people become means for the satisfaction of individual preferences, yesterday and today.

The possibility of exchanging with strangers, and hence the birth of market economy made possible by the contract, was the result of a slow evolution, a century-long transition. From Mesopotamia to the late Roman Empire and through the Middle Ages, this process has come to a total laicization of the law:

> In the concepts of alliance and exchange, which from part of the prehistory of the contract, things and persons are not yet clearly distinguished, and roundabout ways are used to ensure control of time. In the case of *alliance*, things are grasped only through persons.
>
> Supiot 2007, pp. 86–87

As highlighted by Schiavone, Roman law was the first juridical system centred on things as distinct and separate from persons, and for this reason it may well be considered as the invention of law itself. At the same time, Roman law was embedded in a complex system of sacred and religious references, including the complex and yet essential role of the goddess *Fides* (faith) and of the principle of *bona fides* – as well as the categories of *aequitas*. It is in Rome that private law starts to "see" the individual and to give relevance to the subject (especially on the matter of contracts and successions).

Institutions such as the covenant, or the pact, are deeply linked to relations of blood, spiritual and ritual, as well as to relations created through marriage or political agreements. Even the language of the Covenant between God and Israel, as we learn from Deuteronomy, is characterized by the same symbols and structure of political and commercial agreements between nations.[15]

The ancient pact, however, has the limitation (unbearable for the modern man) of being a holistic unity, structurally hierarchical, like the

---

one guaranteed by the Leviathan) to be able to exchange with foreigners and hence may be totally untied from each other as long as they recognize the same authority on the basis of mutual interest and mutual advantage only.

[15] The new covenant of Christianity is established through blood (Christ's), just as the ancient alliance was established through the blood of a lamb during the night of the great passage (Easter).

community it expresses and by which, at the same time, it is expressed: it is never a pact between individuals who are equal in virtue of their being humans; equality is between communities or peoples. Even between God and the people of Israel we may observe a certain kind of equality (a great novelty in the context of ancient religions), but not between single subjects.

The long process leading up to the laicization of the law and the passage from the covenant (or holistic pact) to the individualistic contract as the first means of regulation of social relations, both occurred across *Christianitas*. The latter represented the communitarian universe (*ekklesia*) that supplied the context of spiritual kinship (with the church as Christ's body) in which the contracts could take place. Until the modern age, contracts cannot be clearly distinguished from alliances or pacts[16] (neither in theory nor in practice). In the Middle Ages contracts and exchanges were indeed carried out, *but a stranger, being a Christian, was never altogether different or foreign.*[17]

For a long time, Christian fraternity served as the great cultural mediator that allowed the transformation of the pact into the contract – and it is no coincidence that such transformation only happened in the West.

The contract thus becomes the typical bond of the modern age, since, in contrast to the covenant and to the pact, in the contract and exchange, "persons are grasped through things" (ibid.). At the same time, according to a logic that emerges systematically in the history of mankind, without *Christianitas* we would not have the modern lay notion of contract, for we would be missing a third party: the guarantor of the other's promises and word.

The pact is not just a contract (intended, as we shall see, as a relation between peers and without gratuitousness); it is *also* a contract, but comprehends elements that, in more classic terms, we might call *of philia* and *agape* (like forgiveness, for example). In modern times, the Modern State and the Market become this new "Third Party" that makes the contract possible, whether private or social – outside sacred or

---

[16] Think, for instance, of the role that the sense of sin and divine condemnation play for people who do not keep their word. The sense of sin represented an especially effective form of contract enforcement. Thus Supiot: "It is therefore due to belief in the existence of the one God, who sees all things and before whom no one must speak falsely, that the simple agreement (*nudum pactum*) ended up being identified with the contract" (ibid., p. 93).

[17] A different logic applies to the case of Jews in Europe and to the trading with the East, of which we say more in what follows.

communitarian bonds. On this point Supiot remarks: "The binary and horizontal dimension of exchange or alliance could not have become the homogeneous and abstract plane on which the market economy can flourish without the ternary, vertical dimension of the third party, which presides over the drawing up of contracts" (ibid., p. 93). This does not entail, as Supiot also shows, that modern age acquired its secular character immediately.

We must remember that the function of law has changed radically from the pre-modern to the modern world. The "ancient way", i.e. the Aristotelian–Thomistic tradition, as defined by philosopher of law Italo Mancini (1990), viewed law from a different perspective: as the main tool of justice. This thesis comes directly from the Aquinas:

> It is proper to justice, as compared with the other virtues, to direct man in his relations with others: because it denotes a kind of equality, as its very name implies; indeed we are wont to say that things are adjusted when they are made equal, for equality is in reference of one thing to some other. On the other hand the other virtues perfect man in those matters only which befit him in relation to himself. Accordingly that which is right in the works of the other virtues, and to which the intention of the virtue tends as to its proper object, depends on its relation to the agent only, whereas the right in a work of justice, besides its relation to the agent, is set up by its relation to others. Because a man's work is said to be just when it is related to some other by way of some kind of equality, for instance the payment of the wage due for a service rendered. And so a thing is said to be just, as having the rectitude of justice, when it is the term of an act of justice, without taking into account the way in which it is done by the agent: whereas in the other virtues nothing is declared to be right unless it is done in a certain way by the agent. For this reason justice has its own special proper object over and above the other virtues, and this object is called the just, which is the same as "right." Hence it is evident that right is the object of justice.
>
> Thomas Aquinas, *Summa Theologiae* II,2 q. 57 a. 1

Thus Mancini, after Etienne Gilson, comments on this sentence of Aquinas as follows:

> By practicing the law, man proceeds to improve the world in its most difficult aspect, that is, coexistence. Handing some right to

the weak ultimately obeys a biblical wont, as it demands to protect orphans and widows. Since the world is corrupted and will not turn just as it is supposed to turn, because it is relationships lack inno- cence... the first and most demanding duty of the strange Thomistic neologism, *iustari*, is precisely to adjust, to recompose what has been infringed, to help, to take care, all acts that presuppose the existence of the sick, a being who is not even with himself, someone who is in anguish, in difficulty. The law, when it is just – and there is no law or any of its activities that does not wish to accomplish this – is capable of doing so.

1990, p. 114 [my translation]

This view of law undergoes a profound crisis with the rise of the doctrine of natural law and especially with Hobbes. The "ancient way" of law as justice, i.e. as adjustment (*iustari*), could only gain its full signification in the context of a society intended as an organic entity, as a body of people united by *philia* (Aristotle) or by spiritual bonds (Aquinas). In the ancient law, we never find complete otherness, because the other is either an alter ego (as in Aristotle) or a brother in Christ (as in Aquinas). Therefore the other is never a complete stranger, totally other from me. What is important here is that this attention to otherness coexisted with status, something that justice had no power to *iustari*: if required by justice, law may adjust things, not persons, who continue to be defined by the natural community, thus maintaining their inequality. Ancient justice, from Aristotle to modernity, through Aquinas, was unable to "adjust" a status-related inequality: it could not allow the woman to be "adjusted" and made, in terms of individual rights, like man; or a serf to exit from his condi- tion of inferiority; or a layman to be equal to a priest. Between people so radically different in status, law could only make adjustments in terms of things (in principle even a feudatory could be condemned by a judge to compensate his serf), but the law would not question the radical inequality between them and the lack of freedom existing in their world.

Status-affecting adjustments, i.e. on persons and not just on things, are the result of the invention of the social contract tradition. As Hobbes theorizes the artificial birth of civil society through the social contract, he makes an operation that was unconceivable for the ancient way: he is introducing *iustari* in the domain of status, by adjusting relations between people. Such contractualistic invention creates the possibility of a new society, starting from scratch and annulling personal differences and differences of status in the natural society or "state of nature". In the world prior to the social contract, people are radically different and the social dynamic is founded upon the *iustari* of things and the non-*iustari* of people. At the same time, people are profoundly bound to each other, as suggested by the image of the body (of Christ and of the King, too); but it is precisely this image that shows us the hand is not the heart, and the head not a foot: among the various parts of the body there can be no *"iustari"*. With individuals – who come into the world like mushrooms (Hobbes) thanks to a theoretical device, with no family and no homeland or status – with them begins modernity and the possibility of operating, through the law, on personal differences: by cutting off the heads of kings and nobles, the French Jacobins were putting into practice the theoretical principles of *iustari*, no more and not only on things, but on persons too, on status. "The law is equal for all" regardless of personal status. Differences between people originate from goods, which ultimately refer to human labour (as the first article of the Italian Constitution also recites).

Modern society creates that "artificial" equality (in Hobbes' sense of "non-natural") between people, who now recognize each other no longer through reciprocal status, but through goods – not donated but exchanged. Exchange (both in the economic and political arenas) thereby becomes the main language used by modern individuals to communicate with each other. And goods are not ambivalent; they are not fragile. Hence unfolds the radical process of modernity, which has found in economic science one of its main expressions, well summarized by the great Italian economist Vilfredo Pareto, who re-founded twentieth century economic theory based on the assumption that true science progresses by replacing relations between people with relations between individuals and things (Pareto 1906).

Hobbes introduces a new idea of equality and justice, until then unknown to the ancient way based on the unequal *communitas*. The modern way invents a new view of law, whose primary aim becomes mutual immunization of the participants in the social contract.

The immunizing function of law culminates (since it is already incipient in every ancient juridical system) in modern law (private but also public), a function that has also been illustrated by Simone Weil, Luhmann and, in Italy, by Esposito: "Law is always of a part – never of all. This is the element that determines its fundamental contrast with the very same community whose protection it is dedicated to safeguarding – but in a form that defeats its most intrinsic connotation: in the modern juridical order, the common is only the claim of one owns" (Esposito 2002, p.13, *my translation*). And on Weil he adds: "In its function of immunization – *of* the community and *from* the community – law, whether private or public, has the same aspect of the *proprium*: in any case it is *proprium*, meaning that it "belongs" to the subject, public or private, who declares himself as the bearer of it" (ibid.). Luhmann is even more direct as he argues: *"the legal system serves* as society's immune system" (Luhmann 1990, p. 578, *my translation*).

The idea underpinned by this view of law as *immunitas* recalls the biomedical meaning of immunity and immunization: we try to become immune from a disease through a vaccine that instils in our body a part of the germ to be cured. The conflict that disintegrates the social body is cured by instilling conflict itself within the community, although in homeopathic quantities. Law (like every instrument of immunity) makes the community immune from the outside, immunizing also the inside, sterilizing also the more typically communitarian relations: personal, warm, emotional and certainly painful, but bearers of life. In post-modernity the vaccine is turning into a sort of chemotherapy, since the culture of modernity sees the wounds of the *communitas* as unbearable, as a cancer that must be killed in order not to be killed by it; but what if the disease were only a seasonal illness, one which the body might be able to naturally overcome? In other words, the radical violence, the potentially mortal wound that the introduction of law wishes to sterilize by leaving it outside the community walls, is in fact incorporated into law itself (the poison of the vaccine), which is capable of healing the inner communitarian relations by sterilizing that tragic relational charge that – alas – is exactly the specific character of the *communitas*, by killing the "cum" with the "munus" – a theme that is central for us and to which we shall return often in the following pages.

We must stop here, anyway. In the next paragraph we go back to Greece and to Aristotle to carry on our discussion.

3. The solution based on *philia*

One further attempt was made to reconcile the inextricable knot of wound and blessing life in common always entails. We may ascribe this attempt to Aristotle, whose works on ethics are so deeply concerned with the concept of *philia*, of friendship between equals. *Philia* represents yet another attempt to compose the paradox of the fragility of happiness that Aristotle was partly able to sense. Aristotle's genial insights about the need to have friends in order to lead a good life, considered above, should be read in the social and cultural context where a friend is not truly another *you,* equal to *I,* but rather an *alter ego,* another self, as Aristotle often remarks: "friend is another self" (*Nicomachean Ethics,* Book IX, p.9 1170b).[18] The reading of contemporary philosophers like Martha Nussbaum charges Aristotle's thought on civil life with "tragedy" – a reading that has influenced me and that I have found intriguing in previous works on happiness (in particular Bruni, 2006). But a closer look at Aristotle, considered as a man of his time, immediately reveals that a friend, as intended by the great Greek philosopher, is someone who has been accurately elected and chosen with a view to minimize the possibility of a negative answer, of a "no".

Aristotle believes that one may only have very few friends, because if they were many they would engender a greater heterogeneity and hence a greater risk of suffering the "wound" of reciprocity. In this sense, we may describe Aristotle's *philia* as elective and exclusive. Life in the polis is founded upon *philia* between few equal individuals (male, adults, free, belonging to the same ethnic group – mixed-race, like also peasants and merchants, were generally excluded; cf. Book I, *Politics*). While friends necessarily carry some diversity, for the sake of *eudaimonia* Aristotle encourages the cultivation of a "positive" kind of diversity between similar individuals who complement each other and share a common denominator; between them there is no separating and hurtful "no": *no authentic otherness* (based on diversity), not the kind of otherness that invests every communitarian relationship with tragedy and that will only truly emerge in the modern age. The polis of Aristotle (like the Greek polis in general)[19] *is a community of individuals who are equal,* not different. The art of politics therefore aims at minimizing the suffering and disorder associated with interpersonal dynamics. In the word "community" we should simultaneously read its two etymological precedents (also in line with the Aristotelian tradition), i.e. the

---

[18] Such a "you/alter-ego" has been the subject of several philosophies of otherness (from Emmanuel Levinas to Roberto Esposito) that attempted to overcome it through an exterior "he" who makes relationality open and transcendent: "Despite all rhetorical arguments that present the other as exceeding, in the comparison between two terms, he is only and always conceivable in relation to I. It cannot be but the non-I – its opposite and shadow" (Esposito 2007, p.129, *my translation*).

[19] The Roman *civitas* is instead less based on ethnicity and has a more universalistic vocation.

cum-munus and the *cum-moenia* (i.e. common walls). These are the two fundamental dimensions of the ancient community and they ought to stay together.

The polis is the only place for relations between equals, whereas all other communities within the polis (village and family) are founded on inequality. With regard to family, for instance, Aristotle argues that "the first and fewest possible parts of a family are master and slave, husband and wife, father and children" (*Politics* Book I, part, 2, 1232b), three types of relations characterized by radical inequality. The polis was to be a place of relations between equals, the final stage – and here lies the paradox of this political view – of a process of further aggregation of unequal communities. This is the reason that the State is in charge of education, which "should be one and the same for all " (*Politics*, Book VIII, part I, 1337a). As the space of relations between equals, the polis, not the *oikos*, is the place of ethics; the *oikos* is a place of politics and not economics, where relations are asymmetrical, being always between non-equals.

It is certainly no coincidence that whenever Aristotelian ethics has prevailed over Platonic ethics throughout western history there has been civil development, but also of social exclusion. So for instance, the mounts of pawns (*montes pietatis*), a wonderful institution of Italian civil humanism, mark one of the golden ages of Aristotelian ethics (cfr. Bruni and Zamagni 2007). They were expressions of civil virtue and, simultaneously, of exclusion of the different (of Jews, for instance). When *philia* is the prevailing dimension of life in common, *cum-munitas* and *cum-moenia* coexist.

Today the communitarian movement, from MacIntyre to Etzioni, refers to Aristotle as its main influence; and the ethics of virtue, under-pinning this new (and old) idea of community, is normally associated with a notion of *communitas* as community of equal, not different, individuals: as the *cum-moenia* defending the *cum-munus*. Even the cooperative movement based on mutuality was built, from the outset, on the notion of *philia* as elective friendship between equals, thus leading the Italian neoclassical economist Maffeo Pantaleoni (1898) to criticize cooperation not on the grounds of inefficiency or irrationality, but because of the lack of any difference between the cooperative and capitalistic firm: the latter was founded, as argued by Pantaleoni, on "individual" egoism and the former on "collective" egoism. Although we cannot fully agree with Pantaleoni (mutuality, like *philia*, is not necessarily synonymous with "collective egoism"), the natural evolu-tion of the cooperative movement has identified the need to add to the concept of "mutual benefit", typical of mutuality, the concept of "public benefit" in order to challenge the natural tendency to self-enclosure that is always inherent in *philia*.[20]

The solution of *philia*-between-equals, like modern communitarianism, *remains a form of immunitas*: it consists in surrounding oneself with alter-egos to avoid and lessen the threat arising from diversity, from promiscuity with the other, who is the same as me, but also different. This also partly explains why the various communities of equals historically have always been short-lived: from Robert Owen's "New Harmony" in the early nineteenth century (at the origin of the cooperative movement) to the Anglo-American garden cities. In the next chapter we shall see how, further to the downfall of the ancient *communitas* in the Middle Ages (partly due to the explosion of trades and of the cities), the Christian *philia* will become the new solution attempted in order to make life in common possible: once again we shall find its great potential and blessings, as well as its great difficulties.

First, however, we ought to consider one "non-solution" to the ambivalence of life in common: *agape*.

4. The non-solution of *agape*: the wounded communitas

We have seen earlier in this chapter that as soon as some of the great ancient cultures (Jewish, Greek, Roman) began to see the individual, and with him the possibility of otherness as a source of suffering and death, they started seeking to become immune from the threat of the "wound of otherness". Law (Torah), *jus*, Platonic contemplation and *philia* represent different realities, all of which share the same function: to prevent or reduce the tragedy of otherness from arising inside the *communitas*.

In fact, it is the Christian event that, in continuity with the experience of the Jewish people and with certain elements of the Greek and Roman cultures, allows the ambivalent character of the *communitas* to emerge truly as a dynamic of gift–obligation, of life-and-death. Due to the raging power of the *communitas*, some great ancient cultures (like the Biblical one) could merely sense what would later unfold in Christianity with unprecedented force and potential.

To present this argument we consider a sentence of the Italian philosopher Zanghì. This sentence summarizes the main steps of the

---

[20] I am thinking in particular of social cooperation, which, in its various forms, has affirmed itself in Europe over the last few decades.

discussion carried out so far about the ancient community, and introduces a new central theme in our inquiry:

> In fact, in the great pre-Christian civilizations there is no evidence
> of the social...but only of the political. Of course an intuition of
> the social is always present like a secret vein: think of the highest
> moments of the Roman republican ideal, of Israel at the time of
> the Judges, of some moments in Greek democracy, of the thought
> of some Greek and Roman philosophers, of Jewish prophetism, of
> eastern asceticism, of the Islamic *Ummah*. But such intuition has
> not proved a winning argument, nor could it be otherwise, which is
> understandable. Because the "natural" intelligence, fascinated by the
> Absolute, cannot admit to itself a real difference between the Absolute
> and the world; there can be no difference within the Absolute (so
> it thinks, and not wrongfully, given the elements available to it) –
> hence there can be no difference from the Absolute. The Absolute
> is everything. ... What is left, then, if not organizing the non-real in
> such way that it may, so to speak, be absorbed by the only true Real,
> that is the Absolute? Here, then, lies the denied utopia: here lies the
> political as organization of the illusion to save it from itself.
>
> 2008, p. 253

This view of life in common – which we labelled "sacred" – *truly* fell into
crisis with the arrival of the Christian event. The divine image revealed
by the Christian event was very different from the image elaborated by
the various ancient cultures: *an Absolute in itself manifold* (Trinity) that
represents a huge cultural event, not simply for (and far beyond) religion, and astonishing for the ancient man, for the Jew and the Greek.

Stoicism, unlike Aristotelian philosophy, had already emphasized the
universality of love. In Christianity, however, a new kind of relationship, i.e. *agape*, starts to emerge, whose universalistic nature spurs one
to love even the enemy (the non-friend, who may remain such in spite
of our love), thus breaking the tendency to electivity, which we have
seen being an inevitable aspect of *philia*.

The first Christians use the Greek word *agape* (almost a neologism)[21]
to convey this new dimension of love. This word thus becomes essential in order to express a way of loving that the repertoire of *eros* and

---

[21] The word "agape" already existed in the Greek language, although only as
the verbal form *agapan* and never as a noun, but also in the Greek translation of
the Bible by LXX.

philia cannot express. *Eros*, in fact, operates entirely on the level of desire and exchange; it knows no gratuitousness. *Philia* is by nature non-universal and elective. *Agape* is open to everyone. *Agape* is also not simply marital or maternal love, for these forms of love remain exclusive and non-universal – *agape* includes marital, paternal and maternal love.[22]

However, *agape* – as described in the writings of St Paul and in the four Gospels – is different from altruism. It is always inscribed within a framework of reciprocity. The new law of the community united by *agape* is the new commandment: "love one another; as I have loved you" (John 13, 34–35). The new and only commandment given by Jesus of Nazareth is addressed to a plurality of people: "love one another". The ethics of *agape* is not an individual ethics, nor simply a virtue ethics (even though they share several similarities), but we could instead define it as an ethics *of unconditional reciprocity*. Unlike *eros* or *philia*, *agape* is not *conditional*,[23] but without response from the people in our lives the humanism of *agape* cannot operate to its full extent.[24]

By choosing the Greek word "agape" from among all others,[25] the primitive Christian community chooses a term that was rather bland and rarely used in commonly spoken Greek. "*Agapan*" loosely meant "I like", "I choose", "I look after". It was filled with new and unquestionably broad meaning.[26] This is one of those cases where going back to the etymological origin of a word is not particularly helpful: Christians chose the word "agape" to convey the experience of a new type of love they had experienced by "elimination" of the other alternatives, as a less misleading choice for the concept they wanted to express. They

---

[22] Maternal love, as especially Freud taught us, may also be read through the perspective of *eros* (at least in the case of the mother–child relation). So a mother loves her child, but not necessarily or as much the children of others (unless other forms of love – *agape* – also play a role).

[23] Those who live in a state of *agape* do not condition their choice to love others to their behaviour: *philia* forgives "seven times"; *agape* "seventy-seven"; *philia* loves the friend, *agape* also loves the enemy, the ungrateful, etc.

[24] I believe there is no better definition of *agape* than the one given by Paul in his letter to the Romans (Chapter XIII).

[25] In the Greek language there are at least five different words for "love". Only three of them occur in the New Testament: *agape* comes up 250 times (90%); *phileo* (affection) 31 times (9.9%); *thelo*, only once.

[26] In Latin, *agape* was translated as *charitas*, a word that, without "h" (caritas), was a commercial word used to indicate the paucity of goods (caro = expensive, because scarce). The Latin *charitas* (with the "h") indicates instead a link between love and *charis*, grace, gratuitousness (cfr. Coda 1994).

intended to describe a kind of love that was unknown to the Greeks (and also in part to the Jews).[27]

It is here, within the humanism of *agape*, that *the tragedy of the communitas fully and truly begins*: those who freely embrace the agapic dimension of love realize they have an obligation towards others (the obligation to love them unconditionally and without measure),[28] but also that without reciprocity their life-project may not flourish: it cannot be accomplished in full (precisely because it is based, *by its very nature*, on reciprocity). In addition, the decision to join an agapic community is the free choice of an individual unbound from status, income, sex.[29] The new *communitas* is not initially bound by blood, family, clan, ethnicity, or land: none of the "natural" and elective mediations apply any longer. *Agape* thus creates an unprecedented form of cohabitation: fraternity between brothers who do not share the same blood – brothers we do not choose as "alter egos" (possibly with the aim to lower suffering of authentic otherness) but that we just find next to us; fellow travellers not chosen but "encountered" along the way.

---

[27] In fact, the word *agape* already appeared in the Ancient Testament, in the Song of Songs, in the third century BC. In the Greek translation of the Bible from Hebrew in Alexandria, the Greek translators were confronted with the translations of the Book of the Bible.... There was a kind of love that in Hebrew was expressed with the word *dodim*, which relates to the sphere of desire and was well-translated with *eros*: but for the term that expresses in Hebrew the concept of spousal love, involving eros but also a reciprocal gift, through the term *ahabà*, the Seventy could not find anything better than adopting the word *agape*, also chosen for the assonance from the verb "agapao" which appears already in Homer with the meaning of "taking care of". The story remains nonetheless quite complex. Consider, for instance, that in the only occurrence in the Canticle (5, 1), *dodim* is (erroneously?) translated as *adelphoi*. In the Book of Proverbs (7, 18) it is rendered as *philia*, while in the very same verse *ahava* (plural) is translated as eros, while in Ezekiel, *dodim* is translated twice as a participle of *katalyo* (Coda 1994). *Agape*, then, among the first Christians, also meant the fraternal banquet, which used to take place during the Eucharistic ceremony. This ambivalence in *agape*, as love/banquet, now part of the history of mankind, says more than any other theory about the novelty of this type of love that is communion, reciprocity, new form of life in common. I shall thank Professor Joseph Sievers of the Biblical Institute in Rome for this note (and for his advice on several issues concerning the Jewish and biblical world).

[28] On this point there is an excellent quote by Paul: "Owe no one anything, except to love one another" (Letter to the Romans, 13:8).

[29] Women, slaves, people of low rank (think of the first disciples, fishermen and craftsmen) were the members of the new community that presented itself a social revolution.

This is why *agape is the authentic space of the tragedy of the communitas*, where one lives the *munus* in a truly ambivalent way. With *agape* the fragility of life in common is *truly* exposed.

Originally, the church (in Apostolic times) was the attempt, both philosophical and theological, to translate the novelty of the Christian event and of *agape* into categories.[30]

It is not by accident, then, that civil society and the market slowly mature in western culture (Greek–Roman–Jewish–Christian): a slow process that passes through the entire Middle Ages, as we shall see in the next chapter, and which is still in progress.

For these reasons *agape* poses itself as a radical critique of the various solutions to the ambivalence of the *communitas* we have seen in the first part of this essay:

- The *sacred community*. The "Incarnation" is what culturally ends the season of the sacred. With Christianity the divine stops being an inaccessible reality with which it is only possible to communicate through the mediator. The logos becomes flesh (John, 1) and by becoming man among men it marks the end of the sacred

---

[30] A reflection of this apostolic or primitive stage of the church is the debate on the so-called Trinitarian dogma, which could not but affect also the theoretical debate as well as the "social" life. A Trinitarian view of the Absolute carries within itself the possibility of the social, or, as I prefer to call it, civil, because it succeeds in conceiving the manifold, and hence the story, not in opposition but in harmony with the need of the One. The Greek world, like the Jewish world, had opened to the possibility of horizontal relationality; but the Christian event was needed in order for the civil to really explode: a process that has lasted until the modern age – and still continues. Gurevic writes on this point: "*What the Middle Ages inherited from classical times* – anthropologically speaking – was no straightforward legacy. In the Graeco-Roman period the concept 'person' did not exist. The Greek word *prosopon* and the Latin persona served to denote a theatrical mask. A mask is not only not a person but probably the very opposite... There seems to have been no awareness of individuality in ancient times" (1995, pp. 90–91). At the same time, Christianity and the Uni-Trinitarian view of the Absolute would not have existed without the Jewish world and the encounter with the Greek culture (and, somehow, with the Roman). We must note, in fact, that the Trinitarian theology is the fruit of a long process, whose fundamental steps have included the great Apostolic Councils of the fourth and fifth centuries, which gave rise to a "theory" about the Christian event strongly influenced by the categories of Greek philosophy. In particular, the category of substance (*ousia*) and of person (*hypostasis*), elaborated by the great classical Greek philosophy, were the instruments that allowed to elaborate the Christological and Trinitarian dogmas underpinning the Christian doctrine of God.

community: the image of the "veil in the temple" that gets torn (Mark 15,38) with Christ's death is a metaphor expressing the end of the age of the sacred: there is no longer a "santa santorum" that only the priest may access. Each person may experience the divine without the need for sacred mediators.[31]

- *Law and jus.* Agape challenges even Law and *jus*.[32] The Christian experience is founded on faith *(pistis)*, which is the reception of a gift that, in the wake of Abraham, invites believers to abandon the comfort of their native land to undertake a journey across foreign territories, at the mercy of foreigners, of others. Jesus of Nazareth harshly criticizes a Law that promises salvation and good life by following norms and rituals, without at each moment questioning oneself and without following one single law: *agape*. His harsh critique of the precept of Saturday, of fasting, of social norms and hygiene rules (choosing the company of public sinners such as publicans and prostitutes) says exactly this. *Agape*, furthermore, is the overcoming of the logic of equivalences (Boltanski 2012) on which law is founded. Somehow real *agape* goes further than justice, the great virtue towards which each law is oriented.[33]

- *Philia between equals.* Unlike Aristotelian ethics which sees *philia* as love between equals, where the other is an alter-ego chosen to reduce the frailty of friendship to the minimum, *agape* does not choose the friend but those who live in *agape* find themselves with other fellow travellers who happen to be by their side (in this sense there is an affinity between *agape* and fraternity: both are non-elective). The agapic communitas is not a community of friends closed around

[31] The Christian therefore has immediate access to God, where the only mediator between men and the divine is the person of Christ, who, in his death on the cross, initiates a new figure of mediator: in the *kenosis* of the cross he makes it possible for men to meet directly with God. It is the mediator-nothing that, by disappearing, makes the two parties meet (God and the world).

[32] The Letter of Paul to the Romans is the place of the inevitable writing for anyone wishing to comprehend the Christian critique of the Law. *Agape* becomes the alternative to Law if and when the latter becomes a means of immunitas, a means that ensures salvation without having to question oneself in the relationship with God and the other.

[33] The golden rule of "To each his own" is challenged by *agape*, that suggests giving to those who ask for a tunic, also a cloak; to those who are hit on the cheek to turn the other cheek (instead of appealing to the principles of law); to the worker of the last hour gives the same as the daily worker, that leaves ninety-three sheep for one only, that kills the fattest lamb to celebrate the return of a son who does not deserve it.

itself; it is universal fraternity, in which it is the choice of *agape* that they have in common, not the mutual choice of friends. Indeed *agape* includes friendship, *but it is friendship among all others as equals, not just a chosen few.* The story of Christianity has been also a continuous struggle to fight the self-enclosure that the unavoidable component of *philia* inevitably brings with it. And every time it has closed itself in the safety of *philia*-between-equals, it has lost its profound identity and universal vocation.

The authentic agapic communitas is then a "wounded" communitas, for it is radically exposed to the other's vulnerability, for while the other is unchosen we cannot live without him.

Agape is a kind of relationality founded not on blood, *eros*, or elective *philia*, and for this reason agapic sociality is truly dramatic, founded on reciprocity and exposed to the wound of the other's freedom, for he is brother but also potentially a traitor that *agape* condemns us to love (as an enemy, if nothing else).

And it is also for this radical novelty of which the agapic community is the bearer, that the *new* Christian community lasted for such a brief duration in the first church, and found enormous resistance as it tried to affirm itself in history.

To *agape* and its logic we shall return towards the end of this work.

4
Dawn of the Modern Age

> Life in community enfolds all that is trustworthy and intimate in living closely together. Society is public: it is the world. On the contrary, from birth we find ourselves in community with our loved ones, bound to them for good or for ill. We enter society as a foreign land.
>
> Ferdinand Tönnies

We may interpret the Middle Ages as a process in which individuality slowly emerged at the expenses of the *communitas antiqua*. This process unfolded rather harmoniously until the Tuscan civil humanism in the early fifteenth century, but later exploded in a rapid and irreversible escalation resulting in the Renaissance, the Reformation, the seventeenth century and the Enlightenment. The rise of modern political economy may be situated at some point along this lengthy cultural process.

The ancient community, whose social structure has been described in the previous chapter, at this point undergoes a profound crisis: in a way, it dies. From its death new alternative attempts emerge, some of which are still fully unfolding.

1. The Middle Ages and mercantile civilization

Despite the Christian event and the ensuing irruption in the West of a new form of relationality founded on *agape*, early *Christianitas* (often labelled as "medieval") does not differ substantially in its structure from the ancient community.

In the first century, the first apostles and followers of Christ had founded new communities that were remarkably different from the Greek–Roman–Jewish ones. Already towards the end of the first century

57

and, later, with Constantine and the matrimony between the Church and the Roman Empire, the social dimension of Christianity experienced a long season of "eclipsed fraternity", ending with the Vatican II council. The reasons for this eclipse are many, complex and controversial. An important role was certainly played by the encounter between Christianity and Neoplatonism (with Diogenes, for instance). This encounter not only helped to highlight inside the Church its continuity with ancient hierarchical forms of organization, but also to project a hierarchical view of the world: soul/body; contemplation/ action; religion/laic life; etc. Moreover, the initial failures of fraternity (witnessed also by the Pauline epistles)[1] ultimately encouraged the inevitably hierarchical inclinations of the first communities.

Only very few documents exist that describe the primitive and apostolic church (like the Pauline letters and certain documents dating from the second century) and that can make us appreciate the experimental character of these new communities marked by fraternity and *agape*, in which men, women, slaves and poor, all stood on a plane of equality, non-hierarchical and anti-sacred (Penna 1998, 2007). Among the Pauline letters, the so-called "pastoral epistles" (to Titus and Timothy, written by Paul's followers around the years nineties of the first century) reveal that a change had already occurred inside the first Christian communities: in the authentic Pauline letters (to the Corinthians, to the Galatians and to the Romans...), Paul addressed the community as a whole ("To the Church of God in Corinth", for example); later letters tend to be increasingly addressed to the head of the community or to the head of the church. This change shows a transformation in these first fraternal and horizontally-structured communities that slowly become more hierarchical. After Constantine, they eventually evolved into the medieval church centred on the figure of the Pope and the bishops. The communities founded by Paul were charismatic churches, nurtured by the dynamics of the various charismata (gifts). Despite being all different (from administration to teaching), the latter followed no hierarchical order (in the sense we have specified in the previous chapters), but rather a logic of communion. This experience turned out to be brief: in less than half-a-century, Paul's communities were replaced by the ancient sacred community – although now nourished by an evangelical novelty. In

---

[1] Early signs of tension can be found in Mark 10, 35–45; Matthew 20, 20–29; Acts 5, 1–11; 1 Cor 1, 11. Several controversies and stories of injustice crossing Paul's communities are also frequently reported.

the final part of this book we shall try to say more about this relational and social dynamic.

This early phase of agapic fraternity, culminating in the institutionalization of Christianity, sees the persecution of Christianity by the political power of the time for bearing a new model of life in common: the agapic community. After Constantine, the agapic community becomes a sort of "karst" (underground) river in the landscape of European history: alive, but for long tracts hidden, it only re-emerged in certain great charismatic moments. Despite bringing fecundity to the soil of history, this river never became the ordinary life of *Christianitas* and Europe.

Among the critical and authentically new outcomes of social life were the town and city, as well as the Franciscan movement.

2. Franciscan fraternity and the city society

The great charismatic movements of the Middle Ages deserve our undivided attention. In particular, the Franciscan movement represents a moment of great importance within social and economic history and at the same time a paradox: a charismatic movement at whose heart lies "sister poverty", with the attendant detachment from material goods serving as a sign of a perfect life, becomes the first "school" of economics, from which the modern spirit of market economy will later develop together with the first cooperative banks (the Italian *banche popolari*) and the mounts of pawns (authentic predecessors of modern microcredit institutions).

In fact, as is well known, the earliest systematic inquiries about the economy, about the notion of value and the prices of goods, or about money, are contained in the writings of William of Ockham, Pierre de Jean Olivi, Duns Scotus – all Franciscan scholars. The detachment from money produces a new economic synthesis: the appreciation of real wealth does not pass through one's possessions.

The original Franciscan fraternity is the authentic tragic *communitas* of *agape*, which offers a radical alternative to *immunitas* of the sacred and hierarchical community. The foundational act of Franciscan fraternity, I believe, is Francis' kiss to the leper, the contamination and anti-immunization approach towards the latter, the outcast of the community of Assisi – tempted, like any other community, by the possibility of *philia* between equals, i.e. the *cum-moenia* that literally leaves the misfit outside the city-walls. Even Francis' stigmata, which he received towards the end of his life are regarded, according to the most recent interpretations, as wounds of fraternity, mirroring the disunity and division perceived by Francis in his community. The Franciscan fraternity took *agape* seriously, together with its typical "wounds". Thus says Todeschini on this point:

> The value that Francis highlighted in animals and in outcasts can be described as spiritual and religious, but this definition is not completely satisfying. It is probably more truthful to say that this value, which could not be expressed with money, was mysterious. The enigma of this value consisted in the distance of the creatures from the magic circle of civil humanity and thus in the difficulty citizens had in understanding it. Francis' poverty (and this shocked his contemporaries) seemed to allow him to discover something of this mystery: to reveal some aspects of the value of those things and those people away from the codes of ecclesial, communal, noble, mercantile, and military life.
>
> 2009, p. 65

This "elsewhere", a consequence of *agape*, is what gives rise to Franciscan fraternity, which is not limited to the *moenia* or the *cum-moenia* (i.e. the common walls that guarantee the *cum-munus* between the ones living inside the city), but universally embraces the excluded, the last in the *civitas*.

However, like the early Christian experience, Francis' prophecy and provocation did not manage to establish themselves as the prevailing culture of the time, despite certainly succeeding in contaminating and influencing it.

The communal town and city society, for instance, grows around the Franciscan convent located in the city centre (and no longer in valleys, as in the case of Monasticism),[2] also thanks to the rather paradoxical

---

[2] It must be noticed, however, that despite living in valleys and away from the urban centres, the monks nonetheless played a highly civilizing function: although far from the cities, they operated a deep and vital service towards them, from writing the city statute to various economic and commercial activities that they maintained for centuries (from windmills to the trade of surpluses). Moreover it is possible to read the emergence of the mendicant movements after the year 1000, including the Franciscan order, as a development of monasticism itself (particularly the orders that were more closely dedicated to voluntary poverty: wealthy individuals who made themselves poor in imitation of Christ), as a way to perfection and the sign of an authentic Christian life: in a European world still trying to overcome centuries of endemic misery, the choice of rich and powerful people to voluntarily make themselves poor and vulnerable was in itself a compelling sign, inspiring many to convert. Consider, as highlighted

alliance between Franciscans and merchants – one of the explanations of the incredibly fecund season of the Italian civil humanism.

The Franciscan idea of "value" based on scarcity[3] (think, for instance, of the work of Pierre de Jean Olivi, or later Bernardino from Siena) forms the basis for assessing the value of the actions both of the friars and of the merchants. In the Christian Middles Ages, the figure of the merchant was already characterized in the doctrine of the Church Fathers (if not even sooner in the Gospels) by a radical ambiguity. The merchant is an actor who must be kept under control both by society and morality, for he deals with money, which Jesus counterposed to God by calling it *mammon*. The merchant, who skilfully manages money and business, can always introduce the temptation to exchange even religious values for filthy lucre. On the other hand, the Scriptures and the Church Fathers also made use of similar mercantile metaphors to describe the redeeming act of Christ, "heavenly merchant", whose blood had been the "price" of salvation. Moreover, especially as Christianity became the religion of the Empire, the church itself started to become deeply involved in the management of lands, capitals and money. For this reason the church was unable to avoid having contacts with merchants and their money, finance and trades.

The Franciscans – especially those theologians dealing with economic matters – were well aware of such ambivalence in the moral evaluation of commerce and merchants. In particular they knew that the merchant is the one who makes wealth circulate and who brings about re-distribution (sometimes unknowingly) so that wealth does not pile up in coffers. Only by circulating can wealth produce the common good.[4] The Franciscan critique of the thesaurization of money, or of

---

by Todeschini (2009, pp. 32 ff.), the role of monks like Romuald from Ravenna, around the beginning of the eleventh century, who built their lives around the choice of poverty as a way to "earning souls".

[3] Scarcity is among the notions introduced by the Franciscans. Starting from around the second half of the thirteenth century, Franciscan charisma informs the idea that the value of things is commensurate with their scarcity. The value of a person also depends on the rarity of her function inside the community. Hence the immense value of *agape* and of the action of friars, which, to be remunerated, would require an infinite amount of money. For this reason it is preferable that they remain "unpaid", because each remuneration would cause a depreciation of the action real value, a relational *damping*.

[4] These claims imply an intuition of the so-called "velocity of circulation" of money, that in modern times has been employed in the famous "quantity theory of money" ($MV = PY$), where V (velocity of circulation) is related to the real income Y.

the unfruitful use of wealth even by the church and by a certain type of monasticism, led the Franciscans to state the importance of having wealth circulating rapidly in cities, like blood in a body (a metaphor that thenceforth accompanies all medieval economic reflection, until the founder of Physiocracy, François Quesnay, comes along in the middle of the eighteenth century).

The merchant, moreover, connects the city with the countryside; he generates the encounter of people and goods that without the common denominator of market price might never have met.[5] The merchant, finally, is a pauper (although not indigent), for his mobile and ephemeral wealth is continuously exposed to the twists of fortune, unlike landowners, whose wealth is bound to their status. The city is the fabric of this new European society, which expands itself following the expansion of markets. The complex and dense system of fairs embracing a large part of Europe was this nervous system simultaneously based on trade and Christianity, before, during and after the Crusades.

Thanks to the Franciscans, therefore, a new alliance arises between subjects who might seem like opposites to an external observer today: voluntary poverty and trade. The ethical legitimization of commerce and fair profit were the other face of a movement that, being based on the choice of poverty and on the voluntary renunciation of wealth, could offer – and in fact it did offer – the categories for the comprehension, in a Christian and ethical key, of the market and of mercantile economy. So far, this is nothing new. However, the compelling historical research carried out by Todeschini and his school allows us to refine this account significantly in relation to the concerns of our discussion.

The inclusive and universalistic vocation of the market, well-comprehended by the Franciscans (consider in this respect the encounter between Francis and the Sultanate and its universal fraternity), soon had to face the search for a common denominator to allow trade outside the walls surrounding the city and its institutions. Such a denominator was found in the Christian *fides*, which made it possible

---

[5] The Franciscan "laboratory" of economic reflection, in other words, took place in an environment of close contact between financial professionals and professionals of faith. From Rome to Montpellier, from Paris to Genoa, the Europe of the voluntary poor was also the financial and commercial Europe of consecrated powers, nevertheless managed by merchants who, no longer wandering *pauperes*, now appeared as economic agents and representative of these sacred Lords....Even in this case, poverty, lack, and deprivation appear to Franciscans not as a void to fill but as a starting point for measuring values, wages, and prices" (Todeschini 2009, pp. 106–107).

to cut off the ties of parental bonds, of clan bonds, and even of citizenship (on which medieval commerce had been founded), provided that one remained within the space of *Christianitas*, the great network on which commerce between "different" subjects could rely. Medieval Scholasticism, not just the Franciscans, built a model of market and society that in the long run showed a remarkable power of inclusion. Nonetheless, the "price" that had to be paid for the construction of such a model was the identification of market limits and, therefore, of the identification of the excluded.

3. From fraternity to market (as *philia*)

Franciscan fraternity was one of the main patterns characterizing the development of city society and market economy – two sides of the same coin, as we have seen. The Franciscan *agape* lay at the heart of the charismatic movement in its early stages, but – and this is the point – it later evolved into a form of elective *philia*, thus providing the social framework for the development of market economy within Italian civil humanism.

On the exclusive character of this early form of market economy, Todeschini remarks:

> Franciscans presented the market as a system of relationships based on reciprocal trust and credibility. However, already in the fourteenth century, this had meant that it was necessary to distinguish between those who participated in the common good by dealing and trading and those who substracted wealth from the common good by accumulating only for themselves and their families. Usurers, hoarders, and those poor people who were not useful to the community had been identified as strangers among a population of believers.
>
> 2009, p. 153

In the time of Aristotle, the Greeks already regarded the market as a form of *philia* moved by interests. Unlike unnatural chrematistics, economic exchanges were for Aristotle an expression of *philia*, of reciprocity (*anti-peponthos*) – one of the great bonds underpinning the city's cohesion. Economic exchanges shared the elective character of *philia*: not everyone could take part in an exchange, as is commonly known, but only the adults, male, free, and preferably not involved in the material process of working activities.

This characteristic of *philia* (electivity) is also present in the new mercantile economy of fourteenth- and fifteenth-century European cities. As such, this new mercantile economy ultimately constituted a form of *immunitas*. The experience of Franciscan *fraternitas* had a prophetic character; but, just like *Christianitas*, its transition to history met some critical obstacles. Still, many were the fruits that fraternity actually introduced into the civil dynamic (from the theoretical reflection on the market to the mounts of pawns, for instance). Agapic fraternity, nonetheless, never became the prevailing culture of European trades and cities. The prevailing model was instead more similar to Aristotle's Athens rather than the late thirteenth-century community of Assisi or of any communities in Umbria.

The market requires *fides* – the Romans knew this well – it needs trust; but credibility (and so the market) only works as long as it is mutual. What kind of behaviour should then be adopted towards the non-credible, the untrustworthy? Any parasitic or harmful components had to be cut off from the game of civil life and be left, perhaps, to the care of charitable institutions (be them civil or religious).

Fides is always profoundly vulnerable, particularly in the ancient and medieval world. As pointed out by the great French linguist Emile Benveniste, the Latin notion of *fides* establishes an inverse relationship between the parties as compared to the relation founded on what, in our eyes, is the modern notion of "trust". In the expression "I have confidence in somebody", confidence is something belonging to me, which I can put into his hands and which he can dispose of. In the Latin expression *mihi est fides apud aliquem* it is the other who puts his trust in me, leaving it at my disposal. Having someone's *fides* thus means to have a credit deposited "with" somebody (cfr. Benveniste 1976, I, pp. 131 ff.).

In the ancient and pre-modern world, then, *fides* was the quality of a person who inspired confidence in him and is exercised in the form of a "protective authority" over those who entrust themselves to him (Fontaine 2008, p. 17). Trust necessitated the act of entrusting another.

To function, the market requires a type of reciprocity that must resemble *philia*'s most protective form because, in fact, it was necessary and even.[6]

Therefore, the market functions and generates development only as long as there is good faith, reliability, reputation, *fides* between the

[6] Todeschini again: "indispensable for trust to be concretely based on the membership of individuals in well-structured and civically identifiable groups... professional corporations, guilds, confraternities, or companies... The distance that had already existed in the thirteenth century between usurers and merchants as money-brokers or bankers was now codified by the Franciscan

parties. In the aftermath of the Roman Empire, the Christian religion succeeded in establishing *fides* as a common denominator everywhere in Europe, thereby giving rise to a system of mercantile exchanges revolving around the cities, and even earlier around the seigniors' courts and the abbeys: *Christianitas* always preserved the markets' development from the inside. In practice, such protection took the form of the system of corporations and guilds, where political protection was ensured to merchants in international exchanges though the institution of citizenship. The main actor of the medieval market is therefore the citizen – someone who possesses citizenship (and preferably resides in one of the main mercantile cities of his time). Any foreigner wishing to open a commercial activity in Venice, for instance, had to reside in that city for several years (up to fifteen in certain times) before being granted the status of Venetian merchant. *Fides* was only ascribed to the city's merchants, hence Christians, along with the trustworthiness necessary to carry out economic and financial operations. By contrast, this could not have been the case for non-citizens, who would been seen as operating illicitly. To be convicted for usury was far less frequent for Christian city-merchants compared to Jewish or foreign merchants: for well-known Christian merchants, charging interest on international trades or on public loans was not incompatible with usury, but for them only.[7]

The city and the institution of citizenship guaranteed the role of mercantile ethics as a cornerstone of Christian and city society – the latter founded on an inextricable tangle of faith, reputation, well-being, military power, but also exclusion. As a matter of fact, only

---

representation of the market…The exclusion of a significant part of the city's population from the market, or from the legitimate, legalized sociality, is the price paid to construct a model of market society which is cohesive and morally validated by trust and reciprocity. The Jews present in Italy at the end of the 1300s and in the 1400s are a part of this dynamic" (2009, pp. 154–5).

[7] Between the thirteenth and fourteenth centuries, thanks especially to the work of Franciscan theologians, a distinction was introduced between interest (intended as remuneration for risk and, as such, ethically acceptable) and usury (intended as remuneration for time, hence considered illicit). The theme of the voluntariness of loan and coercion was also crucial for the debate on usury and interest (as in the case of public debt, which made it ethically legitimate to pay interest on securities). Other key themes included the interpretation of interest as free "gift" motivated by one's gratitude towards the lender (more common among Dominican theologians) and the interpretation of interest as a simple remuneration for *lucrum cessans* (which we owe to the Franciscan school).

players considered trustworthy had any chance of being admitted to this game: it was necessary to exclude the infamous, who were unable to enjoy the game of mercantile reciprocity and hence civil life itself, which, in the medieval Communes, extended as far as the markets. To the benefit of those living inside the city, the walls – a means of protection from the alien – guaranteed that the market would produce the circulation of wealth and *fides* (intended both as trust and Christian faith!).

In giving rise to the medieval urban civilization, *agape*, which had previously informed Franciscan charisma, was like yeast: it changed Europe but, in the process, it was itself transformed into *philia*. *Agape* was the price paid for the birth of the market, which would have been impossible without the decisive role of the Franciscans. It seems fair to assume that, had Franciscanism remained true to its vocation of universal and radical love, we would never have known city society or civil humanism. A high price was paid for the birth of the market economy and this was the exclusion of part of the population. Yesterday like today the excluded knock at the door of the trustworthy and, through their destitute presence, they challenge the well-being of the inhabitants of the *civitas*.

An important factor in the transformation and evolution of the Franciscan relationship with poverty, wealth and money, was the existence of the tertiary Franciscan order. This third order was formed mainly by citizens, and particularly merchants, wishing to live Francis' charisma, while simultaneously remaining in the cities and in the business world. This fact (providentially) affected the Franciscan theologians' approach towards money and merchants, thereby producing a kind of spirituality that was consistent with the historical existence of authentic followers of Francis who, while embracing the Franciscan ideal, continued to deal with trade and wealth.

A different choice, partly due to the lack of a tertiary order, was made by the Dominican order, which was closer to the poor and more critical towards money, interests and usury. Mattia Foscesato writes on this topic:

> The development of the concept of poverty within Franciscan mentality, therefore, led on one side to an increasing validation of productive and commercial activities in the city; at the same time, it made clear that some victims were being left behind in the process: the real city's poor

2009, p. 123

4. An unaccomplished revolution

This view of the economic and the civil grew into the more complex reality of fifteenth century cities. This was the case of Bernardino of Siena, a Franciscan scholar who may be rightfully considered (as Schumpeter does) one of the first "modern" economists. In his theoretical thought, we find an increasingly sharp contrast between the Christian and non-Christian (e.g. Jewish) economy. Electivity and exclusion of the different (*immunitas*) became more emphasized and also, somehow, more radical (cfr. his *Vulgar Sermons*). His comparison between Christian "charity" (*charitas*) and the dog-like attitude (*canitas*) of usurers, especially Jewish, is well-documented: "Among you there is no charity, even *caninity*; for one man is the other's dog" (quoted in Bargellini 1980[1930], p. 91 – *my translation*).[8]

The fraternity nurtured and informed by *agape* is what people found unsettling at the time, because it revealed "some aspects of the value of those things and those people away from the codes of ecclesial, communal, noble, mercantile, and military life. The value, but also the importance – that is, the virtue – of outcast and animals in the episodes of Francis's life could vary but in any case Francis's personal existential poverty was the magnifying lens that revealed them" (ibid., p. 65).

Civil humanism, the brilliant first season of the Italian Renaissance (cf. Bruni and Zamagni 2007) will bring that same ambivalence forward – again in line with the thirteenth and fourteenth century culture of the city, and with the Aristotelian *polis*: the city as *philia* for the people inside the city wall, the *cum-moenia*; but *immunitas* for those outside.

---

[8] As we consider the evolution of the relationship between Franciscans and the economy (and politics) over the fourteenth and fifteenth century: "A new combativeness appears in their words and actions. If on the one hand it reinforces a notion of the market as a mirror of civil society, on the other hand it foreshadows some characteristic ambiguities of modern market realities, altogether ascribable to the difficult equilibrium between the expansion of the scope of an economic model and the survival of different economic models. The market starts appearing to Franciscan observants, and first of all to Bernardino of Siena, as a territory to extend and defend. This new combativeness makes their discourse entirely economic and political. However, it also complicates the oldest Franciscan economic vision – that which, in a system of values deriving from economic relationships and daily negotiation, wanted to see a reflection of the incommensurable value of God's creation, men, and their work" (Todeschini 2009, p. 159).

Christian *philia* thus becomes the basis of the economic development of a market that eventually seemed closer to Aristotelian than Franciscan thought.[9]

Friendship is acknowledged as the main economic resource: "The enemy to beat (...) will be (...) *extinctio amicitiae*, the disappearance of friendship among those who make up the market" (Todeschini 2009, p. 189).[10]

Franciscan discourse and lay civil humanism (whose mutual contamination is more extensive than is normally thought and written about – even by Garin and Baron, who coined the expression "civil humanism") – thus created, on the basis of Christian *philia* and trustworthiness, the economic culture and ethics of the market. The writings of Bernardino of Siena or Giacomo della Marca, but also of the humanists Bracciolini and Bruni, as well as the treatises on accountancy and *ars mercatoria* by Pacioli and Cotrugli, continued to be printed both in Catholic and Protestant contexts until the beginning of the industrial revolution and the Enlightenment, when a significant change occurred inside the civil and economic community and to which we shall return in the next few chapters.

In concluding his essay, Todeschini effectively and evocatively sums up the heritage and the unresolved issues left by the Franciscans across European culture at the origin of modern economy: "The wicked, the uncivilized, the poor, infidels, and the disenfranchised would silently, threateningly surround and besiege the city more and more, that radiant city of well-esteemed people, the believers, the saved, and the real and potentially rich" (ibid. p. 196).

---

[9] In the sixteenth century, this alliance between voluntary poverty, citizenship, economic power, political and economic theory becomes stronger and more widespread: "German or Spanish Dominican friars like Gabriel Biel or Domingo de Soto, professors in Heidelberg like Konrad Summenhart, Italian economists like the Florentine Bernardo Davanzati, and balanced humanists like Leon Battista Alberti, exchange with one another and not always consciously, some of the teachings that the Franciscan world, between the practice of poverty and the theory of wealth, had gradually disseminated. In general, the fundamental principle supporting their representation of economic organization is organic, that of the ethical and political functionality of trade among full citizens. Also for them, the key to good sociability consists of the market composed of people of impeccable reputation and, as such, able to recognize each other" (Todeschini 2009, p. 186).

[10] Once more, Todeschini remarks: "clearly the Franciscan economic analysis privileges, especially at this point, the recognizability of the economic operator within a civic contexts." (ibid., p. 164).

In his well-known painting "Pentecost", Giotto painted the church according to the idea of a sacred community, detached from the rest of mankind.

The "infamous", the uncivil, the poor, the infidels, the disenfranchised had been the protagonists of Francis' "agapic revolution". From our point of view, the key question thus becomes: *why* did such "reductionism" occur, turning *agape* into *philia*? And what is its logic? In the previous pages we have proposed several clues, but the question is still radically open and we shall try to outline an answer in the final part of this book.[11]

In the next chapter we look at the Protestant Reformation (another groundbreaking event for economics as well) and then – from a new perspective – we move to Hobbes and the modern age.

Between the medieval market and Smith's market we find Luther, whose passage bore significant effects also on the new ethos of the modern market.

---

[11] More sophisticated considerations may be developed with regard to the inner evolution of Franciscan charisma passing from the "first" to the "second" and "third" times – there is still a lively and controversial debate on this point. Here it is enough to mention the fact that Francis and his movement experienced something similar to the history of Christianity and of the church, and it could not have been otherwise. The prophecy which becomes history, the "salt" which gives flavour to the "mass" looses itself in it, until it can no longer recognize itself as salt. But thanks to it, the human quality of life is improved, and *philia* is enriched with humanity. Modern economics would probably have been less humane and liveable without the great medieval charismata, because *eros* and *philia* would have missed their encounter with *agape*, which transformed them from what they were in Greece or in Rome.

5
Towards a Community of Individuals

> It is true that certain living creatures, as bees and ants, live
> sociably one with another... and therefore some man may
> perhaps desire to know why mankind cannot do the same.
>
> Hobbes, *Leviathan*

1. Not only exclusion: the other face of the Market

The Middle Ages end in the great season of civil humanism, followed
by the Renaissance. These periods are marked by a new civil sentiment, which shows, nonetheless, a radical tendency to read, imagine
and represent the *civitas* and the market – i.e. the civil economy – as
an elitist relationship among subjects considered trustworthy: almost a
sort of happy and sheltered oasis of mutually advantageous and stable
relations, surrounded by the "crown of thorns" of the infamous, the
poor, the untrustworthy, the excluded:

> The 'market', as mirror of society, came gradually to assume the
> fundamental ambiguity that still characterizes it today. Thought of
> as an abstract and global reality, it seems to attract and include the
> totality of the existing population, while in fact it excludes many,
> establishing multiple hierarchies of economic, cultural and cognitive
> nature between people.
>
> Todeschini 2007, p. 7 [*my translation*]

The early forms of market economy in the Middle Ages and throughout
civil humanism show a pattern that may be compared to the model of
elective *philia*. However, one more passage is missing in order to fully
understand the argument developed in the previous chapter.

70

So far, in our attempt to reconstruct the medieval ethics of the market we have mainly followed Todeschini's interpretation of the rise of market economy in relation to elective and exclusive culture based on *philia*. However, we should further observe that during the Middle Ages and until the humanist period, the market also developed a vocation for universality and inclusivity – unlike the electivity of *philia*. This vocation informs the trades between the Christian merchants and the Turks, the Chinese and the Muslims (consider, among others, the importance of Marco Polo's experience), and allows peoples who are far apart and perhaps even enemies (for reasons of religion, ethnicity, etc.) to meet each other and to establish relations of mutual advantage from the economic as well as civil points of view. Ships used to sail from the Mediterranean ports on their way to war against the Saracens, or to the Crusades,[1] and ships loaded with spices from the East and from Arabia used to come and go from those same ports. What this tells us is that even though the dimension of *fides* remains an essential element for appreciating the nature of the medieval market and of civil humanism, the rise of the market had an even greater significance than *philia* and *fides*: the rise of the market was the key element in the transformation of a world still deeply rooted in the culture of the sacred and the hierarchical community into a society of free and equal individuals, a process culminating in the lights and shadows of the modern- and post-modern world.[2]

The ethos of the market was also – and still is – an ethos of inclusion, tendentially universalistic. No other institution but the market has been able to include such an increasing number of people over the centuries without their having to belong to any polis, *communitas*, clan, tribe, or country.[3] The market makes different people meet; its

---

[1] The Crusades were also an ambiguous experience of trades and wars with the "infidels" – without *fides*.

[2] Here are some excerpts from a private conversation with Giacomo Todeschini on the same topic. To my question: "If trust [*fides*] was the basis for exchange in the medieval market economy, how do we explain the major exchange that Venice (like many other cities of the *ancien régime*) entertained with the Arabs, with China and the East?" Todeschini replied: "The question is not easy: I would make it into a different question: what sort of 'affairs' did Venice entertain with the 'outsiders'; or in other terms, what was their weight and significance within the overall Venetian economy in the Middle Ages and until the end of the fifteenth century? And also: which (fiduciary) intermediations allowed society to legitimize (from a political and not just economic point of view) the business dealings with the infidels? This is certainly a problem" (14 December 2008).

[3] About this inclusive dimension of the market, and in particular about the role of mercantile institutions, see Greif (2006).

universalistic vocation was certainly made stronger and more powerful by the Franciscan ethics of "universal brotherhood". At the same time Todeschini (along with other historians heedful also of minorities) has showed us another face of the market, a face that is equally real, but marked by exclusion and electivity, i.e. by *philia*.

Yesterday, and still today, the ethos of the market has lived on this vital tension and ambivalence. Even the mercantile ethos of the modern age, lay and universalistic, is the result of a long period of transition during which trades took place within the city-walls, between Christians, through the mediation of the various craft guilds. In international commercial trades, merchants benefited from political protection and from the mediation of their kin or fellow-citizens, or of city-agencies located in far-away regions, which warranted *fides* even when dealing with infidels. On the verge of modernity several religious conversions (between Catholics and Protestants, or Christians and Muslims) continued to be motivated by commercial rather than spiritual reasons. The dynamics that still take place today within the Islamic economy and banking system (where trading and finance are deeply intertwined with *fides*) closely resemble the centuries-long processes then occurring in Christian Europe.[4]

2. The classical tradition of the political animal (and of the unequal society)

If we wish to comprehend the evolution of critical thinking on the topic of economic social life between the Middle Ages and the modern age, the writings of Thomas Aquinas are too important not to deserve at least a few words. Through an inspired synthesis of Christianity and Aristotelian thought, Aquinas has been the author to exert the greatest

---

[4] The excluded were broadly defined through "categories" and not as single individuals of flesh and blood. Therefore the criterion for market inclusion/exclusion wasn't rigid, but varied according to times and circumstances. The result is a double, and ductile, standard for defining insiders and outsiders: a technical–juridical standard and a "political" one, we might say. So for instance, in the case of usurers (both Jewish and non-Jewish) the principle of condemnation was always latent, potential and not always apt to be used. In other terms, the act of dealing with the Infidels did not contradict the general principle of exclusion, because this kind of exchange was seen as an exception, even though the possibility to appeal to this principle was always latent, un-official, tacit and non-explicit. After the Reformation, gradually, the exception became the rule and *fides* stopped being a pre-condition for commercial exchanges.

influence on Christian views on politics from his day (late thirteenth century) onwards.

In Aquinas, the Christian message of *agape* encounters the philosophical categories of Aristotle's political and ethical thought, giving rise to a theory of politics simultaneously founded on man's social nature and on the hierarchical community. No other thinker has been so determined to keep together the notions of *homo socialis* and *hierarchica communitas*.

At the heart of his understanding of human sociality is not only Aristotle, but also the metaphysical intuition – necessarily absent in Aristotle – *that the relations between the Persons of the Trinity are "subsistent"* (i.e. non-*accidental*):[5] the Three are "subsistent relations". A philosophical genius, Aquinas couldn't fail to realize that the revelation of the Christian God as uni-trinity would necessarily affect the idea of human sociality; nonetheless, the essential distinction between three-theism and Trinity (in which each of the Three is the *unique* God) needed to be preserved.

From the anthropological perspective, the Thomistic theory shows a remarkably lively understanding of the person's relational dynamics, which relies on a different idea of human nature:

> While, according to Augustine and all theological thinkers until Aquinas, sin came from the beginning to alter nature by trapping it in a state of corruption, for him the goodness of nature, including the goodness of politics, which he defines as the very essence of man, is not removed nor substantially altered by sin; it is only hurt and diminished.
>
> Truini 2008, p. 356 [*my translation*]

In Aquinas' words:

> Because man is a naturally social animal; men even in the state of innocence would have lived in society. Social life among many could not exist, however, unless someone took the position of authority to direct them to the common good.
>
> Aquinas, *Summa Theologiae I*, q.96, a.4

This passage well represents Aquinas' view of the human person and social life. His attitude suggests a sort of anthropological "optimism"

---

[5] For Aristotle, relation is one of the accidents of substance.

(different from Augustine's, but also from Occam's and Luther's, as we shall see), which nonetheless co-exists with a hierarchical reading of social life. That is: the natural condition of association (the "state of innocence") is sociability, but at the same time Aquinas conceives political society as hierarchical. Aquinas' preference for the monarchical regime is well known. In particular: "Under the new law there is a higher priesthood, by which men are conducted towards heavenly goods; and so, under the law of Christ, kings must be subject to priests" (Aquinas, *De regimine principium*, Book I, Chapter 16).

This approach is in full continuity with the idea of the sacred community, even though it arises from an inspired combination of *agape* and Aristotelian ethics. Authority doesn't derive from an earthly agreement, but comes from God, and belongs to the law of nature. While the Leviathan, as we shall see, is an artificial authority invented by men for the sake of peace, for Aquinas authority is natural, because the existence of superiors and inferiors, of a hierarchy, is intrinsic to the nature of social life. This genuinely social anthropological attitude thereby coexists with a hierarchical and unequal notion of society, as well as with an organicistic and holistic framework in which the metaphor of the "body" goes hand-in-hand with the metaphor of the naturalness of civil life (as opposed to the idea of civil life as a construction).

Aquinas' starting point is then Aristotle and in particular the famous passage from the *Politics* about the making of the State:

> The first form of association naturally instituted for the satisfaction of daily recurrent needs is thus the family.... The next form of association – which is also the first to be formed by more households than one – is the village.... Formed from a number of villages we have already reached the city.... For this reason every city exists by nature, just as did the earlier associations
>
> *Politics*, 1252–1253

And thus he continues: "From these considerations it is evident that the city belongs to the class of things that exist by nature, and that man is by nature a political animal" (ibid.).

According to Aquinas, just as it was earlier for Aristotle, social life is therefore the natural result of a naturally sociable human being (male, free, adult, citizen). This is what Bobbio has called the "Aristotelian" tradition of social life, of which Aquinas, Marsilio da Padova, and thereby also Bodin, Althusius, Grotius, Vico and Genovesi, form a continuation in opposition to the contractarian position. In another passage from the *Politics*, Aristotle states: "The head of the household rules over both wife and children" (ibid.).[6]

On this point, Bobbio effectively remarked: "It is surprising how lasting, permanent, stable, and vital this way of conceiving the origin of the state has been over centuries" (1993, p. 6). The Aristotelian view was largely accepted prior to Hobbes.[7] Thus Bobbio continues:

> Since individuals live in families from the time of their birth, the pre-political condition is not one of freedom and equality. It is rather a condition in which the fundamental relationships existing in a hierarchical society such as the family is, are between superiors and inferiors. Such are the relationships between father (and mother) and child, or between master and servant.
>
> Bobbio 1993, pp. 8–9

3. The Lutheran revolution and the new foundation of the civil life

The transition from the logic of *fides* to the laicism and universalism of the modern economy was a lengthy one, going from the Middle Ages to Modernity.[8] The Reformation played a decisive role in this transition: as Christian *fides* stopped being the measure of trustworthiness, European Christian society, in which exchanges between cities were based primarily upon *fides* and upon belonging to the church, was compelled to find new foundations and, above all, new institutions – so for instance we may not fully understand the work of Hobbes if we consider it independently of the crisis of *fides* as a precondition

---

[6] In Chapter 7, Book I, he writes about economics and chrematistics: "The rule exercised over the household by his head is that of a monarch (for all households are monarchically governed)" (1255b, p. 20).

[7] In the sixteenth and seventeenth centuries, the School of Salamanca led a post-Lutheran revival of Thomism. With regard to the individual–society relationship, their view was a continuation of the Thomistic themes: *homo socialis* and *hierarchical community*: "it is in fact essential to man that he should never live alone" (Francisco de Victoria); "a time when men wandered about in the manner of wild animals…it is quite impossible that there could ever have been such a time" (Bellarmine) – quoted in Skinner (1978, vol.2, p. 157).

[8] In an illuminating passage of "The Protestant Ethic" Max Weber comments on this spurious process of laicization of market economy: "Anyone can believe what he chooses. But when I learn from a customer that he doesn't attend church, then for me he's not good for fifty cents. Why pay me if he doesn't believe in anything?" (quoted in Supiot 2007, p. 120).

for peace and the common good. Particularly in the case of Northern Europe – from the sixteenth century, the new commercial and financial centre of the world – the scene after the Reformation presented itself as a tangle of different *fides,* all of Christian confession, but no longer capable of creating the basis of trustworthiness necessary in any exchange.[9]

This rupture gave rise to a new *fides,* no longer bound to religion but entirely secularized and based upon the new juridical and financial institutions that – between the sixteenth and seventeenth centuries – re-defined the mercantile ethic of Europe and, hence, of the whole world. It is no accident that the debate on natural law and the social contract (Hobbes), international law (Grotius), finance, central banks, negotiable instruments and stock exchanges all arose in the seventeenth century against the backdrop of religious wars.

As seen, the first commercial and civic revolution in Europe had been made possible through the mediation of *fides,* which served as the social capital of medieval Europe. In this respect, civil humanism, but also the figures of Beato Angelico and Leonardo, Giotto and Torricelli, Dante and Pico della Mirandola, can be regarded as products of this early form of mercantile humanism. The Lutheran Reformation irremediably compromised the order of the European trading-scene based on the Christian faith: after Luther, being a Christian could no longer serve as a guarantee of *fides* on the markets. A new basis became necessary for exchanging and trading in Europe.

It is therefore impossible to appreciate the evolution of market ethics, and of its ethos, without carefully considering the cultural and social meaning of the Reformation. Luther lived in a period that followed civil humanism and preceded the eighteenth-century rise of market economy as well as the creation of modern political economy; hence we now focus on the period after Machiavelli and before Hobbes.

In the context of our discussion, Luther's contribution was decisive for at least two kinds of reasons:

a) in his theological and political thought he was finally able to move beyond the sacred community, thus establishing the possibility, both theological and cultural, of a community made of individuals;

---

[9] The Lutheran revolution induced a strong counter-revolutionary movement, known as the Counter-Reformation, with consequences also in the realm of political thought. Thomism thus returned, toward the late sixteenth and early seventeenth centuries, to dominate the scene of the philosophical and theoretical debate.

b) as a result, the Reformation had the effect of challenging the early humanistic and Franciscan conception that saw the market as tied to *fides* and, hence, with one's affiliation with *christianitas*: after Luther, Christian *philia* will cease to be a suitable foundation; politics, on one hand, and the market, on the other, will need to find a new foundation, in which *philia* will not be replaced by *agape* but by the contract moved by *eros*.

But let us take a closer look at the Lutheran revolution in this double perspective.

Among Luther's main theological and ecclesiological operations is his well-known rejection of the mediating function the church had inherited from the ancient community, and from the idea of the sacred that it never truly managed to overcome. Through the theological reading of the Christian event (particularly through St Paul's theological account), Luther arrives to affirm the uniqueness of Christ, but not of the church or of its earthly hypostases. But Christ is a mediator *sui generis*, who "mediates without mediating" (Cotta 2002, p. 43). He uses no medium to establish a contact between men and God, but from the cross and through his *kenosis* he makes their encounter possible as he disappears to the point of self-annihilation, so that God and mankind may finally meet without veils. He is a mediator whose mediation consists in helping the parts to get closer, but then "disappears" so that they may "touch" each other without mediation.[10] Salvation is operated through the Word announced from one man to another: in this sense there is a mediating value of the word, for it doesn't come directly from God, but from any of the members in the Christian community (not from a priest or minister – that is, not from someone who "administers" the sacred).

In this theological framework there is no room for the church as mediator, or for its instruments of mediation, i.e. the sacraments (except for Baptism and the Eucharist, which do not entail a mediation). Nor is there room for any hierarchy, whose sense lies in the mediated relationship with the Absolute.[11]

This new community is no longer a hierarchy; there are no priests for everyone is a priest to himself: "there is really […] no difference

---

[10] Similarly, Luther's criticism of indulgences may be read as a critique to the mediating function of the Church for the salvation of souls.

[11] In Bruni (2012) I try to show that the different vision of market and hierarchy as developed in the Catholic (community) and protestant (individual) forms of Christianity has deeply affected also the conceptions of Corporate Social Responsibility (CSR) in the Anglo-Saxon context (in the US in particular) and the European one as well (in the Latinate countries in particular).

between laymen or priests" (Luther 1962[1520], p. 409).[12] Luther's view of Christianity is essentially individualistic, reflecting his move away from a community that was unequal, mediated, hierarchical and sacred; and as he distanced himself, the church appeared to him as a community that didn't really ask its members to *graft* into each other as theorized by Paul in the *Corpus Mysticum* and as the (Catholic) Church had intended through the hierarchical community. Therefore, the criticism of the church as hierarchical community resulted partly in a critique of the theological framework of the *Corpus Mysticum* and of the very idea of the church as a body. In Luther's words: "Thus the word Kirche (church) means really nothing else than a common assembly.... Therefore in genuine German, in our mother-tongue, it ought to be called a congregation or holy Chistendom... So also the word *communio*, which is added, ought not to be rendered communion but congregation".[13]

Agapic brotherhood is reciprocity, is being loving each other to the point of giving one's life; it is always a *communitarian* experience, never *'immunitarian'*.[14] As mentioned above, this new community, the *ekklesia*,

---

[12] Only faith leads to salvation. It is a profoundly individual experience, although we should not underestimate the demand, in Luther's theorization, of a certain kind of communion among believers. Structures and institutions (excluding the ministry of the word) are exteriority, unaffected by Christ's saving action; therefore they may be left to political power, because they do not belong to the "city of God", but only to the "city of men" – a typically Augustinian theme that Luther recalls, develops and radicalizes well beyond the thought of Augustine. Moreover for Luther the city of God is essentially a local community, a community of preachers of the word, the true place for the sacred encounter with Christ. The church is ultimately an "inner church", a communion between one's soul and Christ, without mediators.

[13] Luther, *The Large Catechism* (1580[2008], p. 61). The distinctive ecclesiological signs in Luther's thought which will become critical in modern politics are identified by Gabriella Cotta (2002) in the "loss of consistency in the idea of *Corpus Mysticum*; the impoverished sense ascribed to the sacraments which become pure signs of God's will; the drastically reduced role of priests, turned into simple ministers" (p.110, *my translation*). This citation represents a classical *locus* in the Lutheran literature and has become a crucial passage in our discussion. Christianity had introduced into the history of humankind a new type of communion, agapic brotherhood, in which one *grafts into* the other, thus forming a new body, i.e. Christ's *Corpus Mysticum*.

[14] In his works, Luther repeatedly claims that the Christian is a servant to all and is subject to all, but to no-one in particular: in a way, by being subject to all, he is only subject to God (a concept that closely resembles one of the tenets of Smith's market theory: by depending on many customers, the seller does not ultimately depend on anyone in particular).

attempted over the first two centuries to create a new form of fraternal, non-hierarchical and non-sacred cohabitation founded on *agape*. But as we've seen, from the third century, as the Church was grafting onto the Roman Empire, the frailty of this cohabitation caused it to assume a hierarchical configuration, almost as a continuation of the ancient community. This *hierarchica communio* spans through the Middle Ages – in spite of the vigour of the great medieval charismata – and arrives at Luther in the sixteenth century. The Reformers (not just Luther) do not see in this medieval *ekklesia* the church of Christ, but essentially the ancient hierarchical and sacred community. By reacting to a non-fraternal community, their proposed reform turned into the elimination of the very idea of the church as mediator in favour of a church decidedly egalitarian: thus began the community of individuals, then members of an assembly – a direction more emphasized by nineteenth-century Lutheranism.

This "revolution" in the idea of community is rooted in Luther's anthropological pessimism, partly inherited from Augustine. Man, even when he has been redeemed and inhabits the city of God, remains anthropologically ill and unable to do good in the absence of Christ, even when he intends to do so. A human being who is so sick cannot be left to encounter another without mediation, because he would cause too many wounds and murders against others. Thus the mediator that Luther's purely theological formulation had removed is brought right back into the frame.

The "kingdom of flesh" extends to the "city of God" because true Christians cannot be distinguished from the "sons of darkness" and because the corruption of human nature makes it is easy to go back and forth from one "city" to the other: in fact, not only are "true" Christians few, but "above all they cannot be recognized as such by human judgement, which can sustain the wickedness of all. Therefore the reign of flesh is the reign for all, the only one man may truly know and comprehend" (Cotta 2002, p. 127; my translation). We may thereby explain the apparent paradox which Luther seems to incur as he rejects mediation at the theological level, while at the same time advocating a strong political power on the political level, preceding Hobbes' political theories. Unnecessary mediation is harmful to the spiritual Christian. On the contrary, for those men, including Christians, who are attached to exteriority, it is *irreplaceable* in order to achieve that peace and serenity that allow one to pursue his inner life; given the wicked nature of the post-adamitic man, this pursuit would be impossible in the absence of political and social mediators.

a) Unmediated relation in the sphere of faith:

b) Mediated relation in the sphere of politics:

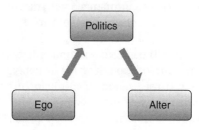

Therefore, every individual may have a direct (un-mediated) relationship with God in the religious sphere; the same cannot happen with the human "you", because sin makes the inter-human relation "sick" and mediation by the political power becomes necessary. From Luther's theological and anthropological conception thereby derives his political position:

> All who are not Christians belong to kingdom of the world and are under the law. Since few believe and still fewer live a Christian life... God has provided for non-Christians a different Government... and has subjected them to the sword so that, even though they would do so, they cannot practice their wickedness and that, if they do, they may not do it without fear nor in peace and prosperity... so a wild, savage beast is fastened with chains and bands... If it were not so, seeing that the whole world is evil and that among thousands there is scarcely one true Christian, men would devour one another, and no one could preserve wife and child, support himself and serve God; and thus the world would be reduced to chaos.
>
> Luther 1962[1523], p. 370

We are far from the anthropology and the view of social life of Aristotle or Aquinas, but also from Augustine's,[15] who, despite acknowledging a

---

[15] Augustine realized the ambivalence that is inherent in social life, but did not negate the political vocation of man, even if clouded and tempted by his sickness, which is also a relational sickness (sin). Cfr. Skinner 1978, Vol. 2.

sort of dialectic, both internal and external, between the "two cities", also proclaimed the real and positive nature of a Cain-like politics.[16]

At the same time, Luther's position (mediated most likely by Calvin and other reformers who influenced the English Reformation, like Butzer or Nox) is among the great sources of the argument of *bellum omnium contra omnes* and of its remedy (the social contract and the Leviathan).

The acknowledgement of the ambivalent quality of social life in the Greek–Judaic–Christian world never entailed the denial of the existence of the *appetitus societatis* that is part of human nature. The awareness of the ambivalence inherent in human relations, and of the potential pain and fear involved in human cohabitation, introduced the need for *mediation* in the forms we discussed in the previous chapter (Law, *philia*, contract), but never had the vocational commitment to the *communitas* as the way to true happiness been negated. Throughout the Middle Ages, including the period of civil humanism, the socio-relational nature of man had never been questioned; during the humanist phase *philia* served with its "exclusions" as a way to control such ambivalence without negating the vocation to human sociability. Those mediations may then be seen as attempts to *preserve* social life, though at the cost of preventing the emergence of the individual. The rupture with this tradition occurred with Luther.

On one hand, Luther's radically negative social anthropology determines a rejection of the "sacred community", because he recognized that the sacred community, including the *Christianitas* of his day, creates inequality and servitude. On the other hand, there is the acknowledgement of man's corrupted nature, hence of the need for politics to govern these corrupted men through an absolute power and thus secure peace.[17] Luther, therefore, deserves the merit of inducing the "death" of the sacred community from within Christianity (and Western culture); but it is also to his arguments that Hobbes goes back, albeit perhaps indirectly, when laying the anthropological foundation of the political theory of the social contract. The "secularized mediators" produced by

---

[16] Augustine is among the first Christian authors to interpret Cain's foundation of the first city as a "vocation" for politics, but in his anthropological view the human person never loses the relational vocation toward others (despite being "sickened" by sin).

[17] Luther's political views were deeply affected by his experience of the German "Peasants' War", where he learnt about the tendency towards the "war of all against all", and chose to side with the Princes, that is, with the political order.

politics in the modern age ("the mortal God" of Hobbes) serve to govern individuals who are irremediably anti-social. By this time the process leading up to the Leviathan is already in motion.

The new mediator, i.e. the contract – both social (*politics*) and private (*market*) – is no longer thought of as a form of "protection" and "salvation" from the ambivalence of social life, but it becomes a new form of relationship, which is a guarantee of immunity for individuals now facing each other on a common ground that is no longer truly communitarian. This is what happens with Hobbes.

In the following section we shall look more closely at Hobbes' project, while in the remaining chapters we shall see how that form of market humanism based on Christian *philia* did not completely disappear from the horizon of modernity, but survived in the Neapolitan school of Genovesi's Civil economy.

4. Hobbes and the "new" social life: the social contract for the uncivil animal

The view of social life overthrown by Luther, and later by Hobbes, corresponded to the model of the ancient sacred community in which human beings only exist insofar as they are "seen" and "mediated" by a third subject holding a higher position in the hierarchy: the king, the father, the priest. In the classic Aristotelian–Thomistic tradition the kind of social life emanating from the *natural* sociability of man as "political animal" was achieved at the cost of renouncing the existence, and hence to the freedom, of man as individual. The birth of man-as-individual required the death of the community-as-individual. This is what Luther had announced and what Hobbes later postulated through his coherent and fundamental political theory. Hobbes' theory of the social contract differs from Locke's, or Grotius', or Rousseau's. In a way we might say that all contractualist theorists from Hobbes' time onward (arriving at Rawls' original contribution combining Hobbes and Kant) have attempted to build a theory of the social contract and civil society capable of overcoming the anthropological pessimism, the anti-sociability inherent in the state of nature, and the foundations of politics as absolute power. At the same time, we ought to remember that Hobbes' theory was the first decisive step toward the foundation of that civil dimension, which on one side determined the rupture with the Aristotelian–Thomistic tradition and with the ancient community, and on the other led up to modern society. For this reason, while it might perhaps be possible to propose a reading of modern economics independent of Rousseau's writings, the same cannot be said of Hobbes, for all post-Hobbesian theorists of society (including all classical economists) have seen in Hobbes a starting point and, in the perspective of modern individualism, a point of no return.

The theory of the social contract, although intuitively anticipated in the ancient and medieval thought, is ultimately a ripe development of the Protestant Reformation, of the birth and discovery of the individual. This is where Aquinas' and Althusius' positions, otherwise quite similar, substantially depart: it is no accident that almost every contractualist author (including the more "social" ones, like Grotius and even Althusius) ultimately operates within the Lutheran and Calvinistic culture and within its anthropological framework.

By now, it should be clear why Hobbes represents such a crucial figure in our discussion. Thomas Hobbes provides an explicit and radical alternative to the Aristotelian view of sociality: in his eyes the kind of sociality that humankind (in Europe, at least) had known until then was incompatible with the acknowledgement of man's individuality, of his freedom and equality. In other terms, Hobbes considered the classical natural *communitas* to be illiberal, because it was radically unequal and hierarchical. The rise of the individual meant moving beyond that tradition and discarding it so as to found a new order in the wake of Luther's contribution. The theory of the social contract was this new order, a new artificial (non-natural) foundation of social life, leading to a point of no return for all modern age.

First in *De Cive* (1642) and later in the more discursive and polemical style of the *Leviathan* (1651), Hobbes outlined his new theory of social life, built on the popular distinction between the *state of nature* (the natural result of un-mediated relations between individuals) and the *civil society* (an artificial order founded by agreement).[18] In Hobbes, as in later contractualist thinking, the state of nature *prior to* the social contract, and the civil state *after* the social contract, are counterposed as two ideal types. The social contract marks the limit between civil society and the non-civil community. Obviously, behind Hobbes' idea of the

---

[18] As is well known, two are the social pacts (that Hobbes summarizes as one): the pact among rational individuals, through which each individual freely decides to give up his absolute individual freedom ("give up my right of governing myself", *Leviathan* XVII) to create a new association and make peace and life possible (*pactum societatis*); and the pact between this new association and the Leviathan (*pactum subjectionis*).

state of nature, dominated by the war of all against all (*bellum omnium contra omnes*), is a radically pessimistic anthropological view, similar to Luther's. Human beings are "wolves" to each other – an expression that is remindful of the "dogs" of Bernardino of Siena. In their spontaneous interpersonal encounter, which occurs without mediation, there is no friendship, nor love; but conflict, fight, war, unhappiness (in the state of nature life is "solitary, poor, nasty, brutish, and short", *Leviathan* (ch. 13, § 9)).

Civil society, then, is not a natural condition, but the artificial product of human beings that willingly abandon the warlike state of nature and freely establish an unnatural association, egalitarian and free. The *natural* for Hobbes is synonymous with the slave–master relationship (as Hegel will observe), domination, and even murder. The individual realizes that in the state of nature life shall never be good but constantly exposed to danger; for this reason he rationally decides in his own interest to found a state on the basis of individual cost–benefit calculations.

The core of Hobbes' humanism emerges from the very first lines of *De Cive*:

> The majority of previous writers on public Affairs either assume or seek to prove or simply assert that Man is an animal born fit for society, – in the Greek phrase *zòon politikòn*. On this foundation they erect a structure of civil doctrine, as if no more were necessary for the preservation of peace and the governance of the whole human race than for men to give their consent to certain agreements and conditions which, without further thought, these writers call laws. This Axiom, though very widely accepted, is nevertheless false; the error proceeds from a superficial view of human nature…. By nature, then, we are not looking for friends but for honor or advantage [*commodum*] from them. This is what we are primarily after; friends are secondary.
>
> 1998[1642], p. 22–23

We are a long way away from Aristotle, Francis of Assisi, Aquinas, and from the civil culture of the cities and from the civil humanism in which the market was based on *philia*.

What arises from the dynamic of naturally social individuals is not a civil-society but a state-society, whose existence is only possible if established by an artificial contract and if an impersonal "Leviathan" maintains it through the monopoly of force and violence. This result arises from a notion of the state of nature as inhabited by subjects who come into the world "like mushrooms" and, as such, need no help from others and have no obligation toward anyone. As Esposito remarks:

> If the relationship between men is in itself destructive, the only route of escape from this unbearable state of affairs is the destruction of the relation itself. If the only community that is humanly verifiable is that of crime, there doesn't remain anything except the crime of the community: the drastic elimination of every kind of social bond.
>
> Esposito 2009, p. 27

For Hobbes the society of free and equal individuals is only compatible with a weak relational bond, which we call here, with Esposito, mutual "immunitas". And actually, if human beings are *naturally* incapable of friendship and positive relationships, how are they supposed to change *after* the contract? In fact after the contract they do not turn into "relational" individuals; they just build a new form of communal life in which everyone obeys the Leviathan's absolute power and has no contact with anyone else. Here again we are confronted with the same sacral structure we encountered in the ancient community (now in a secularized form), despite the attempts to negate and destroy it, as depicted in Figure 5.3 below.

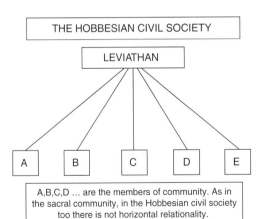

What binds A, B, C...is the social contract, which requires no *philia* or sympathy between individuals, but only mutual indifference and absence of war: *immunitas.*

The new contract-society is not therefore the evolution of the natural community; it is rather, as we have now seen, its opposite, its negation.

6
Between Hobbes and Smith

> The strongest is never strong enough to be always the master,
> unless he transforms strength into right, and obedience into
> duty.
>
> J. J. Rousseau

1. A preliminary formal representation

In this chapter we push the analysis one step further by comparing the
projects of Hobbes and other modern-age authors. This comparison will
allow us to comprehend the cultural and anthropological meaning of
the birth of modern political economy.

We may start by representing the theory of the problem of the social
contract as a "game".[1] In lieu of the Prisoner's Dilemma (a game often
employed to describe the social contract), we shall use the "Stag Hunt"
game.[2]

Increasingly adopted in the social sciences today, this game may also
be seen as a formalized version of the story told by J.J. Rousseau in his
Discourse on the Origin of Inequality, which forms part of his theory of the
historical evolution of life in common:

> In this way, men were able gradually to acquire some rough idea of
> mutual commitments and the benefits of keeping them, but only as
> much as clear and present interests might require, for men had no

---

[1] By the word "game" I refer here to its use in the social sciences, which is
different from its ordinary meaning.

[2] In a more generalized version, this game is also known as the *Assurance
Game*.

A/B	Stag	Hare
Stag	4,4	**0,3**
Hare	**3,0**	2,2

Figure 6.1   Stag Hunt

foresight, and far from concerning themselves with a distant future, they hardly thought of the next day. *When it came to tracking down a deer, everyone realized that he should remain dependably at his post; but if a hare happened to pass within reach of one of them, he undoubtedly would not have hesitated to run off after it and, after catching its prey, he would have troubled himself little about causing his companions to lose theirs.*

2009[1755], pp. 57–58, my italics

This kind of situation may be translated into the matrix below, perhaps somewhat twisting the letter but certainly not the spirit of Rousseau's passage:

Hunting a stag[3] is riskier because hunters have to coordinate with each other; each of them has to do his part. Hunting a hare, on the contrary, involves no risk and no need of coordination. But the stag (or rather the share of it due to each hunter) is more valuable than the hare. When both hunters (A and B) independently choose to go on hunting the stag (even when the hare is within reach of their arrows or rifles), they achieve the best outcome, both from an individual and social point of view – 4 is the highest payoff in the game and, if we take the sum of the payoffs for each outcome as a measure of social well-being, the combination Stag–Stag returns the highest sum (8). When each of the two hunters decides to chase the hare, they each obtain not the lowest, but the intermediate outcome (2,2). In turn, when they do not coordinate and A decides to hold on to the initial "pact" of hunting the stag

---

[3] I apologize for using the metaphor of hunting, which many including myself hardly regard as...civil. We are shortly to abandon this metaphor, anyway.

(pacts are not binding in this game), while B decides to give in to the temptation of hunting the hare (hence obtaining 3),[4] the hunter who keeps faith to the stag hunt receives zero points (under the assumption, held by Rousseau, that hunters may only succeed in hunting a stag if they stick together, and that, alone, one hunter may only catch a hare). A symmetrical situation (0,3) occurs in case B decides to hold on to the pact, but A does not. This simple game has two "Nash equilibria", i.e. two stable outcomes, which for either player it is not convenient to abandon, unless they move together (in this case from Hare–Hare to Stag–Stag).

Why is this game such a good representation of the dialectical relation between the State of Nature and Civil Society?

First of all, unlike the Prisoner's Dilemma[5] where only the non-cooperative outcome (Hare–Hare) constitutes an equilibrium, in the Stag Hunt the cooperative outcome too (Stag–Stag) is an equilibrium. In the classical version of the social contract, both the state of nature and civil society, the latter artificially created by the contract, are two stable situations; they are two Nash equilibria (for A it is rational to choose "Stag" if B chooses "Stag", and "Hare" if B chooses "Hare"). By stipulating a social contract, they make a "leap" from the lower, less risky, equilibrium (2,2), to the highest (4,4).[6]

---

[4] In this version of the game (where the numerical payoffs are equal to 4,3,2,0), we are assuming that if one hunter hunts a hare but the other hunter doesn't, the probability of caching a hare (or of catching a bigger hare) is higher compared to the case in which both hunters go after the hare (this is why Hare–Stag returns 3, while Hare–Hare returns 2). The logic of the game would remain unaltered if a payoff of 2 were paid in both cases (Hare–Stag; Hare–Hare). See Skyrms (2004, pp.3 ff.) for a discussion of this point. It is standard practice in game theory to give an ordinal meaning to the numerical payoffs (4>3>2>0; a>b>c...); any transformation of the numerical payoffs which maintains the same order still describes the same "game".

[5] The Prisoner's Dilemma is possibly the most popular game in economic theory: it is a non-cooperative game characterized by having non-cooperation (e.g. 2,2) as its only equilibrium and as the only rational choice for each player, even though mutual cooperation (e.g. 3,3) would yield an outcome preferred by both players. Hence the "dilemma".

[6] Someone might object that the social contract also presents a free-riding issue, given by those who wait for others to stipulate the social contract and then enjoy its benefits without contributing (as if the social contract were a sort of public good: differentiating between 3 and 2 allows us to partly capture this issue). In fact, the spirit of seventeenth- and eighteenth-century authors goes in another direction: those who don't take part in the social contract are excluded from the game and cannot enjoy the benefits of social life, as explicitly stated

There is also a second aspect that makes this game particularly suited to depicting the kind of situations we are discussing, including the Hobbesian case.[7] The two outcomes and equilibria in the game are characterized by the fact that one (4,4) is superior to the other (2,2) in terms of payoffs (the cooperative equilibrium is actually "Pareto superior" compared to the non-cooperative one); but the non-cooperative equilibrium is *risk dominant* compared to the cooperative one. What does this mean? If a cautious player chooses to hunt the hare, he will never go home empty-handed; if, on the other hand, he chooses to hunt the stag, he might well go home without a prey (0). Metaphor aside, by not cooperating I risk nothing, I need not entertain any form of relationship with others, and I depend on no one. Of course, I receive less (2 or 3) compared to sharing a stag (4), but my result is certain, without need to enter a relation based on trust, which is always fragile and vulnerable to the choices of others.

Mutual distrust (or, to use Hobbes' language, "fear of risk") renders the state of nature a state of non-cooperation (2,2). The social contract thus allows us to "leap" from (2,2) to (4,4). But how? Simply by re-designing the rewards of the game (payoffs) after the social contract: since the two (or *n*) players are rational, they know that mutual fear would land them in (2,2); for this reason they make a pact and simultaneously consign to the State the absolute power to punish those who don't respect the contract (in Rousseau's story they are the ones who abandon the stag hunt to chase the hare). One way to represent this dynamic in the previous matrix is to imagine that a certain sanction (set for instance

---

by Hume with his "sensible knave" and by Genovesi (in his "catechism", as we shall see). In reality, if we take the Stag Hunt as a game representing the social contract, we ought to explain the outcomes (3,0) and (0,3), and also explain why hunting alone (0) is worse than the state of nature. An intuitive explanation may be given by the situation of a lamb surrounded by wolves: the state of nature is a situation in which all are wolves to each other (2,2). An even worse situation occurs when one player unilaterally decides to cooperate within a hostile environment, because in this case he or she cannot even rely on the minimal prudential measures typically adopted in situations of conflict.

[7] Hobbes' theory is more articulated and may also be defined in terms of the Prisoner's Dilemma: cooperation (civil society) is not a "spontaneous" equilibrium of the interaction among individuals, but the social contract establishes an enforcement system (the Leviathan), which makes the cooperative outcome stable. The game may be redesigned by introducing penalties for non-cooperation so as to make cooperation the rational choice. I discussed the Prisoner's Dilemma in the context of the cooperation analysis carried out in Bruni (2008) and in Bruni and Smerilli (2011).

A/B	Stag	Hare
Stag	4,4	0,(3-3)
Hare	(3-3),0	(2-3),(2-3)

Figure 6.2 Leviathan's Game

to -3) is applied by the Leviathan in case of non-cooperation: in this new game, which we may call "the Leviathan's game", the only equilibrium becomes 'forcible' cooperation (4,4).[8]

As showed by Robert Sugden (2004, p. 169), Hobbes (*Leviathan*, chap. 15) does not dispute the existence, even in the state of nature, of spontaneous conventions of cooperation between people (like paying a debt, for instance); what he does dispute, however, is the possibility that such conventions may form a generalized practice capable of sustaining the entire civil society. For this to happen in a society where individuals give up their freedom to not cooperate for the sake of avoiding a generalized war, the Leviathan is needed. On this point Sugden remarks: "I have to confess that I cannot understand Hobbes's argument" (2004, p. 169); and thereby presents his own "Humean" account of the creation of civil society and of the exit from the state of nature.

But first, in the next section, we take a look at the difference between Hobbes' and Locke's respective versions of the social contract, which I believe will offer relevant insights into our discussion.

2. Hobbes and Locke (and Grotius)

In Hobbes' theory the only equilibrium that individuals are able to achieve in the "state of nature" is the *risk dominant* one (2,2) because they are dominated by fear. They are rationally aware that there is a possibility of improvement, both generally and individually (don't

---

[8] We may also represent the social contract in a different way: instead of redesigning the game's payoffs, we could think of the social contract as an agreement made before the start of the game, which allows us to select the Pareto superior equilibrium (4,4).

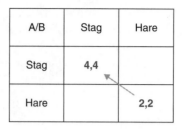

A/B	Stag	Hare
Stag	4,4	
Hare		2,2

Figure 6.3   Hobbes and Locke

forget Hobbes considers human beings rational and self-interested). At the same time, individuals are unable to spontaneously reach the higher equilibrium (corresponding to the birth of civil society). An artificial act is needed to reach the equilibrium in (4,4): the institution of the social contract and of coercive power. This event is represented in the table below: from the state of nature (2,2) the social contract allows the shift (arrow) to the equilibrium in (4,4) (in the table I maintain the original payoffs without sanctions).

The social contract thus enables a "Paretian" improvement (i.e. an improvement in efficiency) for each individual and for society as a whole. It is the social contract that artificially "creates" a new form of sociality (civil society), otherwise absent in the state of nature, where people are unable to spontaneously keep promises and pacts:

> Outside the commonwealth is the empire of the passions, war, fear, poverty, nastiness, solitude, barbarity, ignorance, savagery; within the commonwealth is the empire of reason, peace, security, wealth, splendour, society, good taste, the sciences and good-will.
>
> *De Cive*, p. 116

Such a commonwealth is not spontaneous but artificial:

> An association [*societas*] formed only for mutual aid, does not afford to the parties to the accord or association the security which we are looking for, to practise, in their relations with each other, the laws of nature given above [...]. But something more is needed, an element of fear, to prevent an accord on peace and mutual assistance for a *common good* from collapsing in discord when a *private good* subsequently comes into conflict with the *common good*.
>
> Ibid. pp. 70–71

Both the social contract and the Leviathan are necessary in order to achieve the cooperative equilibrium. The Leviathan prevents men from surrendering to the temptation of chasing the hare ("when a private good comes into conflict with the common good").

Such a radical argument can best be explained in light of the anthropological conception endorsed by Hobbes, who, in the wake of Luther, deemed "natural" human beings incapable of friendship (at least in the public sphere), because they are sickened by cupidity (*concupiscientia*), egoism and power.

Locke's theorization of the social contract and of the state of nature appears certainly different from this perspective.

In brief: war is for Hobbes the natural condition (the state of nature) and the social contract is entered into for the purpose of ensuring peace (civil society); for Locke, on the contrary, the state of nature would be dominated by peace and concord, but conflicts arising from the scarcity of resources and from private property make it *necessary to resort to the social contract to avoid ending up in war.*[9]

We read in Locke's *Treatise*:

> And here we have the plain difference between the state of nature and the state of war, which however some men have confounded, are as far distant, as a state of peace, good will, mutual assistance, and Preservation, and a state of enmity, malice, violence and mutual destruction are one from another.
>
> *Treatise*, § 19

This depiction of the state of nature is an oblique, yet sharp, response to Hobbes. Thus he continues:

> To avoid this state of war (wherein there is no appeal but to heaven, and wherein every the least difference is apt to end, where there is no authority to decide between the contenders) is one great reason of men's putting themselves into society, and quitting the state of nature.
>
> Ibid., § 21

Every individual is willing to take this step, for "though in the state of nature he hath such a right, yet the enjoyment of it is very uncertain and constantly exposed to the invasion of others" (ibid., §123).

---

[9] Binmore (2005, p. 25) regards the "optimistic" view of Locke as an unrealistic "pastoral idyll", the product of an ideology aimed to morally justify the newly-born commercial society.

Locke's account is informed by a different anthropological conception, not too far in this respect from the Aristotelian tradition. As we
read at the beginning of Chapter VII:

> God having made man such a creature, that in his own judgement, it
> was not good for him to be alone, put him under strong obligations
> of necessity, convenience, and inclination to drive him into society.
> The first society was between man and wife.
>
> Ibid., §77

At the same time Locke promptly remarks (here in line with Hobbes)
that family "which what resemblance soever it may have... with a little
Common-wealth, yet is very far from it" (ibid., § 86).

Thanks to Locke we can see that no structural inconsistency exists
between "Aristotelian" anthropology and the social contract. The State
therefore emerges either to "preserve" and protect what is already part
of the human nature (Locke), or to create a new kind of sociality otherwise absent in nature (Hobbes) – but which kind?

Even farther from Hobbes, but in some respects closer to Locke, is
Grotius' formulation of the social contract, which shows direct connec-
tions with the Aristotelian–Thomistic tradition, but also with Althusius
and with the tradition of natural law. According to Grotius, the human
being is characterized by dignity and sociability, by the "impelling
desire for society, that is, for the social life – not of any and every sort,
but peaceful, and organized according to the measure of his intelli-
gence, with those who are of his own kind" (1979[1625], pp. 34–35). For
Grotius the emergence of the social contract is due to the fact that, in
the state of nature, natural rights are unsecured and fragile; its function
is therefore to guarantee and permit sociality, rather than inventing it:

> Grotius argues explicitly that we must not attempt to derive our
> fundamental principles from an idea of mutual advantage alone;
> human sociability indicates that advantage is not the only reason
> why human beings act justly. Grotius evidently believes that a
> society based upon sociability and respect rather than upon mutual
> advantage can remain stable over time.
>
> Nussbaum 2005, p. 37

If we wanted to illustrate Grotius' or Locke's view of the social contract
by continuing to employ the language of the stag hunt, the matrix thus
obtained would be symmetrical to the Hobbesian case:

A/B	Stag	Hare
Stag	4,4	
Hare		2,2

Figure 6.4   The social contract *à la* Grotius–Locke as a Stag Hunt

A/B	Stag	Hare
Stag	3,3	1.4
Hare	4,1	2,2

Figure 6.5   The social contract as a Prisoner's Dilemma

In this table, the dotted line of the arrow (now inverted) signifies a virtual, not a real shift: the social contract is a device that protects social life in a context of potential conflicts generated by private property and by the scarcity of resources. Without the social contract, conflict would ensue (2,2).

To produce a more faithful representation of Locke's original formulation, the problem of the social contract may be illustrated through the Prisoner's Dilemma in lieu of the Stag Hunt game (though the latter is still possible nonetheless): as noticed, while in the Stag Hunt there are two equilibria, in the Prisoner's Dilemma there is only one (non-cooperative) equilibrium and a single dominant strategy, i.e. non-cooperation. The cooperative outcome, still more rewarding in terms of payoffs,[10] is not an equilibrium in the Prisoner's Dilemma game: cooperating is never rational from the individual's point of view. If we chose to illustrate Locke's social contract with a Prisoner's Dilemma (either dynamic or repeated), we should observe that cooperation in the state of nature is not stable but exposed to the temptation of unilateral opportunism (free riding). The social contract turns the cooperative outcome into an equilibrium.

---

[10] Or "Pareto superior", where superiority is assessed in terms of efficiency, as defined by the Italian economist Vilfredo Pareto (1906).

In Locke, the social contract results in the cooperative equilibrium; but the underlying anthropological framework is substantially different, and so is the nature of the social contract. In this version, which we may call classical or Aristotelian–Thomistic,[11] the contract is *subsidiary* to sociability, which is the natural dimension of human life. In Hobbes, instead, the social contract is a *substitute* for natural reciprocity; it is a new form of social relationship based on mutual *immunitas*.

In the next chapter we shall consider whether and in what way the rise of political economy might be seen as either a continuation or a rupture with Hobbes and with the tradition of contractualism.

3. The invention and simultaneous "killing" of the community of individuals

We are coming to one of the first "poles of attraction" in our discussion. The Modern age – a label that fails to capture the continuity with the process that originated in Greece and Israel – is nothing short of a paradox with regard to common life: *in the very same moment as it salutes the community of individuals, it simultaneously proclaims its death.* This twofold process is especially clear and radical in Hobbes' work, even though it represents a common tendency of the entire tradition of 'natural law' (as Norberto Bobbio called it), which will become dominant in the West starting from the eighteenth century.

There is one particular aspect of this process that it is useful to consider and that has not been sufficiently emphasized in the literature about Hobbes.

If civil society is for Hobbes an artificial creation, we ought to remember that the *state of nature* he describes has an equally "artificial" or ideal-typical nature. Men at the time of Hobbes, or in any time before then, were not equal and free individuals and certainly not in a position to realize the convenience of a pact, let alone to actually subscribe to one: real men in the *ancient régime* were not individuals, but subjects still embedded in the sacred community dominated by "status", not by "contract". We noticed in previous chapters how the ancient sacred community continued to exist throughout the Middles Ages in spite of the disrupting force of the Christian event and of the new signs of

---

[11] Here I do not wish to defend a *general* continuity between Locke and the Aristotelian–Thomistic tradition (we know Locke's conception of society differs from it in many ways; the very idea of the social contract is something we do not find in Aristotle, or in the Thomistic school).

Greek, Roman and Jewish culture. Indeed, Luther had well interpreted the climate of his times and on these grounds he built his Reformation, whose nature was religious as well as political.

The artificial civil society described by Hobbes has its origin in a state of nature that is no less artificial. Not only because human beings are not as radically selfish and anti-social as Hobbes portrayed them, but also because human beings in the seventeenth-century *were yet to become individuals*. These male, adults, heads of family, politicians, ecclesiastics or merchants (the only human beings we may consider "individuals" in the sense Hobbes intended) were hardly in the condition of equality and freedom required by Hobbes' theory: for the most part they were the products of the community in which they were embedded (tribe, city, church, empire, etc.), and their freedom was, at best, limited and conditioned.[12] Of course we cannot argue (nor do we wish to) that no individual ever existed in the Greek polis or in the medieval cities; but, among men, they were the exception, not the rule. The culture of the *ancient régime* was not the culture of the individual.

This point is crucial for our discussion. Just *before "killing" the individuals' community,* modernity – of which Hobbes is the greatest expression in the political sphere – *invents its possibility.*

The ability to discern individuals before their actual appearance is a major strong point of Hobbes' theory.[13] Toward the individual

---

[12] Real freedom did exist in certain contexts like economic exchanges; less so in marital choices, while it was virtually absent from choices concerning religion and status. Women's freedom and equality were close to inexistent, but for abbesses or duchesses.

[13] Rousseau wrote extensively about the "historical" mistakes in Hobbes' theory (even though his perspective is different from mine – *si parva licet!*). He criticized Hobbes' state of nature, not quite because real human beings did not fit Hobbes' description of the state of nature, but because the state of nature was not "natural" but the product of a human nature that was "artificial" and corrupted by the market economy. Rousseau's anthropological conception is more optimistic, even though, after all, his theory of the social contract is not substantially different from Hobbes' as both defend the need to pass from the state in (2,2) – not a state of nature, but a state already of decay – to civil society (4,4). An observation similar to the one I make about Hobbes is contained in Locke's *Treatise on the Government* (§ 95). Interestingly, recent studies in cultural anthropology have highlighted a reality not dissimilar from Rousseau's theory of the "three stages". These studies (for a survey see De Waal 2001; some interesting hints are also in Binmore 2005, Ch. 9) suggest that before the agricultural revolution in the Neolithic (about 11,000 – 10,000 years ago in the Fertile Crescent) small communities of hunters and gatherers had a loosely hierarchical order and lived substantially in peace. With the agricultural revolution

Hobbes performed almost a sort of abortion (please forgive the strong analogy): the relational individual was still at a stage of gestation but was destroyed before he was even born. Hobbes imagined a city inhabited by free and equal individuals as incapable of positive relationships and constantly in a state of civil war. Indeed, he could infer the possibility of such an *uncivil city* from the battles of religion of his day (at the time Hobbes was elaborating his political theory, the "Thirty Years' War" was raging in Europe); yet those battles were not fought by free and equal individuals – they were, rather, the swan song of the sacred communities that had dominated Europe for thousands of years. Hobbes had conceived the possibility of a free and equal individual in relation with other free and equal individuals; but he prevented his birth. In fact, partly as a result of Hobbes' thought, it is not the relational individual that will make his appearance in the modern age, but an individual who is alone and whose relations with others are merely instrumental. The Middles Ages could have carried the person, but instead gave life to the individual alone.

Hobbes more than any other was able to envision, prophetically (and herein lies his greatness), that the world was changing: the sun was setting on the sacred community and rising on something new. Once the sacred mediator had been eliminated, that is, once the Sun had set on Christianity, the modern man, disoriented, looked around himself and discovered the existence of another individual, another-who-was-not-himself. In the pre-modern world, man had been able to recognize the transcendent Absolute and to put himself on a level of inferiority in a relation of submission to Him and to his historical mediators. This new individual, that Hobbes could barely distinguish, found himself for the first time in front of another individual, in a generalized and radical way; another individual similar to himself, but different: every "I" represents for his similars another "I", a "non-I", and hence a problem. He has found himself in front of someone who is neither above nor below him, but beside him.

On this point Todorov remarked: "As one studies the broad currents of European philosophical thought on the definition of what is human, a curious conclusion stands out. The social dimension, the very fact of life in common, is not generally conceived of as being necessary to

---

and the emergence of the great ancient empires a new phase of scarcity and conflictive sociality arose, marked by extensive empires informed by a strongly hierarchical and sacred character. This phase, as seen in previous chapters, will last throughout the Middle Ages.

human beings. This "thesis," however, is not presented as such; it is a supposition that remains unformulated" (Todorov 2001[1995], p. 1).

Above all the other is a "wound" and therefore an evil we ought to avoid, if we can. Modern man cannot see the "blessing" associated with this wound. This is why we try to escape the other, to find some escape route. The two main escape routes Modernity has been able to provide have been the Leviathan and the Market, the new mediators introduced to escape the pain that accompanies the kind of relationality occurring between individuals who are free and equal, but also potentially murderers.

Modernity, in fact, regards and invents the other as equal, thereby leading to a rude awakening – that is, to the discovery of the negation that other-ness necessarily entails. The enthusiasm induced by the discovery of one's own existence as individuality has been accompanied in the modern age by the fear of the other's existence. In the very same moment the modern man utters the word "I", he fearfully says "you". Discovering the other does not lead to mutual recognition but opens up to a season of research – still very much in a phase of development, in an increasingly tighter alliance with technique and technology – of escape routes to avoid meeting the other's eyes. Hobbes, more than any other, understood this groundbreaking shift. He was able to anticipate it and, through his influential work, he gave shape to its modern evolution.

Confronted with the negation that the discovery of the other entails, Hobbes decided that the risk deriving from this kind of horizontal sociality was too high a price to pay (life in common itself): thanks to him, European society found itself passing *from containing communities without individuals to featuring the individual without community.*

The sacred mediator was replaced by the Leviathan (and by the Market), once again delaying the journey over the distance that divides "I" from "You". Western culture was not offered the possibility of a community simultaneously free, equal and fraternal; instead it experienced either the fraternity, illiberal and unequal, of the sacred community, or the free and equal individual without community.

It is my strong impression that Hobbes' theory was profoundly prophetic, for it seems to be much more fitting today than it was in the mid-seventeenth century. In this respect, the success enjoyed today in social theory and in the praxis of contractualism applied to society and firms appears emblematic (as in some versions of stakeholder theory).

In order to be *fair*, the great free and pluralistic society has a vital need of individuals who are not bound by ties and passions and who are capable of restraining their personal notions of goodness to the private sphere. Therefore the diversity between "I" and "You" is handled, quite simply, *by removing it*, by protecting oneself through social and private contracts that show an increasing level of sophistication and require no dialogue, nor any inter-human encounter, but rather *mutual indifference*, to say it with J. Rawls (1971); such contracts produce a society that is all the more free the less people cross paths and touch each other.

The reciprocity of the contract has thus become a new form of reciprocity, whose power is fully expressed in the economic sphere. For this reason, from the next chapter we shall delve further into the origins and traditions of political economy, which perhaps more fittingly than political theory incarnates the *immunitarian* project of modernity. The latter is only fully revealed when observed from the perspective of the individual, without the mediating community, at the mercy of others who are equal to him but incapable of *philia* and of any positive and immediate relationship: was this not the sort of life in common that emerged in the setting of civil and religious wars of sixteenth- and seventeenth-century Europe? Once the Christian *fides* became un able to provide a foundation for life in common any longer, the Market became the new lay *fides*, the new ethos of life in common.

7
Relationships and Vaccinations

> The idea of wealth is not always the cornerstone of civilization,
> for often it is a consequence, other times it is among its partial
> objectives, other times still it is a means ... Therefore one may
> be rich by way of accumulating many goods, and yet not be
> civil.
>
> Ludovico Bianchini (1855)

1. A market without face

The Middle Ages were the great incubator of the market economy.
Markets and merchants have always existed in the history of man (and,
to some extent, even in the prehistory). In the Middle Ages, however,
something new came to light: something we call today the *market
economy*. Although the latter will only appear in the second part of the
modern age, all its elements are already present in the late Middles Ages,
like seeds that will later germinate.

With the protestant Reformation (initially championed by Luther and
later by Calvin and other reformers), *fides* and medieval *philia* exhausted
their common function of mediator in commercial and financial
exchanges in Europe. In the Middles Ages and during the period of
civil humanism, the market had basically been a network of personal
relations, and hence not anonymous. People in flesh and blood, their
identities and personal stories were the actual parameters for trustworthiness. Florence, Venice, Marseille and Bruges had built their fortune
on such mercantile ethics.

In the aftermath of the civil and religious wars between the Christians,
starting from the mid-sixteenth century, Europe sought to create a new
basis for exchanges, i.e. a new *fides*, which, as Genovesi would later

observe, also means "cord": a new cord was needed, a new social bond for a new Europe.

Personal trust based on identity and citizenship could no longer suffice: identity and citizenship now stood as reminders of confessional divisions, stories and situations that had to be confined to the background in order to secure peace and to favour the return of trade flows. In the seventeenth century, merchants and countries were forced to create a new market economy that became increasingly anonymous and financially driven (at least for the exchanges between cities and between countries): it was not people and their identities that were now circulating across Europe (and in the New World), but in their place credit notes, paper money, shares. From the seventeenth century the market started to become depersonalized and turned into a form of relationship capable of mediating between strangers. It is at this point that Capitalism emerged in Europe, as the goods exchanged began to lose their connection to the identity of their makers.

This extraordinary invention led to an enormous expansion in exchange flows and to the inclusion of millions – today billions – of people, thanks to the disempowerment of any element of diversity and identity (whether religious, ethnic, national, etc.) in human relations. In order to take part in an exchange, I do not need to regard the other tragically in his otherness: the price system acts as a "third party" sterilizing any potentially harmful elements. From this the modern market – and the post-modern market even more – takes its ambivalent character: by disempowering and levelling human diversity, the market makes it possible to take part in an exchange with anyone (with Muslims in the East, for instance): *fides* is no longer a requirement and neither is *religio*; mutual needs and desires are enough. This type of relationality may be assimilated to *Eros,* whose character, we will see, is equally universalistic (Marion 2006). At the same time, such universalism does not correspond to a network of *encounters* among different subjects, but rather to a relationship of mutual indifference among subjects whose diversity has been evened out in order to make possible exchanges without diversity. The highly innovative and inclusive power of the market as well as its incredible ability to generate loneliness and anonymity are both products of the modern economy. Deep personal relationships are a source of potential suffering; for this reason it is best to confine them to the increasingly narrow private sphere, since "fraternity" (non-electivity) would be overly dangerous in the public sphere: it's a question of whether we can content ourselves with equality and freedom.

2. More about the origins of modern political economy

I wish now to introduce the argument that I will develop over the next few pages. Going back to the metaphor of immunization through vaccination described earlier, we will see how that tiny bit of sociality that the modern economy (Smith) brings into the "new community" (the commercial society) is, in fact, poisonous: its aim is to sterilize the community's typical and vital relations, while at the same time protecting itself against the virus of personal and dangerous relationships with others. This kind of sociality that penetrates into the market is the antidote injected into the body to kill the "evil" that is ascribed in the modern age to unmediated human relations, considered illiberal and unequal. From this point of view, Smith sides with Hobbes: unmediated horizontal relations are negative and uncivil; they must be sterilized by introducing a small "dose" of relationality into the market, a vaccine against the great evil that is the harmful charge of relationality.

Like for Hobbes, civil society is not the "state of nature", but an artificial construction, i.e. the Market – which must be created intentionally so that the individual's self-interested actions may unintentionally realize the common good (the wealth of nations).

It is important to remember that according to Smith, and to the founders of political and modern civil economy (from this point of view there is no radical difference between the Scottish and the Italian traditions), the market is not the natural outcome of human aggregation into societies: it is a natural instinct to "barter and exchange", Smith observes, but only with well-designed institutions, just laws and uncorrupted judges can such natural instincts produce the common good, i.e. civilization. Hume, for instance, believed that justice, an essential virtue in the commercial society, is artificial and not natural, because justice is too impartial to be governed by natural sentiments; sympathy, on which benevolence depends, is natural, but depends on social and affective closeness and does not apply to strangers, with whom it is necessary to maintain the sense of justice (cf. Bruni and Sugden 2000).

In Naples, Vico (1744) already argued that the transformation of individual vices (greed and ambition) into the common good (wealth and politics) may only occur within civil society and especially within the city society, where it is possible to achieve "civil happiness" (here the word "civil" is essential).

The market is an artificial creation in the sense that its ability to operate and to generate economic development depends on the selection of some features in human sociality (think of the "vaccine" metaphor) while leaving others aside (or restricting them to the private sphere). For instance, the market works by banning from itself friendship and benevolence, which nonetheless remain among the natural traits of human sociality, but which would jeopardize the mechanism of price signals. At the same time, the artificial quality Smith has in mind is not identical to the one Hobbes has in mind: for the latter civil society is created by a double pact (between the citizens and between them and the Leviathan), which nullifies the statuses of natural society and domesticates with absolute authority the anti-social instincts of man–wolf.

In the wake of Hume, Smith describes society as artificial, because it functions by taming and sterilizing the "riskier" dimensions of human relationality and by artificially establishing institutions (from property rights to tribunals). But in a more radical sense and according to an interpretation with which the founders of political economy would most likely be uncomfortable (and that I will not follow further), Smith's commercial society may only work within a civil society à la Hobbes, where there is a social contract which artificially establishes the institutional conditions that allow the alchemical transformation of private interests into the common good. To work, the "invisible hand" requires institutions that are very visible and for a large part artificial, which may guarantee the enforcement of contracts and/or the right incentives for the enforcement among the parts of the contract itself (reputation, in particular).

There is, therefore, a sort of continuity between Hobbes' and Smith's projects. Hobbes was perhaps the most radical author to have theorized the necessity of the death of the *communitas* in order to allow the birth of the modern *societas* founded on the social contract between free and equal individuals. Smith has been less explicit in this respect, yet no less radical.

Their anthropological approaches are different: Hobbes, following Luther, looks at the human ability to naturally create a positive kind of sociality with his peers with radical pessimism; on the other hand, particularly in his *Theory of Moral Sentiments* (1759), Smith offered a view of the human person as fundamentally relational and open to genuine relationships with others: *sympathy, fellow-feeling, correspondence of sentiments*: these are all absolutely social categories, on whose basis we can consider Smith as one of the authors who most engaged with the psychology and sociology of inter-human relations. At the same time, Hobbes and Smith have a common enemy: the ancient social relation, the pre-modern social relation, which is for them radically negative and alternative to the *free-society*. The anti-feudal polemic in fact was fundamental in Hobbes as much in Smith (and in Hume and Genovesi, as we are about to see): it was a radical polemic that, although springing from different anthropological conceptions, led both the authors of *Leviathan* and of the *Wealth of Nations* to formulate very similar theories with regard to the kind of sociality necessary to the new society, finally free and virtually egalitarian. In the *Wealth of Nations* we find one crucial passage concerning the anti-feudal polemic:

> A revolution of the greatest importance to the public happiness was in this manner brought about by two different orders of people, who had not the least intention to serve the public. To gratify the most childish vanity was the sole motive of the great proprietors. The merchants and artificers, much less ridiculous, acted merely from a view to their own interest, and in pursuit of their own pedlar principle of turning a penny wherever a penny was to be got. Neither of them had either knowledge or foresight of that great revolution which the folly of the one, and the industry of the other, was gradually bringing about.
>
> 1976[1776], p. 440

Just a few pages earlier, Smith refers to Hume (and indirectly to Hobbes) with regard to the origin of his insight:

> Commerce and manufactures gradually introduced order and good government, and with them the liberty and security of individuals, among the inhabitants of the country, who had before lived almost in a continual state of war with their neighbours, and of servile dependency upon their superiors. This, though it has been the least observed, is by far the most important of all their effects. Mr. Hume is the only writer who, so far as I know, has hitherto taken notice of it.
>
> 1976[1776], p. 433[1]

---

[1] In fact, Hume was not the first to understand these mechanisms. Just a few years before Hume, Vico had already fully comprehended the mechanism that lies at the heart of Hume's historical and social analysis – although the Scottish scholars could not have known that.

At the heart of the cultural manoeuvre that Smith operated as the founder of political economy, we thus find an intention that is similar to Hobbes': selfless commercial exchange has to replace the *munus*. In other words, the form of reciprocity that the contract entails (deriving from the act of *cum-trahere*) is regarded as a form of reciprocity or relationality that is opposite to the *munus*, which in the eighteenth century is only (and rightfully) seen as obligation, not as a free gift. The *munus*-obligation is an expression and a reaffirmation of the dependence on the benevolence of others: it obligates and binds; whereas the contract frees and renders the individual independent from all in general, and from each single individual in particular.

We shall now examine some key theoretical passages of Smith's thought.

3. Smith: common good without benevolence

There is one sentence by Adam Smith that has become, and not by chance, so hugely famous over the last two centuries as to basically have become commonplace in the imaginary of political economy. It's the one about the "butcher", that we shall take as a starting point in order to approach Smith's thought about the market and the interpersonal relations within it: "It is not from the benevolence of the butcher, the brewer, or the baker, that we expect our dinner, but from their regard to their own interest. We address ourselves, not to their humanity but to their self-live, and never talk to them of our own necessities but of their advantages" (1976[1776], pp. 26–27).

This passage embodies the basic logic of all classic liberal economy, but at the same time offers an important key to understanding the optimistic humanism that informs the phenomenon of trust in markets' expansion and in globalization. Smith emphasizes the independent character of the "benevolence of his fellow-citizens", which he regards as a positive virtue associated with the new sociality brought about by market economy. Market relations allow us to satisfy our needs without having to depend on others in a hierarchical system, since by depending on all in an impersonal and anonymous way, on the Market's "invisible hand", we depend personally on no-one, we must have no personal (and potentially harmful) encounters; we depend on many, none of whom has a face:

> Each tradesman or artificer derives his subsistence from the employment, not of one, but of a hundred or a thousand different customers.

Though in some measure obliged to them all, therefore, he is not absolutely dependent upon any of them.

Ibid., p. 420

One depends exclusively on the market, not on ambivalent friends. This is why, according to Smith, the market economy is an immediately civilizing factor, it is itself civil society, civilization; and this is also why there is no civilization outside the market's sphere of action.

Hence the ethical justification of Smith's humanism of independence, well-summarized in this one sentence which is hardly ever quoted and comes right after the passage of the butcher in the *Wealth of Nations*: "Nobody but a beggar chooses to depend chiefly upon the benevolence of his fellow-citizens" (1976[1776], p. 27).

We thus arrive to another key moment in our discourse.

The "benevolence" of citizens is what the Aristotelian–Thomistic tradition had in mind when addressing the Common Good, which they saw as arising from the *intentional* action of those willing to give up something in terms of private good (i.e. their personal interests) for the sake of fostering the common good. According to this ancient tradition there could be no common good without *intentional benevolence*. After Hobbes, Smith states, on the contrary, that the common good is the unintentional result of the action that is intentionally directed at one's private good: the direct pursuit of private interests indirectly produces the common good. Not only does the latter require no benevolence from others, but it is even more and better served the less benevolence is imbued in the intentions and actions of those taking part in the new market relation. Furthermore, the search for self-interest comes from the stoic *virtues* of prudence and independence. The impartial spectator approves of the individual search for self-interest because of the civil fruits it bears; but, unlike for Mandeville, the private action of prudent men all looking for interest is not a vice (Hirschman 1977, McCloskey 2006).

In his *Theory of moral sentiments*, Smith reminds us that the human being has a natural tendency to sympathy, benevolence and a direct relationship with the other. At the same time, such anthropological and psychological traits are not necessary for the smooth running of the market: "Beneficence, therefore, is less essential to the existence of society than justice. Society may subsist, though not in the most comfortable state, without beneficence: but the prevalence of injustice must utterly destroy it" (1984[1759], p. 86). On this ground Smith can argue that "Society may subsist among different people ... from a sense of its utility, *without any mutual love or affection"* (ibid., pp. 85–86, *my italics*). In order for the market to function, the participants must respect the artificial principles of justice (a sense of justice may arise out of concern for one's own reputation, or out of one's inner sense of justice, or else, out of fear of punishment: all of these different mechanisms are present in Smith's theory and each of them plays an important role). But the impersonal principles of justice are quite different from the ones regulating the most intimate sociality in the private sphere.

This is a critical argument, not far from the opinion many have of market ethics today. But in fact, this line of argument entails a complication, engendered by the idea that civil society may function and progress even in the absence of gratuitousness – a word that is very close to Smith's notion of *beneficence* – or, in other terms, that the market contract may be a good (and even more civil) substitute of the gift: this is an argument that is gaining increasing support in today's globalized society. Gift and friendship are important matters in the private sphere, but in the market, as well as in the civil, economic and organizational life (in firms, for instance), we can – must, even – do without them; and it is good to do without them precisely because of their being charged with suffering and vulnerability.[2]

For Smith, then, benevolence or beneficence expresses, strengthens and nurtures the *munera* that in the feudal society were indissolubly linked to status and it is definitely not an expression of gratuitousness and reciprocal freedom. The "other" that Smith has in mind as he imagines life in pre-modern societies is not someone with whom we may freely create relations of friendship, let alone *agape*; but here too, like in Hobbes, the other is someone who stands "above" or "below" me, not "by my side" as an equal. In other words, in the public sphere the relation with the other, direct and personal, is for Smith synonymous with the feudal world and, as such, must be overcome by way of a new sociality, anonymous and mediated; the latter is all the more civil as it is freed from benevolence and from the gift–*munus* of others. It is not possible to comprehend Smith's humanistic vocation – nor Genovesi's or Verri's – unless we look at their enthusiastic attitudes towards the market together with the indignation for the suffering and humiliation

---

[2] Even though some part of the literature (think of Bobbio, for instance) counters the freedom of market humanism with the equality of the socialist–communist project, it is worth remembering that the liberal project is also strongly committed to a certain idea of equality, with which this essay is concerned.

inflicted by the few feudal masters to the multitude of serfs in the pre-modern *communitas*.

It is for these reasons that in Smith there is not only the realization that in the large-scale society friendship is not enough to get by, as he writes: "In civilized society he stands at all times in need of the coop-eration and assistance of great multitudes, while his whole life is scarce sufficient to gain the friendship of a few persons" (1976[1776], p. 26). In his thought there is something more that is even more radical: even if we had enough friends to gather the things we needed (as it could happen in small village communities), the commercial society still allows a more civil relationality, a new form of *philia* of a higher moral level, because chosen freely and because we have been freed from the ties of status, which are illiberal and hierarchical.

In summary, Smith resorts to the market's mediation (in a way, he even invents it, at least in theoretical terms) because in his view the unmediated relation is synonymous with an uncivil, feudal, asym-metrical, vertical relation, and not so much because he wishes to avoid a situation where the market remains harnessed by tight liga-ments (such as family, clan, friendship, etc.) – a concern that will arise later in economics (in Wicksteed (1910) it is already present and clear, as it will be in Luigi Einaudi and in the liberal thinking of the twentieth-century). The market allows us to avoid this imme-diate and uncivil relation and to create one of higher human quality. Back to the image of the butcher and of the beggar: we could illus-trate Smith's claim by imagining that the beggar, after entering the market (for example by finding a paid job), went back into the butcher's shop, no longer to beg, but to buy some meat: this new rela-tionship, for the exact reason of its being mediated by the market, is for Smith more humane than the relations of dependency typical of a world without markets, i.e. of the feudal world. The imperson-ality and mutual indifference that characterize mercantile relations are not negative aspects in Smith's eyes; on the contrary, they are positive and civilizing: this is the only way in which the market may produce the common good.

Friendship and market relations thus belong to two separate and distinct spheres; we can even argue that it is the very existence of market relations in the public sphere (and here only) that guarantees the possibility of experiencing relations of friendship in the private sphere that are authentic, freely chosen and unconcerned with status: if the beggar goes to the butcher to beg, he shall never be able to share with him a relation of friendship outside the market. If, on the contrary, the ex-beggar goes one day to the butcher's shop or to the brewery to legitimately purchase the goods, in the evening the ex-beggar will be able to meet his providers at the pub with greater dignity and perhaps they could even become friends. On this ground, Silver argues: "According to Smith replacement of *necessitudo* by *commercial society* brings with it a morally superior form of friendship – voluntary, based on *'natural sympathy'*, unconstrained by necessity" (1990, p. 1481).

This way it will be possible to set the conditions for the development of civil society, built on the category of indifference or non-involvement. The stranger is not a friend to me, nor an enemy or an ally; I am simply unconcerned with strangers: "The stranger is not a friend from whom we can expect any special favour and sympathy. But at the same time he is not an enemy" (ibid., p. 1483). The market lets individuals entertain authentic relations of friendship, although it is not in itself the place of friendship, but the place of mutual indifference. It is a "tool" of genuine sociality (friendship), but not a "place" of friendship.

Smith does not wish to deny (and neither do the economists who today we may count as his heirs) that in private life there may be room for a non-mediated, face-to-face relationality, like in a family or in a restricted circle of friends. On several occasions Smith stresses the radical distinction between "justice" and "beneficence and humanity" (1976 [1759], pp. 78–91, 152–153, 174–178). In fact, it is significant that when Smith portrays the "social passions" ("generosity, humanity, kindness, compassion, mutual friendship and esteem, all the social and benevolent affections"), his most relevant examples are derived from the family environment. In order to illustrate such social passions, he paints an idyllic, and even romantic, picture of what in his view is the ideal family, characterized by "cheerfulness, harmony, and contentment" (ibid., pp. 38–40).[3] For Smith, *social passions* are practiced in the more "soft" and (Smith seems to be saying) accidental contexts of family and intimate friendship. Such domains are non-essential and separate from the less delicate but more essential, even indispensable,

---

[3] The distinction between "justice" and "humanity", which is highly significant, in TMS is related to genre: "humanity" is 'the gentle virtue', 'the soft virtue' (p. 153), 'the virtue of a woman' (p. 190); it "consists merely in the exquisite fellow-feeling", which, as "the most humane actions require no … self-command" (pp. 190–191). 'Self-command', on the other hand, is identified with 'manhood and firmness', while the 'useless outcries' of men unable to show their virtues are for Smith 'womanish lamentations' (p. 244). It shall be remembered, however, that "humanity" is exactly what we should not appeal to turning to the "butcher" for our meal.

worlds of economics and politics (together seen as informing the public sphere). At the same time, Smith – as a man of the Enlightenment – does not see the family as the "model" for society.[4]

Very few ideas, perhaps none, have remained as central to the economic science as this one by Smith. Today, Smith's economic theory is no longer taught in universities (except for some brief mention of the "invisible hand"), but the idea of economic exchange as reciprocal indifference and the idea of the market as the place for anonymous and interpersonal relations still supports the whole framework of contemporary economics, which, from this point of view, can be seen as a legitimate heir of the "Adam" of economic science.

In summary, the "disease" that Smith perceives and wishes to cure is not the "wound" that friendship and horizontal relations between peers inevitably produce, but rather the one generated by the asymmetry of power that is typical of a world that was not liked then (and that is still not liked today). For Smith, the mediated relationship, self-interested and anonymous, is a means of growth and liberation for people (we have seen this in the opening chapters and we still see it today in those regions where there is too much *communitas* harnessing people through all sorts of ties).

In order to defeat the disease of feudal relations, he injected an antidote into the organism (i.e. civil society), a small "bit" of those relations, i.e. only the ones characterized by indifference, instrumentality and anonymity. Human relationality (for Smith non-civil) could have been eliminated by injecting into the social body a small dose of that relationality, i.e. market relationality, that in the last two-and-a-half centuries has become the new social relation.

Unlike Hobbes, who – to remain within our medical metaphor – resorted to a harsh treatment, a sort of chemotherapy, in order to destroy the disease of the *lupus–lupus* relation, Smith adopted instead almost a homeopathic approach, softer and less invasive, but that ultimately bore the same result: the expulsion of a well-rounded relationality, along with its contradictions and its potential for happiness. Then – and this in short is my argument – the market relationship is not a new kind of relationality (if by this we refer to the inter-human encounter), but in fact it reveals itself as a sort of vaccine capable of immunizing from the complete and dramatic human relation.

---

[4] The most original and relevant author, in this respect, will be J.S. Mill (1869), who will see in family life a residual of the feudal world embedded within modernity, still anchored to the serf–master paradigm.

I realize this is a radical argument, but given what has come about after Smith, especially in this era of globalization and technology, it shows that Smith's operation was entirely successful. Obviously, the point is not to condemn Smith, who – it is worth stressing this aspect – saw the human relation in the public sphere as something radically uncivil, as a result of the asymmetrical and hierarchical kind of relations prevailing in his time. This kind of relationality probably had to disappear in order for human beings to be able to experience in the public sphere *liberté* and a certain *egalité* (in terms of abstract rights, not in terms of points of arrival or departure): but the market relationship that originated out of the introduction of modern political economy was not informed by *fraternité*, as perhaps the fathers of the philosophical, political, and economic Enlightenment would have hoped. Instead, the result was an inter-human relation characterized by mutual indifference, perhaps the opposite of fraternity.

The history of the west (and today of the whole world) might have been different if the market sphere had been confined to a precise domain and if the private sphere had grown as a place in which to experience the kind of happiness that can only be produced by relations between peers, but also intimacy and affection. In fact, the history of the last two centuries has shown a different trend: the market sphere has increasingly invaded the space of the civil, and even the private sphere (consider, for example, of the evolution of family law), and we now find ourselves with market "relationality" as the new relationality of the twenty-first century. The fascination it was able to exert on postmodern man has been too strong, due to its promise of a new relationality without the obligation of the *munus*, without the "poison" hidden in every gift, without the "wound" that every inter-human "blessing" carries along (Bruni 2012).

If, then, we wish to recover an authentic relationality even inside the markets – and I believe this will be a decisive challenge in terms of quality of life over the next few years – then it becomes necessary for economic theory to move beyond Smith and to imagine a science capable of gratuitousness and of relationality, not merely one contractual and immune.

3. The evolution of market logic

As in previous chapters, we shall conclude by switching to another literary genre and language, but not to another theme.

In order to understand better, or just differently, Smith's originality (and continuity) in comparison to the Hobbesian project, we start by looking once again at Hobbes and at the game of the stag hunt, which here we read according to an evolutionary perspective. We shall ask, in particular, what happens *over time* in a Smithian perspective (in spirit, of course, not in the technicalities or language), in a given population (group, community, society) if a certain share (or percentage) of its members plays "stag" and the remaining part plays "hare".

This analysis of the evolution of the market should be called "Humean–Smithian", with Hume's Treatise being the real source of inspiration for Smith's idea of cooperation in society as well. In line with Hume's and Smith's philosophy, we can say that if the players can "see" the "higher" equilibrium of the game (4,4), they will *evolutionarily* reach it on the basis of individual interests of mutual advantage and on the instrumental value of the reputation of justice.

The existence of the market in a civilized society, based on the division of labour and hence seen as a great cooperative work, is the essential requirement for economic development and hence for the wealth of nations and for their well-being. The existence of the market depends on the existence of the notion of justice inside people and on their ability to honor promises and contracts (for this reason, when describing the market and its ability to produce, by evolving, a spontaneous order, Hume and Smith normally have in mind the repeated interactions between the market's participants, where reputational effects are also in play). These are for Hume and Smith essential market characteristics, but in order to evolve they only require "self-interest" (and the repetition of interactions, from which conventions spontaneously arise).

As underlined by Sugden (2004) and Bruni and Sugden (2000), according to Hume, "self-interest is the original motive to the establishment of justice" (1978[1740], p. 499). He tries to show that the three laws of justice would emerge spontaneously out of the repeated interaction of self-interested individuals. The whole of Hume's analysis of the emergence of justice is modern, prefiguring many features of game theory. Hume explains promising as a practice that (in particular in small-scale societies) evolves out of bilateral practices of mutual assistance, based on reciprocal self-interest:

> Here I learn to do a service to another, without bearing him any real kindness; because I foresee, that he will return my service, in expectation of another of the same kind, and in order to maintain the same correspondence of good offices with me or with others. And accordingly, after I have serv'd him, and he is in possession of the

advantage arising from my action, he is induc'd to perform his part, as foreseeing the consequences of his refusal.

Ibid., p. 521

Around such practices there grows up a convention, that emerges from individual self-interests, of marking promises:

> When a man says he promises any thing, he in effect expresses a reso-
> lution of performing it; and along with that, by making use of this
> form of words, subjects himself to the penalty of never being trusted
> again in case of failure...After these signs [of promise-making] are
> instituted, whoever uses them is immediately bound by his interest
> to execute his engagements, and must never be expected to be trusted
> any more, if he refuse to perform it.

Ibid., p. 522

In this argument are all the essentials of the modern explanation of cooperation in terms of the value of reputation.

To say something more about this Humean (and Smithian) evolutionary approach, although with a high degree of approximation, almost by way of a parable, we shall resort to the so-called evolutionary games, whose characteristic is to extend the use of several elements from the field of biological evolution to the evolution of human behaviours and cultures. *Fitness* – which in evolutionary biology is typically measured on the basis of the relative survival rates of offspring in the following generation – in evolutionary games becomes expected utility. While the basic mechanism in biology is the reproduction and survival of the fittest, in the social sciences this role is played by imitation:[5] the assumption is that in a given population a strategy with an expected

---

[5] The metaphor of evolution allows evolutionary game theory to operate without the notion of rational and maximizing behaviour so critical in "traditional" game theory, since a strategy may take the form of any norm of conduct, not necessarily "rational" (e.g. any mutation within the same species). Several precautions must be observed as the methodology of fitness-based evolution is extended to cultural evolution (cf. Cavalli-Sforza and Feldman 1981). For instance, whereas in biological evolution Lamarck's theory (which contemplates use or disuse as an explanation for mutations: e.g. the neck of giraffes) does not work (as explanation of improvements transmitted to children), today we know that in cultural evolution improvements are transmitted by imitation and "horizontally", which would then lead to prefer a Lamarckian approach as opposed to a purely Darwinian one (Corning 2005). The frontier of evolutionary theory today has become considerably rich and sophisticated compared

utility lower than average will not be imitated and will gradually tend to disappear; conversely, the strategy with the highest relative success will instead be imitated and therefore will grow.[6]

Let us begin by considering a hypothetical and hyper-simplified world, where only two people exist and only two strategies: one person plays "always Stag", the other plays "always Hare". The evolutionary history of such a population is extremely simple: the strategy that reports the highest expected utility (the expected value of the payoff) tends to grow over time and to spread through the population (by imitation), whereas the other is reduced until it disappears.

If we consider the numerical payoffs of the matrix we used in the previous chapter, the threshold value for the share of cooperative subjects in the population (p_c),[7] above which cooperation (the "stag" strategy) will emerge over time, is $\frac{2}{3}$.[8] If therefore $p_c > \frac{2}{3}$, "Stag" will be the strategy to prevail over time; if, on the contrary, at the start we are not above this level of cooperation in the population, "hare" (non-cooperation), will be the prevailing strategy. It is straightforward to notice that under these conditions,[9] the "basin of attraction" of non-cooperation ("hare") is two times larger than in the case of cooperation ("stag"). In fact, more than $\frac{2}{3}$ of the initial population must follow a cooperative strategy in order for cooperation to evolve.

Graphically, we could illustrate the dynamics of the population as follows. If p_c is exactly equal to $\frac{2}{3}$, then the two strategies will

---

to its first-generation models, which were adopted in evolutionary game theory. Bearing in mind these methodological concerns, we now start telling, almost as a sort of parable, our evolutionary story, which we shall use as a form of language, or rhetoric, in order to refine and enrich our discourse.

[6] Those who disappear are the ones who are not imitated (by others, horizontally or in space, or by their children, vertically and over time), while the ones more widely imitated grow within the population. This is the kind of technology that governs the most basic versions of evolutionary games.

[7] The share of cooperators (p_c) may also be interpreted as the probability an agent has of encountering a cooperator (stag).

[8] As proof, consider that the expected utility of playing "stag" in the case of a population with only two pure strategies (stag, hare) is equal to $U_c = 4 p_c + (1 - p_c) 0$, that is, the weighted average between the payoff received by an agent who plays "stag" when confronted with another agent playing "stag" and the payoff received when confronted with an agent who plays "hare". Analogously, the expected utility of playing "hare" (Non-cooperation) will be: $U_n = 3 p_c + (1 - p_c) 2$. By comparing the two expected utilities, we can find the "threshold value" of p_c: hence $p_c > \frac{2}{3}$.

[9] If the payoff for hunting the hare by oneself had been 2 (instead of 3), it can be demonstrated that the threshold value for p_c would have been $\frac{1}{2}$.

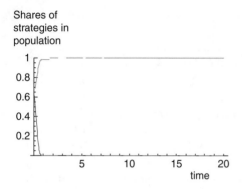

Figure 7.1   Shares of Strategies in a Population

coexist. If, instead, the initial share of "S" strategies is below $\frac{2}{3}$, evolution leads to the affirmation of "H" (non-cooperation) as shown in Figure 7.1 above.

In the graph the blue line represents the share of cooperative agents, "stag", while the red line represents the "hare" subjects. We have time on the horizontal axis and the share of cooperators in the population (p_c) on the vertical axis.

In Hobbes' thought the impossibility of cooperation is due to the fear and consequent lack of mutual trust, which gives rise to the social pact and, consequently, to the Leviathan. We have seen that this solution is always available each time a hierarchically superior mediator is established, along with his sanctions, for the purpose of creating cooperation where it would not otherwise emerge. In this case too the higher equilibrium is eventually achieved, although this happens at the cost of a significant amount of individual freedom.

In comparison to Hobbes, the tradition of political economy relies on a different notion of cooperation that has its origin in Hume. This tradition, recalled today by some "evolutionary" authors such as Sugden (2004) or Binmore (2005), explains the emergence of cooperation (in the market, but not exclusively) in evolutionary terms and on the basis of individual interests without the need to resort to the Leviathan or to a hierarchy external to the relation itself.

Fundamental, in this respect, is a well-known passage from Hume's *Treatise on the Human Nature* that goes together with the contiguous one we have already quoted a few pages ago:

> Your corn is ripe to-day; mine will be so tomorrow. It is profitable for us both, that I should labour with you to-day, and that you should

aid me to-morrow. I have no kindness for you, and know you have as little for me. I will not, therefore, take any pains upon your account; and should I labour with you upon my own account, in expectation of a return, I know I shou'd be disappointed and that I shou'd in vain depend upon your gratitude. Here then I leave you to labour alone: You treat me in the same manner. The seasons change; and both of us lose our harvests for want of mutual confidence and security.

1978[1740], p. 520

The following year, on account of the previous experience, the two self-interested farmers, who mutually distrust each other and share no friendship or mutual interest, learn that it is simply rational to cooperate, without need for any form of positive active sociality or benevolence.

Back to our terminology: if the subjects "see" a better equilibrium (cooperative: 4, 4), sooner or later they will reach it through evolution, without need of relations of benevolence, mutual trust, friendship, let alone love.[10]

This is an important dimension in terms of market humanism and of its ethos: in order to trigger market cooperation, so that it can produce its fruits of civilization, it is not necessary to restrict individual freedom, nor to create political systems that can punish opportunistic behaviours from above: it is sufficient to give people the right incentives and to put them in the condition to learn from past experience, to be able to recognize, directly or indirectly, their own partners, and to appreciate the story of their own interactions with others. Individual rationality, and personal interests (including the concern for one's own reputation) will do the rest, without need for any existing relation of friendship or proximity between individuals.

We have just seen, in fact, how the higher equilibrium (4,4) may be achieved without the Leviathan, but through a stable strategy in an evolutionary game. One condition applies, however: *that the initial share of cooperators in the population must be above a certain critical threshold,* (whose value will depend on the structure of the payoff matrix). In order for market cooperation to affirm itself through evolution within a given population on the sole basis of self-interest and

---

[10] In fact a more thorough reading of Hume reveals that his view of the market and of civil life is more articulated. It could be summarized as follows: the market, and life in common in general, is normally a "stag hunt", in which some circumstances, such as the Prisoner's Dilemmas, present an incentive to free riding: these very circumstances lead Hume to not exclude the importance of law and political authority.

without Leviathan (from this point of view the approach of Smith and Hume truly is the liberal approach of spontaneous order and of diffidence towards the cumbersome presence of the State), a certain civic culture must be present from the start (of the population, given our structure of payoffs); and that basically amounts to saying that in order for the market to develop through cooperation, some cooperative dispositions and civicness need to be already embedded in the population and that fear and difference must not prevail, otherwise market cooperation cannot start and it cannot evolve from the bottom, as Hume and Smith had intended (something that happened in large part in the Anglo-Saxon world).[11]

We are coming to a significant conclusion for the purpose of analyzing the development of the market and its ethos.

The kind of sociality underpinning the official tradition of this science is still deeply Smithian in character and it is based ultimately on the assumption of mutual indifference: the intention behind A's action is completely independent from B; A satisfies B's preferences only as a means to achieve his or her own individual objectives: it is not necessary to assume any form of participation to a communitarian reality, to an "us". From this point of view, if we apply the traditional distinctions of love and human relations to the categories of *eros–philia–agape*, the economic science of Smithian inheritance may be wholly defined within the repertoire of *eros*.[12]

In Modernity, the immunity of the contract replaces the immunity of *philia*, on which the civil humanism of the fourteenth and fifteenth centuries was founded. In the new commercial society one can trade

---

[11] In fact if we introduced less "radical" (and less realistic) strategies than the two we have so far considered, cooperation could be reached with less demanding conditions. It would suffice, for example, to move from two to four strategies, adding to our world strategies of the "tit-for-tat" kind in order to make the initial condition less demanding, and to favour the spontaneous emergence of simple cooperation. On this point, see Bruni (2008).

[12] As observed in an another work (Bruni 2012), erotic love, for example, also indirectly produces the common good (if well ordered and regulated by institutions), which consists in the creation of strong bonds between people, the care of children, the growth of the population (where this is good), etc.; but this result (this common good) is not normally the aim of those who act moved by passion and erotic desire. What makes the entrepreneur undertake a project is, especially in the beginning, the will to fill a lack (of honor, wealth, power), an erotic urge that in Smith's perspective (but not only his) produces the common good even when the market works within civil society or, as Genovesi will say, "where the arts are protected and trade is free" (*Lezioni*, I, cap. 10, § XVIII, p. 419).

with anyone, there is no need to be citizens, Christians, Catholics, Protestants, or even believers: the law and contracts are enough; it is sufficient to build social contracts (Hobbes) and commercial contracts (Smith) that anonymously enable the exchange. Until Luther and Calvin, *"bona fides"* played a "credibility" function in medieval *christianitas* and this was the basis for exchanges. The Protestant Reformation had the effect of complicating the matter in a radical way by creating the first significant crisis, since Christian *fides* was no longer capable of ensuring "credibility", not even within Europe. With the new re-foundings of politics and economics, *fides* becomes no longer necessary: it is enough to consider one's own interests so that both the good of the other and the common good will emerge indirectly from their interplay. The market thus discovers its universalistic vocation (typical of the Enlightenment), and now that it is no more limited by *philia* or *fides* it can open itself to anyone, thus creating a new humanism, egalitarian and liberal, in which each individual potentially encounters everyone, without truly encountering anyone but him or herself. Freedom and equality, but without fraternity!

In the coming chapter we shall get to know another tradition and another market ethos: I am talking about the Neapolitan school of Genovesi and of its attempt to rescue a certain *philia* and a certain fraternity and to infuse these into a new commercial society.

8
The Neapolitan Tradition of Civil Economy

We address ourselves, not to their humanity but to their self-love, and never talk to them of our own necessities but of their advantages.

Adam Smith

We have come to this public square but we do not wish to sell these goods to you for the sake of our interest, nor for our need; because need – God bless – we have way too much in our home.

Reported oral tradition from a 19th century fair in Southern Italy.

1. The economy of civil virtues

The "classic" tradition of sociality, here referred to as Aristotelian–Thomistic, found another significant expression in economics within the Neapolitan tradition – in a sense Italian and Latin – of civil economy (Bruni and Zamagni 2007), which represents an important attempt to keep alive within modernity the tradition of civil life based on *philia*.

To learn more about this tradition, we shall first of all examine the works of Antonio Genovesi, a Neapolitan philosopher and economist who lived around the same time as Smith: Genovesi and Smith are surprisingly similar in many key aspects of their thought.

A few biographical notes about Antonio Genovesi to begin with: born on the 1st of November 1713 in Castiglione (now: Castiglione del Genovesi) near Salerno, from a noble but modest family, Genovesi becomes involved in the ecclesiastical way of life very young, until officially becoming a priest in 1737. After living in Buccino (Salerno) for a few years, he moves to Naples in 1738. There he studies philosophy and attends the lectures of Gian Battista Vico, whose thought will remain for him a constant source of inspiration. In 1739 he establishes a private school, teaching philosophy and theology and thus gaining some experience in pedagogy. During these very years he meets Celestino Galiani, thanks to whom he is offered his first university teaching position and thus becomes professor of metaphysics in 1745. Meanwhile, in 1743, he publishes the first part of *Elementa Metaphysicae*, a philosophical work that is strongly disputed in the ecclesiastic sphere. In the same period he meets and befriends Ludovico Antonio Muratori, another important figure of the so-called "public happiness" school. He thus becomes a member of the circle of Bartolomeo Intieri, an academic from Florence whose Galilean approach was significant for Genovesi's transition from metaphysics to economics, *"da metafisico a mercadante"* (cf. Bellamy 1987). In 1753 he publishes the circle's reformist manifesto: *Discorso sopra il vero fine delle lettere e delle scienze* ("Discourse on the true end of letters and sciences"). Between 1765 and 1769, his most important works are published: *Lezioni di economia civile*,[1] *Logica* (1766), *Diceosina o sia della filosofia del giusto e dell'onesto* ("Diceosina, that is the philosophy of right and honest", 1766) and *Scienze metafisiche* (1767).[2]

The civil economy tradition that was affirmed in the eighteenth century should be seen as the *modern expression of the civil tradition that originated in the Middles Ages*. Like the first civil humanists, not only does Genovesi regard civil life as not in conflict with the good life, he sees it as the place where happiness may be fully realized thanks to good and just laws, to trading and to the civil bodies where men are free to practice their natural sociability: "Even if companionship can bring evils, on the other hand it also assures life and its goods; it is the source of the greatest pleasures, unknown to the men of nature" (*Diceosina*, p. 37). And like the civil humanists and the Franciscans, Genovesi also thinks the market is a matter of *philia*.

---

[1] The *Lezioni* appeared in three editions between 1765 and 1770, here simply referred to as *Lezioni*, which is in fact a further development of his manuscript *Elementi di Commercio*, recently republished as part of the *Critical Edition of Lezioni*, Naples 2005.

[2] See Bruni and Sugden (2000, 2008). We know that Smith and Genovesi lived in the same time period, although they never entered in contact with each other directly; nor is it likely that they ever learned about each others' existence. Still we cannot exclude the possibility that Genovesi was aware of Smith's *Theory of Moral Sentiments*, given his extensive knowledge of the Scottish Enlightenment.

On the natural (and non-artificial) character of sociality and on its essential role for a fully humane and happy life, Genovesi is also in line with the ancient Aristotelian–Thomistic tradition:

> Every person has a natural and inherent obligation to study how to procure her happiness; but the political body is made of persons; therefore, the entire political body and each of its members has an obligation to do what is on their part, i.e. all that they know and can for the sake of common prosperity, as long as that which is done does not offend the rights of the other civil bodies. From the civil body, this obligation returns with beautiful and divine ties to each family and each person for the common pacts of society. Each family and each person is therefore under the obligation to procure, for what she knows and can, common happiness, due to two obligations, one of which is within nature, and the other is among the first pacts that subsequently continue with posterity ... for the sake of living in a community. A third obligation may be added, that of one's own utility. What Shaftesbury proclaimed (*Inquiry of Virtue and Merit*) will be eternally true, that true utility is the daughter of virtue for it is eternally true that the great depth of every man is the love for those with whom he lives. This love is indeed the daughter of virtue.
>
> *Lezioni*, I, chap. 1, § 34, p. 29[3]

Only a few decades earlier, the Neapolitan Paolo Mattia Doria argued in the introduction to his *Della Vita Civile* (1710):

> To this rather impossible goal of men to possess all the virtues and to the property for which they each possess only a few, the invention of civil life aspires to offer a solution ... which reveals the true essence

---

[3] Explicitly recalling Genovesi, and especially Vico, the Neapolitan Mario Francesco Pagano makes, few decades later, a similar point: "More than any other animal, man is made for society, and his natural state is sociable. ... Thus, that horrid beast running through the woods naked and alone, covered only with hair, armed with a long club, belting out horrible roars and indicating the profound dullness of soul to his stupid and senseless face, does not deserve the name of man. The savage can be said to be only a sketch of a man". And with clear reference to Aristotle's famous phrase that only a beast or a god can live without society, he concludes: "When the solitary man is sufficient to himself, when he can attend to his own needs by himself alone, then either he must have no knowledge of anything ... or he must be a god himself" (Pagano, in Actis-Perinetti 1960, pp. 43–44).

of civil life as a mutual help of virtues, and of natural faculties, that men lend to each other in the attempt to attain human happiness.[4]

However, at the heart of the view of life in common held by the authors of the Neapolitan school of civil economy (not only Genovesi) is the idea that "mere" sociability, man's character of being a "political animal", cannot suffice to distinguish the human from other animals. The kind of sociality that is typical of human beings is a *qualified* type of sociality – which we must call reciprocity, friendship, mutual assistance or fraternity – all basically synonyms in the vocabulary of Genovesi and of the other authors belonging to this tradition:

> Man is a naturally sociable animal: goes the common saying. But not every man will believe there is no other animal on earth that is not sociable. ... In what way then is man more sociable than the others? ... [in] the reciprocal right to be assisted and consequently his reciprocal obligation to assist us in our needs.
>
> *Lezioni*, I, chap. 1, §§ XVI, XVII, p. 283

This passage contains something that we do not find in Aristotle or in Smith: for Genovesi, *reciprocity* (not only *relationality*, nor simple sociability) is the typical element of human sociality. For Smith, instead, what constitutes the typical character of human sociality is

---

[4] Thus also his fellow-citizen Gaetano Filangieri in his *Scienza della Legislazione*, one of the most influential texts of the European Enlightenment: "The Author of nature ... would have performed the most perfect and august of its productions vain, if man had not been formed for social intercourse and mutual connexions. It has given him reason, which develops and expands by communication, and in the concourse of society. In addition to imperious feeling, from which the cry of other animals is wholly derived, he has the exclusive blessing of speech ... He is susceptible of a multitude of passions useless to a solitary being. For what purpose is he warmed with the ambition of pleasing, of acquiring the esteem of others, or establishing an empire over their affections and opinions? Why are the germs of friendship, compassion, benevolence, planted in his breast, or the seeds of those amiable sentiments sown within his bosom, which ripen in every well-disposed mind? Why has he the singular desire of sharing with another a part of his existence; or why, in a word, are not his natural appetites confined within the narrow limits allotted to those of every other inhabitant of the globe, the satisfaction of physical wants? They frequently return to him, though but for a moment, and in the void they leave him after their enjoyment, they prove their insufficiency to procure his happiness, and proclaim to him that he has intellectual, as well as corporeal wants, which are only to be gratified in society and its relations" (Filangieri 1780[1806], p. 3).

the "propensity in human nature...to truck, barter, and exchange one thing for another" (*Wealth of Nations*, p. 25), founded, as we have seen, on the power of persuasion.

Genovesi pictures economic market relationships as relations of mutual assistance, hence not impersonal or anonymous. In fact, the market itself is conceived as an expression of the general law of society, i.e. reciprocity.[5] This is both clear and important, especially in his analysis of trust, or "public faith", which lies at the heart of his *Lezioni di economia civile*.

2. Public Faith (*fede pubblica*)

Like for the Franciscans in the fourteenth and fifteenth centuries and for the civil humanists, the market is for Genovesi a matter of *fides*. One of the key elements in Genovesi's theory of civil economy is "public faith", which he considers (alongside the tradition of civil economy) as the true precondition for economic development; "confidence is the soul of commerce, and without confidence all the component parts of this mighty structure would crumble under it" (Filangieri 1806[1780], Vol. 2, p. 145). In his thought there is a substantial difference between *private* and *public* trust: while the first can be assimilated to reputation, i.e. a private good which can be "spent" on the market, the latter is not the sum of private "reputations"; rather, it entails the genuine love for the common good. This concept is similar to what modern theorists have called "social capital", that is, the fabric of faith and civil virtues that allows human and economic development to get into motion and preserve itself over time (Bruni and Sugden 2000).[6]

According to Genovesi, the lack of "public faith" is what has determined the lack of civil and economic development in the Kingdom of Naples – an argument that more than two-and-a-half centuries later has lost none of its currency. In the Kingdom, as denounced by the tradition of civil economy, "private trust" (intended in particular as blood ties or bonds based on feudal pacts of vassalage), or honor, was

---

[5] Genovesi's theory of reciprocity as the fundamental law regulating human relations originates from a sort of morally-oriented Newtonian approach, which also informs his scientific views. Like Hutcheson, he associates Newton's law of gravity with the concept of reciprocity, because this law indicates that mutual body attraction decreases as "social" distance increases.

[6] For the same reason, as Ludovico Bianchini will point out almost one century later, inspired by Genovesi, public faith is not just a means, but it is "part of the wealth" of a nation (1855, p. 21).

abundant; but public and generalized trust, the kind that originates from the cultivation of civil virtues, was too scarce. Some decades later Gaetano Filangieri similarly maintained that no civil and economic development can be achieved without man having "confidence in the government, the magistrates, and his fellow citizens" (1806[1780], Vol. I, pp. 10–11), who are the first and most important resources for any kind of collective and individual development.

If on one side market development brings civil and economic development, for the Neapolitan school it is even more important to stress that *cultivating* public faith is the precondition for any possible discourse concerning civil and economic development: "nothing is more necessary than public trust in a wise and easy circulation" (*Lezioni*, II, chap. 10, § 1, p. 751). Very significant is also this footnote by Genovesi: "This word *fides means rope that ties and unites*. Public faith is therefore the bond of families united in companionship".[7]

We need to make one further step. In the *Lezioni* (chapter X, book II), Genovesi explains to his students and fellow-citizens that public faith is above all a matter of authentic reciprocity, and not only a matter of contracts. According to the Neapolitan economist, public faith is not the kind of capital that can be built outside the market and later be used on the market: on the contrary, the market is conceived as part of civil society, which produces what today we would call social capital and relational goods. For this reason his discourse on public faith is directly economic: "Where no trust exists – not in the part that constitutes the reciprocal confidence of citizens in each other, nor in the certainty of contracts, or in the vigour of laws, or in the science and integrity of judges...there is no certainty of contracts, no power of laws, no trust of man towards man. Because contracts are bonds and civil laws are also themselves *public pacts and contracts*" (ibid., p. 752).

3. Trade as mutual assistance and reciprocity

The category of reciprocity is also critical to Genovesi's notion and theory of the market. In his analysis of trust ("public faith"), he systematically ties the concept of trust to those of reciprocal confidence, mutual assistance and friendship, arguing that these concepts are essential to the economic and civil development of society.

---

[7] The same note appears in the second Neapolitan edition (1768–70) in an extended version with a stronger emphasis on the meaning of trust as bond of society (*Lezioni*, p. 751, footnote).

In line with the thought of Montesquieu and with the Scottish school, the Neapolitan tradition regards economic activity as an expression of civil life; it sees *trade as a civilizing factor*. Like for the civil humanists, for Genovesi and the Neapolitans not only is civil life not in contrast with virtue, but it is seen as the place where virtues can find their fullest expression. The thought of Montesquieu is certainly present in the writings of Genovesi (who was among the first to translate and address the works of Montesquieu in Italian language); it runs through the whole Enlightenment movement, including its Neapolitan offspring: "Every form of government... has its own predominant principle of action; and *fear in a despotic state, honour in a monarchy, and virtue in a republic*, are these ruling principles" (Filangieri (1806)[1780], Vol. I, p. 138). Virtue, not fear (as Hobbes and Machiavelli instead argued) is the basis of civil society – a concept that we examine here more closely and that has been key to the entire tradition of civil economy.[8]

Giacinto Dragonetti, whose works we discuss extensively over the next chapter, also has a fascinating theory and understanding of trade (clearly in tune with Genovesi), in which we can feel the echoes of the Medieval Franciscan polemic against gold stagnating in the coffers and not circulating among people creating wealth:

> A thousand proofs convince us that man was made for society, but above all, the mutual dependence on mutual wants, that basis of all union.... The bareness of one place is to be supplied by the fertility of another.... A state without trade is a carcase... The gold that stagnates in the coffers of the rich, is lost to circulation, is a robbery committed on the public. No heap of wealth ever made a nation great.... To make each individual participate of the benefits of nature, and to give to the body politic all the strength it is capable of, ought to be the effect of commerce.
>
> 1766[1769], pp. 110–123

Furthermore, for Genovesi and for many Illuminists of his generation in Italy and elsewhere, one of the fruits of commerce is the ability to

---

[8] Such awareness emerges already in the title he chose for his lessons, namely *Lezioni di commercio o sia di economia civile*, or in English, the *Lesson of commerce, or of civil economy*, where that "or" highlights the civil character of commerce: "I heard it said amongst us that we do not have commerce. This either means that the 800,000 families of this Kingdom do not form a civil body, or else he who says this is without a head" (*Lezioni*, I, ch. 16, § VI, p. 243).

"bring the trading nations to peace. ... War and commerce are as opposite as motion and quiet" (*Lezioni*, I, chap. 19, § VII, p. 290).

Yet, the praise of commerce and civil wealth does not make the Neapolitan authors forget that happiness does not come from goods themselves. Both Filangieri and Bianchini, as well as many civil illuminists, strongly believe that civilization entails a fair distribution of wealth: "Exorbitant riches in particular individuals, and luxurious idleness in others, are symptoms of National infelicity, and suppose the misery of the bulk of people. They are civil partialities prejudicial to the public interest; for a state can only be rich and happy in the single instance, where every individual by the moderate labour of a few hours can easily supply his own wants and those of his family" (Filangieri 1806[1870], Vol. I, p. 10).[9] Giuseppe Palmieri in his *Reflections on public happiness* wrote: "No society can exist without commerce; yet, one can say that society springs from this need" (1805[1788], p. 147).

Strictly related to the issue of commerce there is an interesting dialogue at distance between Genovesi and Montesquieu. Genovesi edited the Neapolitan edition of the *Esprit des Lois*, writing some footnotes with his own annotations and comments. In one of his footnotes Genovesi wrote something on commerce that seems at first glance going in a direction opposite to all the other theses on commerce present in his previous works.

In commenting Montesquieu's well-known thesis "The natural effect of commerce is bringing peace", Genovesi wrote:

Commerce is a great source of wars. It is jealous, and the jealousy arms men. The wars of Carthaginians, and of Romans, of Venetians, Genoese, Pisano, Portuguese, Dutch, French, and those of English witness this. If two nations trade for reciprocal needs, these are needs that are opposed to war, not the spirit of commerce

Genovesi 1777, II, p. 195

---

[9] Filangieri then goes on to offer an argument that still maintains its currency today: "Constant labour, and a life supported with difficulty, can have no pretensions to the title of a happy life. It was the miserable doom of Sisyphus! No single instant could be called his own. The whole of existence was incessant toil, and endless exertion" (ibid.). Almost one century later but still within the same theoretical tradition, Ludovico Bianchini will remark: "Without too much amassing of goods, the idea of civility naturally brings with it the best distribution of comfort and ease" (1855, p. 12).

From this passage is clear that Genovesi criticizes the spirit of commerce if it is intended in the mercantilist meaning (that was the vision of commerce dominant in his time), according to which commerce was deeply linked to the predatory spirit of conquest of the Nations, a "zero sum game" rather than a form of mutual assistance. Then, Genovesi and the whole Civil Economy praise commerce and market when they emerge among persons and peoples on the basis of mutual needs in a spirit of reciprocity.[10] A thesis that is not less relevant nowadays than it was in the eighteenth century.

4. Market as *philia*

The general view of Genovesi and his school about civil life and the market centres on *philia* as its main paradigm, because their discourse is entirely played within the repertoire of friendship, mutual assistance and reciprocity. Its underlying logic is well summarized in Genovesi's "little catechism of natural law", which provides a rational demonstration addressed to his students of the importance of virtue in the pursuit of private and public happiness, which is key to his discussion of "public faith" in the *Lezioni*. I report this passage almost entirely because it offers an overview of the way in which this school envisions the rational foundation of life in common as *philia*:

> All of you who have had the chance to learn how far-reaching virtue is and what merit and enchantment it possesses, as well as those of you who would love to get accustomed to it and to put it into practice, will often have to remind themselves of this little catechism of natural law, whose usefulness for the general human experience is both necessary and constantly verified.
>
> 1. Nature and reason both push us to live on this earth and to lead ourselves in such a way as to have the least unhappy life possible....
> 2. No human condition is to be considered more unhappy than being alone, separated from any dealings with others. There is

---

[10] Actually this thesis is present in the whole chapter XVII of the *Lezioni*. Thanks to the critical edition of the text and also to the annotation of the editor (M.L. Perna), it is possible to follow the evolution of Genovesi evaluation of the spirit of commerce from the first draft of his treatise (*Elementi di commercio*, 1758) up to the *Lezioni* (1767). His evaluation was much more positive at the beginning of his career as an economist, and much more elaborated and critical at the end. In fact, in the secondneapolitan edition of the Lezioni (1769), we find some new footnoteswhere this critical attitude towards the spirit of commerce are moreemphasised: cf. Bruni (2011).

a beautiful and true saying by Aristotle, according to whom a solitary man content by himself must be either a divinity or a beast. What would he do without the life and bliss-giving breath of his fellows?

3. We must find a way to be sociable with one another, to cultivate the virtues and qualities that enable us to be reciprocally united with each other and to live a companionable and friendly life.

4. Not just any society of man with man be our case, not in the way as even beasts are to some extent sociable, but in a way founded upon reason, for which the members know their reciprocal rights and not only do they not think of violating them, but they even study ways to be benevolent and helpful to each other.

5. Such reasonable society cannot exist unless those who compose it and give it form are reciprocally and sincerely friends to one another, so that men's reciprocal friendship in political bodies be the equivalent of what the mutual attraction of component particles is for natural bodies. Without such mutual attraction in nature there are, nor can there be, large bodies, just like without that friendship there can be no political body.

6. Men are not and shall never be sincere friends to each other, unless they do have sincere and reciprocal trust in each other, for each suspicion is a morally repelling force, capable of intoxicating and compromising true friendship.

7. Men cannot sincerely trust each other and rest their faith upon others, unless they are deeply convinced of their mutual virtue and piety; which, as we have said, is the one foundation of faith.

8. Men cannot trust each other's virtue for a long time, unless they truly are virtuous...

9. As soon as a man is recognized as wicked and impious, ready to offend and deceive others, and as one who gains pleasure from the troubles of others, due to a force that is inherent in human nature, all others will regard him as a ferocious and poisonous animal, with whom it is impossible to communicate or to deal in a friendly manner....

10. A man in such state is excluded from all social relationships and cannot expect from anyone any of those comforts that make life lighter or pleasurable, except those he might be able to get out of others by dint of physical power, by astuteness and shrewdness, either with great fear or danger.

11. A man in this state cannot resist for long...

Lezioni, II, ch. 10, § XI, pp. 762–3

In this "catechism of natural reason" (to which Genovesi adds many similar remarks, which he draws from religion: *Ib.*, XIV, p. 765 ff), the central message is clear: rational considerations about our own happiness suggest that we shall cultivate those civil virtues that allow us to experience social relations informed by reciprocity. In addition we can find one more cardinal point (see especially points 7–8-9) of that humanism based on *philia*: the exclusion of the non-friend, in order to safeguard *fides*, i.e. the reliability of the agents in the market. We are therefore in a zone of full continuity – from this point of view as well – with Aristotle, Aquinas, Francis, and civil humanism with its shining lights and with its shadows.

To sum up, we see that the Smithian idea of market is well expressed through the category of "mutual advantage" considered in strictly individual terms (nothing in Smith's thought suggests the existence of a collective subject, of a "we") and, from this point of view, Smith shares with the social contract tradition the idea that life in common is justified by reciprocal interest, by the mutual advantage of the single individuals taking part in the contract. Genovesi's view, aligned with the classic tradition and with Grotius, is instead characterized by the concept of "mutual assistance". We must observe, however, that the difference, small as it may appear, is in fact a decisive one. In an exchange motivated by "mutual advantage" each party benefits from the transaction, a transaction that is only possible as long as it is also beneficial to the other party. Hence, trading is *objectively* mutually advantageous: each party acts in a way that the results are advantageous to the other. Yet, as we have seen, none of the two parties has any concern for the interests and well-being of the other; no "we" is required. Market exchange, intended à la Genovesi, as "mutual assistance", requires something more and different from the notion of mutual advantage.

The concept of "assistance" entails an intention, on the part of the person who "assists", to benefit the person "assisted". Assistance supposes an action that is intentionally directed towards another person for the purpose of helping her with her needs, i.e. an intention to be helpful to each other. If assistance is mutual – as Genovesi intends it – then these intentions are reciprocal. But mutual assistance is not played entirely in the field of contracts (despite not excluding this field); in this perspective it stretches beyond the idea of mutual interest: a good society must be based on something deeper and different than just interests. The needs of some do not always correspond to the interest of others, but those needs still ought to be satisfied in a decent society. Citizens are not only and not always *stakeholders*, but also *needholders*, and Genovesi's notion of assistance picks up precisely on this point.

5. We-rationality

Once again, let us go back to Genovesi's pages. These may also be read – as already proposed in Bruni and Sugden 2008 – from the perspective of a "we-rationality".

Reading his *Lezioni*, we discover that one of the paradigms that best explains the general sense of Genovesi's civil economy is about a kind of rationality that we may define "collective" (by which term we do not refer to a holistic kind of account, unconcerned with the freedom and existence of the single individual). Today, this theory is nicely summarized by the so-called *team agency* or *team thinking*, developed by authors like Sugden (1993), Hollis (1998), Bacharach (2007), Toumela (1995), and more recently Smerilli (2012). Martin Hollis, and especially Robert Sugden, have developed a particular version of this theory, which has been termed "we-rationality". The basic idea of this theory consists in the construction of a notion of rationality according to which, in making a decision about which action to undertake, a person is able to think not just that "this action shall have good consequences for me", but rather also that "this action is *my part* of *our* action which shall have good consequences for [all of] *us*".[11]

We have seen already that the logic of Genovesi's argument always refers to the idea of rationality and friendship. These categories are normally seen in today's debate within the framework of an individualistic paradigm;[12] but in Genovesi go back instead to the idea of a "we", as is clear from the *Lezioni*. In the final paragraph, Genovesi summarizes the message and central thesis of his treatise to which, no wonder, we will constantly come back in the next chapters:

> Here is the idea of the present work. If we fix our eyes on such beautiful and useful truths, we will study not for stupid vanity, nor for the pride of appearing superior to ignorant people, or for the wickedness of cheating, but to go along with the law of the moderator of the world, which commands us to do our best to be useful to one another.
>
> *Lezioni*, II, Conclusions, § XVII, p. 890

---

[11] Thus Robert Sugden on this point (2000, pp. 182–183): " 'In relation to a specific decision problem, an individual may conceive of herself as a member of a group or team, and of the decision problem, not as a problem for her but as a problem for the team. In other words, the individual frames the problem not as "What should I do?", but as "What should we do?" ' ".

[12] Friendship as person capital is à la Becker, for example; or reciprocity as an individual behavioural strategy.

The law given by the world's moderator (God), according to Genovesi, does not ask that "each of us seeks his own interest in the expectation that the interests of others and those of society will be assured by the invisible hand of the market". And neither that "everyone individually seeks to second the interest of others". His "general law" of civil behaviour is different: "*we* have to have as goal to be useful to one another". The 'commandment' is: "be helpful to one another" and *addresses us collectively*. As far as the interpretation of the market in the perspective of this "we-rationality" is concerned, we shall return to it later in this work.

6. Culture as a game

In light of our discussion so far, we can imagine a non-conventional way of looking at the discourse of Genovesi with his students with contemporary eyes, or as a way of expressing the meaning of his actions as a reformer of the Enlightenment. We could, for example, regard Genovesi's discourse as an attempt to show that the "game" of the market is not a Prisoner's Dilemma, but rather a Stag Hunt.

In the eighteenth century the Kingdom of Naples was well known in Europe as an example of nation characterized by a deep sense of mutual distrust (Herreros 2008). In such civil context, when one thinks of the market or life in common in general, one tends to picture such relations as a game where the lowest payoff goes to the agent who chooses cooperation when the other chooses non-cooperation; and the higher payoff corresponds to opportunistic behaviours, to free-riders, to the cheeky ("birbi" in Italian argot) as Genovesi used to call them:

> I am about to have my *Lezioni di commercio* printed in two volumes. I recommend my work to the Divine Providence. I am now old, and I neither hope nor demand anything more from this earth. My aim would be to see if I could leave my Italians a little more enlightened than when I found them, and perhaps also a little more devoted to virtue, who alone may be the true mother of all good. There is no point in thinking about art, trade, government, if we do not think about reforming morality. As long as men will find it convenient to be cheeky, we should not expect much from the fatiche metodiche. I have too much experience of this.
>
> Genovesi, letter of 1765, in Genovesi 1962, p. 168

In fact, it is fairly easy to show that if the subject who cooperates (or wishes to cooperate, like perhaps Genovesi's students) pictures the market according to a relational structure similar to the one in the Prisoner's

A/B	Coop	Non-Coop
Coop	**3**,**3**	**1**,4
Non-Coop	4,**1**	2,2

Figure 8.1 The Prisoner's Dilemma

Dilemma, he or she will read such relational structure as part of a "frame" (in the language of M. Bacharach) in which non-cooperation always prevails over cooperation (Smerilli 2012). In this case he or she can find no logical justification to his or her cooperative action. In fact, if we consider a Prisoner's Dilemma, we obtain the following matrix:

The agent who pictures the market according to the relational structure of the Prisoner's Dilemma ends up thinking of the market as a place where the sly one, who takes advantage of the other's cooperation, is better off (4), while the one who cooperates by himself or herself is then worse off (1). As it is well known, this game has only one equilibrium, i.e. the one involving mutual non-cooperation (2,2): the fear of being exploited and the hope of getting away with a "cheeky" move result in mutual non-cooperation and in the traps of poverty, just as happened in the Kingdom at the time of Genovesi.

Given a person who sincerely wishes to cooperate but pictures the market and civil cooperation as a Prisoner's Dilemma, what does this person expect? If we apply the same evolutionary methodology to the analysis of a world à la Smith, we shall immediately observe that those who choose a cooperative strategy in an evolutionary game of the Prisoner's Dilemma type are destined to become extinct.[13] This is pretty much the same situation as the one where an honest athlete competes in a doped environment. In a Stag Hunt, instead, we have seen that there is a certain threshold value of the share of cooperators (p_c) for which cooperation can emerge over time.

The first message Genovesi wants to share with his students can be summarized as: *"never read trade and exchange as a Prisoner's Dilemma"*,[14]

---

[13] We can see in fact that the expected utility of those who choose to cooperate shall be: $U_c = 3p_c + (1-p_c)1$, hence: $U_c = 2p_c + 1$. The expected utility of non-cooperation is instead: $U_n = 4p_c + 2(1-p_c)$, hence $U_n = 3p_c + 2$, from which U_n (the expected utility of non-cooperation) is always greater than U_c (the expected utility of cooperation) for *every value of p_c*. The situation remains unchanged if instead of using numbers we adopted just ordinal payoffs (with letters).

[14] In fact, we know that even in a context which is perceived as a Prisoner's Dilemma, it is possible that cooperation might emerge (i.e. that a certain cooperative strategy may not become extinct over time) if the game is repeated (and only if it is an evolutionary game) over an indefinite horizon, i.e. if there exists

but as a different game, like a Stag Hunt".[15] Why? As we have already seen in part, if I regard the market (or any interaction) as a Stag Hunt, I associate the higher payoff (4) to a joint action: I do not achieve the best result by exploiting others, but by cooperating with them, although there is a risk that others may not keep their promises. Moreover, looking at it from a different perspective, from the point of view of the individuals considered separately, the Stag Hunt doesn't have a single equilibrium (but two).We can imagine a single equilibrium if we place ourselves in the perspective of a "we", typical of Genovesi's discourse: if the players read the game in terms of the best possible answer to the question "what would it be better for *us* to do?", cooperation evidently becomes the only equilibrium in the game.[16] It is therefore necessary that the players reason in different ways: it is such a "different way of reasoning", called a culture, that creates the *frames* through which we read the various games of life and thereby make our choices.

In other words, faced with the same "objective" situation, some subjects may interpret it as a Stag Hunt, while others may read it as a structure of interaction that is more rewarding for the "cheeky" ones (the ones Genovesi called *birbi* in the passage from the letter reported above) and where cooperation is always "dominated" by opportunism (4 > 3), i.e. as a Prisoner's Dilemma. In this second case, rational persons will never decide to adopt a cooperative strategy. If, on the contrary, the world is substantially assimilated to a Stag Hunt, where cooperation (although fragile because exposed to the opportunism of non-cooperative players) receives the highest payoff, it is possible that people may decide to undertake a cooperative strategy. The frame therefore

---

a recognizability between the players and if the players adopt strategies that are more complex than just "always cooperate" and "never cooperate", but rather "tit-for-tat" (in Genovesi's thought there are elements moving in this direction, even in the 'Catechism' we quoted). In order to rescue Genovesi's logic, I prefer not to complicate the analysis any further, but to spend some time on each of the main steps of the journey we are outlining in the essay. For a more refined and complicated version of this analysis, see Bruni (2008).

[15] In what sense can we read the market as a stag hunt? It will certainly not work to define the market as a collection of negotiations between two people (often affected by asymmetrical information and different degrees of market power, which may be better represented through other types of games), but rather as a sort of social contract, where, if we manage to create a market, we will then all be better off compared to a situation where there is no market ("state of nature").

[16] According to Smerilli (2012), for example, in a we-perspective the only equilibrium is "stag-stag".

has *a value in itself*, independent of the fact that the world may be "objectively" a Stag Hunt or a Prisoner's Dilemma. Our representation of the world (which is a matter of culture or education) is essential to our choices, because depending on the type of game I envision I shall expect certain countermoves from my fellow-citizens and on this basis I shall decide upon my strategy. The interpretation of the world is as real as the world itself, because my perception of the game affects the objective structure of the game. Moreover, if I read life in common as a matter of being "cheeky" or "foolish", I will not subscribe to cooperative behaviour and I will not even have the chance to figure out what the "actual" game of life is. The success of ecological policies, for instance, depends for a large part on the way in which we interpret the world. Personally, I believe that many "civil games" are "objectively" a Stag Hunt, but especially in certain regions that are characterized by distrust, we tend to read them as a Prisoner's Dilemma and for this reason we do not undertake cooperative practices, but remain trapped in *risk dominant* equilibrium (2,2).

In such contexts, culture and educational activity consist above all, though not exclusively, in creating the right "frames" that the citizens will use to interpret the games of life.

9
Virtues and Awards

> Several hundreds of books are concerned with crimes and punishments; only few with merits and rewards.
>
> Melchiorre Gioja, *Del merito e delle ricompense*

1. Giacinto Dragonetti

Central to the eighteenth century was the rich issue concerning theories of action and its motivations. Hume, Rousseau, Smith have written complex theories of action where the motivations in the social and economic arena were much more complex than just the search for self-interest. In Italy there was also lively debate, and thinkers like Pietro Verri and Antonio Genovesi made important statements on the unintended consequences of actions, imitation, emulation, desire for distinction, and so on.

A stream of this debate is the dialogue (at a distance) between the well-known writer Cesare Beccaria and Giacinto Dragonetti, a Neapolitan author much less famous than his Milanese contemporary. This paper aims to demonstrate the relevance of Dragonetti's work for both the history of economic thought and (potentially) the roots of the Law and Economics tradition. There are many reasons for the renewed interest in Dragonetti: he was one of the representatives of the Civil Economy school; Dragonetti's *Delle Virtù e de' Premi* ("On Virtues and Rewards," 1766[1]) was for some decades directly associated

---

[1] In English, Dragonetti's book was called "Treatise on virtues and rewards." In contemporary language (and economics), and for the reasons that will follow later in the paper, I prefer to use the term "awards" instead than "rewards".

(also by publishers[2]) with Beccaria's *On Crimes and Punishments*; and finally, because of the original and forgotten topic of his research.

Contemporary economic theory of action is based on individual *incentives*. Dragonetti advanced a theory of action based on *awards*. Such a theory proceeds from the hypothesis that good (or virtuous) citizens act also for intrinsic reasons. Unlike modern incentives, "awards," in fact, are not the ex-ante "motivation" for a given action but an ex-post recognition or prize. Contemporary economics registers a new tiny interest in the issue of awards or rewards, a further reason for a re-evaluation of Dragonetti's forgotten book. The work of Bruno Frey, in particular, is bringing the issue of awards back to the attention of economists (Frey and Neckermann 2008; Neckermann et al. 2009), although the economics community has not yet recognized this branch of research. This paper aims at contributing to a reconsideration of the forgotten issue of rewards and awards in the social sciences.

Giacinto Dragonetti (1738 1818), a lawyer and disciple of Antonio Genovesi, was born in L'Aquila. Under Genovesi's supervision the young Dragonetti published *A Treatise on Virtues and Awards* ("Delle virtùe de' Premi"), in Naples in 1766, shortly after Beccaria's *On Crimes and Punishments* ("Dei delitti e delle pene," 1764).[3] By 1769 an edition of

---

[2] In most of its European editions, Dragonetti's *Delle virtù e de' Premi* was published in a single volume with Beccaria's *Dei delitti e delle pene.*

[3] In the preface to the 1768 Modena edition, the publisher Giovanni Montanari introduces the author with these words: "The author of this treatise, Dear Reader, is Mr. Giacinto Dragonetti." The preface to the 1769 English edition reads: "Jacinto Dragonetti is the author of the following treatise first published in Naples, and received an applause little inferior to that which had celebrated the name of Beccaria" (1769, p. 4). Giacinto Dragonetti was educated first in Rome and after 1760 in Naples, where he read jurisprudence and became a student of Genovesi. In a private letter of 1767, Genovesi referred to *Delle virtù e de' premi* as having been written by "a friend" (1962, p. 205). In 1947 the Italian philosopher Benedetto Croce mentioned Dragonetti's Treatise in a note published in the literature journal *Biblon,* dismissing it as "rather insipid and adding nothing to the debate" (Croce 1959[1947], p. 235), without providing any further explanation to support that statement. Even more interestingly, the same note by Croce includes the transcription of several extracts from a three-page manuscript that he had discovered among the pages of a first-edition copy of the book that appeared anonymously in 1766 (as did many reformers' books of that time, such as Beccaria's *Dei delitti e delle pene*). Croce ascribed the manuscript to Domenico Cotugno (celebrated professor of medicine and friend of Genovesi) and, on the basis of the content of the manuscript, Croce disputed Dragonetti's authorship of *On Virtues and Awards* (referring to Giacinto's brother as its true author). Now, archival research reveals a set of unpublished letters by Giacinto Dragonetti that

Dragonetti's book with the original Italian text and an English translation was already circulating.[4] In 1776, in his influential *Common Sense,*
Thomas Paine cited the book, referring to Dragonetti as "that wise
observer on governments" (1923[1776], p. 30).

Interestingly enough, in one of the very few papers dealing with
Dragonetti, Wootton (2000) shows the influence of Helvétius's *De l'esprit*
on both Dragonetti's *Delle virtù e dei premj*[5] and on Paine's *Agrarian
Justice* (1797), in particular their common call for a more egalitarian
land reform. In fact, although Dragonetti's work makes no reference to
Helvétius, his private correspondence (now published in Bruni 2010,
appendix) contains an explicit mention of *De L'Esprit.*[6]

---

provide evidence that Giacinto Dragonetti is in fact the authentic author of the
book (although his brother Gianbattista had some influence on him).

[4] Just like Pietro Verri and the *Accademia dei Pugni* are thought to be behind
the young Beccaria's of *On Crimes and Punishments*, it is likely that Genovesi
and the *Accademia delle scienze* might have been behind the young Dragonetti.
Dragonetti's book is undoubtedly the result of a dialogue with Genovesi and
the Neapolitan Economia Civile school, and *On Virtues and Rewards* may
well have been written under Genovesi's supervision. This was the opinion
of Alfonso Dragonetti, who in a short biography of his great-uncle Giacinto
writes: "In 1760 he came to Naples to receive an education that would prepare
him for a career in the practice of law and he engaged in the study of jurisprudence in the spirit of philosophical inquiry (...). The illustrious Genovesi
was then a master of reasoning, not just in Naples, but in Italy, and it was
under his guidance that the young mind from l'Aquila was educated to mature
reflection and exact thinking" (1847, p. 113). Dragonetti did not pursue an
academic career, first working as a lawyer in fiscal matters and later (in the
1780s), as *Magistrato* (judge) of the Monarchy of Sicily. In 1788 he published a
second book, *Origine dei feudi nei regni di Napoli e Sicilia*, where he continued his
intellectual battle against the feudal system and its unjust system of rewards.
In fact, in 1799 he participated in the Jacobin party during the Neapolitan
revolution and, after the Bourbons' repression, he was exiled to France where
he remained up to 1803.

[5] Wootton wrongly defines Dragonetti as "Beccaria's disciple" (2000, p. 325).
Two unpublished letters from Dragonetti to his brother (now in Bruni 2010)
suggest that Dragonetti learned about Beccaria's book only in 1765, when he had
already begun to work on his own treatise.

[6] A letter to Dragonetti's brother Gianbattista (1736–1819) dated 1765 reads:
"Always you suggest that I read *L'Esprit* de l'Helvétius, because according to
you my work has to be modeled according this author's thought." And then
Giacinto asks his brother, who was a scholar of philosophy and humanities,
to amend his book in order to include some elements of *De l'Esprit*. Wootton
notes this about Dragonetti's chapter "On agriculture": "Following in the wake
of Helvétius, he argued for a redistribution of land and an increase in wages"
(2000, p. 325). In fact, in that same chapter Dragonetti wrote, "The small

After his early fame, Dragonetti was almost forgotten even in his homeland, and the issues concerning the relationship between awards and virtues were likewise neglected.

2. Not only punishments: awards

The Introduction to Dragonetti's book provides a clear point of entry to his vision of virtues and awards: "We have made numberless laws to punish crimes, and not one is established to reward virtue" (1769, p. 13).[7]

Although the title of the book (*On Virtues and Rewards*) may be interpreted as an attempt to counter Beccaria's argument (*On Crimes and Punishments*),[8] an accurate reading of the two books reveals the same specific intention – to address an aspect that had been overlooked. Furthermore, Beccaria was not totally oblivious to the positive implications of rewarding virtue, but he does confine this topic to the margins

---

number of proprietors, and the crowds of simple labourers, are the heaviest [cause of the] misery of the those last" (1769, p. 73). Actually, Dragonetti's egalitarian thesis comes, most probably, from the Neapolitan reformation program in agriculture in which Genovesi was also actively involved: "If some part of the old constitution will not be reformed and if a better division of the lands will not be implemented, the books of the philosophers and all the sovereigns' goodwill are just mocking upon the misery of the State" (Genovesi, *Lezioni*, I, ch. VIII, § 17). Dragonetti expanded and developed his vision of land distribution in his second book (1788). In a previous work, Wootton defined Dragonetti as an "unknown Italian" (1994, p. 37), that "not a single Paine scholar has ever read" (ibid.).

[7] The quotations from Dragonetti's *Delle virtù e de' Premi* come from the English 1769 edition. All the other translations of Neapolitan authors (Genovesi, Filangieri, Palmieri) are mine.

[8] Dragonetti's book was hardly an imitation but rather a different approach to matters of law. As Giacinto's nephew, Alfonso Dragonetti remarked: "Those who claim that the treatise was written to contradict or confute Beccaria, most likely ventured their judgement on the basis of the only apparent opposition of titles" (1847, pp. 113–114). The title of Dragonetti's book was unlikely to be an idea of the author's, but most probably of the publisher Gravier in order to profit from Beccaria's success, and possibly by Genovesi (De Tiberis 2010). What it is sure is that when Dragonetti was almost finishing his book, he did not know Beccaria's *Dei delitti e delle pene* (see Bruni 2010). And in the aforementioned note Croce states, "It ensued some following in Italy and abroad a small book published in Naples in 1766, not in opposition but as a complement to the famous treatise of Beccaria, *On Crimes and Punishments*" (Croce 1959 [1947], p. 235).

of his inquiry. The theme of rewards arises towards the end of *On Crimes and Punishments*, in a section about crime prevention:

> Another means of preventing crimes is to reward virtue. I notice that the laws of all nations today are totally silent on this matter. If the prizes awarded by academies to the discoverers of useful truths have increased both knowledge and the number of good books, why should not prizes distributed by the beneficent hand of the sovereign likewise increase the number of virtuous actions? In the hands of the wise distributor, the coin of honor will prove a lasting investment.
>
> Beccaria 1995[1764], p. 109

Beccaria's analysis of "prizes" contains yet another remark about the importance of education: "Finally, the surest but hardest way to prevent crime is to improve education" (ibid.), an instrument closely linked to the reward of virtue, an issue dear to most Enlightenment thinkers (especially Genovesi). Beccaria and others only mentioned the reward of virtue without exploring it further,[9] whereas Dragonetti, inspired by a more radical and far-reaching approach, devoted his analysis entirely to this disregarded issue. Dragonetti envisioned an entire system of laws built around the idea of rewarding virtue ("political virtue" in particular): *a code of virtue* to go alongside the penal code. "The Roman lawgivers knew the necessity of recompenses, but contented themselves with hinting at them, without courage to form their code"[10] (1769, p. 13).

---

[9] For example, Montaigne, Hobbes, Rousseau, Montesquieu, and later Diderot, Bentham, Gioja, and others; or, in ancient times, the Roman philosophers and legal experts who Dragonetti also recalled. The issue is also present in the Civil Economy tradition in the Kingdom of Naples. In his own theory of crimes and punishments as outlined in *Scienza della Legislazione*, Gaetano Filangieri, a leading figure of the Italian Enlightenment, acknowledged the importance of rewarding virtue ("the object of those laws concerning instruction, customs and public education is to mould the hearts and spirits of individuals within society; to exhort them to virtue through passions; to assume next to the fear of punishments for crimes, the aspiration of rewards for virtue" [Italian version, 1780, p. 283]), but made no mention of Dragonetti. Neither did the Apulian Giuseppe Palmieri in his influential book *Riflessioni sulla Publlica Felicità* (1788), despite dedicating an entire chapter to the subject of virtue, with several passages closely resembling the writings of Dragonetti. It is also interesting to note that the Neapolitan Constitution after the Revolution of 1799, written by Mario Pagano (a Genovesi disciple), mentions the issues of *premi* together with the punishments (AA.VV. 1852, p. 65).

[10] In a note Dragonetti recalls the famous phrase from the Digest, Lib. I.*l*.I § I. Tit. I: "Endeavouring to make men good, not by the fear of punishment only, but likewise by the incentives of reward" (ibid.).

It is also clear that Dragonetti's point wasn't to deny the importance of punishment; like Genovesi, he recognized its crucial role. But Dragonetti was convinced that concentrating on punishment principally or exclusively wouldn't be enough to get the Kingdom of Naples back on a path of civil and economic growth.

More generally, the different positions of Beccaria and Dragonetti can also be explained in terms of their respective philosophical traditions. In fact, while Beccaria's framework is essentially consistent with the first elements of the utilitarian doctrine, Dragonetti has to be interpreted within the classical tradition of virtue ethics (in line with Aristotle, Cicero, and Thomas Aquinas). And if Beccaria echoes Hobbes in his characterization of the state of nature ("Laws are the terms under which independent and isolated men come together in society. Wearied by living in an unending state of war and by a freedom rendered useless by their uncertainty of retaining it, they sacrifice a part of that freedom in order to enjoy what remains in security and calm" [Beccaria 1995[1764], p. 9]), the vision of sociality and the essence of the social contract that emerge in Dragonetti follow the works of Genovesi and the Thomistic–Aristotelian view of civil virtues as natural to humankind. Dragonetti hoped to revive interest in the reward of civil virtue that had characterized the Roman republicanism of Cicero and Plutarch and that emerges also in certain expressions of the Lockean tradition.[11]

In this classical tradition, a virtue (*arête*) is a disposition or character trait of an individual, defined generally relative to a particular domain, according to the *telos* or, in today's words, the intrinsic nature of that domain. Furthermore, the logic behind the classical view of virtue diverges from both the instrumentalist and the consequentialist accounts. A virtuous person pursues *areté* for an intrinsic reason, and not for the sake of pleasure or other material rewards. At the same time, a virtuous action may also indeed yield pleasure and material rewards, but they are an indirect result, a sort of by-product of the virtuous conduct (Bruni and Sugden 2011).

Therefore, there is nothing in the classical theory of virtue that impedes considering in the market also *virtues* (dispositions or character traits that help to promote excellence–*areté* and approval in the economic domain), as Dragonetti does (and as most of the communitarian literature today does not). And if that's the case, how can virtue truly be rewarded? More to the point – how does Dragonetti's book suggest we reward virtue?

---

[11] Echoes of this tradition can be found in the notion of "social pacts" in Genovesi (2005 [1765–67], vol. I, ch. 1) and in Filangieri (2003[1780], book III).

First, with more emphasis than is present the classical theory of virtue, Dragonetti associates virtue with the direct and intentional pursuit of the public good (which is distinct from, although not in contrast to, one's personal well-being). In Aristotle, for instance, the way to search for the common good is to perform individual virtuous actions, so there is no contrast between the individual good and the public good. Dragonetti, instead, emphasizes the intentional search for the public good, even when this requires the sacrifice of individual gains. His approach to virtue, which is very close to the ethics of Republicanism, was surely influenced by the history of Europe and by the circumstances in the Kingdom of Naples at his time, where free-riding and the pursuit of individual privileges were jeopardizing public wealth and happiness. "Hence the name of Virtue to every action that respects the interest of others, or the preference of another's well-being to our own" (ibid., p. 19).

So, according to Dragonetti, the sheer pursuit of personal interest, despite being natural and, unlike Mandeville, not to be disparaged as a vice, should not be called "virtuous" per se. Virtue requires effort to reach results that go *beyond* one's private interest. In the Italian edition of 1768 (in Modena), Dragonetti suggests that God is *good* rather than *virtuous*, because doing good takes God no effort. The 1769 English edition states something similar:

> Virtue can only be the attribute of a being weak in nature and strong in will; this is the effort of human morals; a generous effort in behalf of another, independent of the laws, is therefore virtue; its points are the sacrifice which the virtuous offers in himself, and the advantages that hence arise to the public.
>
> Ibid., p. 19

Serving the common good therefore is a *sufficient* condition for virtue, whereas effort and sacrifice are *necessary* attributes (they are also non-spontaneous, unlike the pursuit of pleasure and self-interest). Thus, according to Dragonetti, "Many have ambiguously given the name of Virtue to actions that result from mere natural, religious, or civil laws, and whose proper title is Duties" (ibid.).

His vision of virtue is consistent with his view of rewards:

> He, therefore, who measures his actions by the standards of law, deserves (however commendable) no other recompense than the advantages arising from social compact. He, on the contrary, who

extends his benevolence beyond what the laws strictly enjoin, merits a particular reward; for if he contributes more than others towards the general welfare, it is just he should enjoy more sensible benefits. Virtue disappointed of its proper recompense must become the prey of drones, the scourge of the virtuous, and its own destruction.

Ibid., p. 23

The "recompense", therefore, is a reward for an action that goes "beyond" what private and social contracts normally assign; it's the prize awarded for a free act deliberately intended for the common good: "It is true, that all the members of a state owe it those services which the laws ordain; but it is as true, that its citizens ought to be distinguished and rewarded in proportion to their *gratuitous services*. Virtue *sufficient for itself* is not the virtue of man" (ibid., p. 27, *my italics*).

Expressions like "gratuitous services" or "virtue *sufficient for itself* is not the virtue of man" present clues about other elements in Dragonetti's view of civil virtue. Virtue is a matter of freedom, and its recompense cannot be set by ordinary social and private contracts. At the same time, Dragonetti is stating that an ethics of civil virtues in which awards are not publicly acknowledged, or where they are exclusively intrinsic ("virtue sufficient for itself"), is not sustainable because "it is not the virtue of man"; the latter would require us to be super-human, and hence unfit for civil life (this passage contains an echo of the "god or beast" of Aristotle). Unlike most contemporary accounts of civil virtue, which seem to favour an intrinsic notion of rewards,[12] for Dragonetti the reward of virtue has a civil and "public" nature, and is somehow external to the virtuous agent: "Nor ought it to be objected, that virtue, in proposing its price, loses its dignity and becomes mercenary" (ibid.).

In other words, it is possible to reward civil virtues without the risk of reducing the gratuitousness of virtuous acts to a mere counter-service of a ("mercenary") exchange, which would otherwise compromise the spontaneous, genuine, non-mandatory, essentially free character of virtue – this issue has arisen frequently (and controversially) in the lively debate over the proper reward of "vocational" activities.[13]

---

[12] Consider, for instance, the various theories of intrinsic motivational crowding-out, beginning in economics with Frey (1997).

[13] For a review and debate see Bruni and Sugden 2008.

3. Rewards and awards

These ideas are close to – but have not yet reached – an understanding of what Dragonetti really has in mind by invoking the importance of rewarding – or awarding – virtue. Contemporary economists will immediately recall the notion of incentives, a tool used in economic theory – mostly in monetary or material form – to induce an effort from agents by aligning their interests with those of the organization (principal) for which they work.

Actually, the (still preliminary) contemporary research on awards demonstrates that awards are something different from the contemporary idea of incentives or rewards. Bruno Frey and Susanne Neckerman underline the main characteristics of awards (and their main differences with the standard incentives in economics), including, among others, the low "objective" cost of awards and their high subjective value, their relational and symbolic value, and the complementarity between awards and intrinsic motivation (Frey and Neckerman 2009). These features of awards or prizes (i.e. medals; academic, artistic, civil, or military awards), however, do not help much in illustrating Dragonetti's theory of awards, as this discussion will reveal. But this lack of contemporary literature on awards offers the chance to observe one aspect that has been waiting, up to now, in the shadows – the difference between the English terms *rewards* and *awards*.

As mentioned in the Introduction, the first 1769 English edition chose to translate the Italian word *premi* as "rewards." In contemporary English and in economic culture, however, "rewards" does not convey the entire meaning of what Dragonetti intended. *Premi*, in fact, does contain in part what the contemporary term "rewards" signifies (as will be shown); but other connotations of *premi* are better captured by the term *awards*. Generally, awards are acknowledgements of intrinsically good activities which are not perceived as an expected counter-action within a reciprocal or contractual relationship where recompenses have been established ex-ante (a *quid pro quo* or synallagmatic structure).

Rewards – and the prefix "re" (*re*ciprocity, *re*turn, *re*stitution etc. from the Latin *rectus*, "straight," or "right"*) reveals this –instead are expected and anticipated ex-ante if one individual has performed a given action. Of course, any human social act is somehow an act of reciprocity: when we do something towards others we pretend, expect, desire, hope for some form of return or reciprocity. In rewards, especially monetary or extrinsic ones, not only can the reward be calculated and fully foreseen ex-ante, but, generally, the reward is (totally or principally) the *motivation* for performing a given action. On the other hand, in the case of the awards (i.e. civil, artistic, or scientific awards), when a given activity is performed that may be associated with a possible award, receiving the award is not generally the motivation for the activity, also because it cannot be foreseen and calculated ex-ante in a rational cost–benefit analysis.

For these reasons, the meaning of *premi*, the eighteenth century Italian word Dragonetti chose for the title of his book, can be better conveyed in English by "awards" (in Latin, in fact, *premi* literally means "prizes"), even though Dragonetti's use of the term also conveys in certain dimensions "rewards" as it is currently used.[14] Actually the connotation of "awards" as it is used today is very present in Dragonetti's use of *premi*, although his emphasis is much more "social" (or civil) than in the modern analysis of both rewards (as incentives in economics) and awards (in Frey and Neckerman's sense).

In fact the main difference between the modern economics term "incentives" and Dragonetti's *premi* is the contrast between the individual and social. Incentives are individual-based, designed around private self-interest (only as an indirect or unintentional effect might they also yield benefits of some sort for the common good). The nature of an incentive scheme is purely extrinsic, by nature a private principal–agent relation. *Premi*-awards, instead, are public or civil by nature; they are given when someone has performed intentionally an action for some form of common good. They must be assigned publicly, in the presence of an audience, and the value of an award is directly proportional to its publicity and social approval. This social approbation and recognition is the greater part of the value assigned to an award.

There is another crucial element in Dragonetti's notion of *premi*. In harmony with the Civil Economy tradition, he claimed that actions whose aim is the public good are not in contrast, at least in principle, with self-interest (despite these being two separate objectives, and not necessarily interrelated); nor is the public good in any way incompatible with individual interest or incentives. *Awards go hand in hand with rewards*. In considering the Roman republic or the Greek *polis*, Dragonetti notices that "Public grandeur was not concentrated in a few, but expanded itself with such power, that each private interest was dissolved in the public, and each ray of the public reflected on its members" (ibid., p. 29).

---

[14] "Rewards" is instead an accurate translation of Melchiorre Gioja's *Sui meriti e sulle ricompense* (1818), i.e. "On Merits and Rewards."

Hence his own definition of rewards: "Rewards alone tie the wayward interest of individuals to the public, and keep the eye of man intent on general good" (ibid., p. 31).

Therefore, despite acknowledging the distinction between acts motivated by virtue and those motivated by self-interest, Dragonetti never saw these two kinds of actions as opposed or in any way incompatible. It is fair to say that, in his view, a good society ought to be able to reconcile self-interest and virtue, rewards and awards, contracts and gratuitousness.

Consider one further step.

The structure of his book also provides other significant clues to Dragonetti's idea of rewards (not only awards). Its central section contains several specific recommendations for rewarding virtue. He sets them out in order to avoid attributing high rewards to conduct only marginally virtuous or beneficial to society; and, conversely, emphasizes that truly virtuous conduct receives too modest a reward. In the words of Dragonetti, "It is more pernicious to reward improperly than not at all" (p. 39).

It is worthwhile to note that the treatise was conceived against the backdrop of animated anti-feudal polemics,[15] which Dragonetti clearly had in mind and which form the central theme of his later work, *On the Origin of Fiefs in the Kindgoms of Naples and Sicily* (1788), his work that formally assessed the juridical controversy over the inheritability and alienability of fiefs in Sicily and Naples, at the same time maintaining the reformist aspirations typical of the Civil Economy tradition.[16] This broad cultural perspective provides the backdrop against which the deeper meaning, still relevant today, of the theoretical debate concerning rewards and virtues can be unfolded.

At the heart of Civil Economy thought lies the conviction that feudal society could not lead to prosperity or civil development. The feudal system promotes the *perverse reward* of acquired privileges and discourages genuinely virtuous behaviour. This point is clearly illustrated in the following passage:

The distinction of ranks has been struck out to reward the good: if it was continued to their descendants it was on the presumption

---

[15] A circumstance that had a remarkable impact on the Neapolitan Enlightenment, including authors like Filangieri and Pagano (but also on the entire era of the European Enlightenment culture in the rest of Europe).

[16] Franco Venturi (1972, p. 212) remarks that Dragonetti's book "caused the powerful feudal lords...to cry aloud."

that they would not degenerate. In supposition it is easy to pass from probability to falsehood: Hence an implicit faith in noble virtue distributes often considerable favours to birth only. The experience of every day evinces that the titles, dignities, honours, and other advantages merited by the sires serve merely to shelter the dishonoured escutcheons of the sons. Let Europe scorn the illusion, nor permit the supported virtue to prey on what is due to the real.

1769, p. 41[17]

A key consequence of these anti-feudal polemics is an attitude of praise towards the arts and commerce, a trait that can be truly appreciated only in the light of the overall project of the Neapolitan and the whole European Enlightenment, whose mission was to build a post-feudal liberal society where the proper reward of true virtue (and the discouragement and punishment of false virtue) might eventually provide an impetus for a new phase of civil life and economic development. Many remarkable pages by Genovesi, Filangieri, and other authors of the European and Neapolitan Enlightenment reveal this common anti-feudal sentiment.[18]

In line with most of the European Enlightenment, the Neapolitan tradition considers economic activity to be a genuine expression of civil life. It sees commerce as a *civilizing factor*. Like the Italian civic humanists of the fifteenth century, Genovesi and the Neapolitans see commercial activity as an expression of civic virtue, and civil life as the place where virtues could be expressed to their fullest. Montesquieu's theses are present in Genovesi's writings, although the Neapolitan and the French authors do differ in some ways, including in their concepts of commerce.

Dragonetti's praise for the virtues of commerce has to be read in a Genovesian spirit. Dragonetti never formulated an actual and complete theory of the relationship between virtues and awards/rewards, and nor did he ever lay out the theoretical mechanisms for rewarding virtues – which is the greatest limitation of his work. Nevertheless, he has provided several insights which can be read and appreciated within the general framework of Civil Economy.

---

[17] A remark which maintains its revolutionary appeal even two-and-a-half centuries later.

[18] Genovesi's vision of commerce was probably also influenced (including, I would add, his critique of Montesquieu) by John Cary: see Reinert (2005).

4. The market and commerce as proper rewards for virtues

A key point that makes Dragonetti's ideas relevant in the contemporary ethical debate concerning markets is the connection he makes between markets and civil virtue. As he uses the term, *premi* conveys a meaning associated with both *award* and *reward*, although in an unusual and original way.

Both Genovesi and Dragonetti, and the tradition of Civil Economy as a whole, regarded commerce as a key opportunity for cultivating and *rewarding* civil virtue. If the market is construed in the Civil Economy tradition as a form of "mutual assistance," then commerce itself becomes a virtue because by trading and contributing to developing the market, individuals are ultimately contributing to the common good. Moreover, starting a commercial activity in eighteenth-century Naples required the ability to take risks, and this gesture too may be interpreted as a token of public virtue since the entire community benefited from its results. From the perspective of Civil Economy thinking, the market is a place where virtues can be encountered and cultivated. The market and trade are both essential to public happiness. As Dragonetti notes, "Commerce is the reciprocal communication of the produce and industry of various countries. ... The citizens of earth carry on a war of industry against each other, and where that ceases, there the supports of life decay" (1769, pp. 113, 121).

For this reason, society ought to recognize commercial virtues and publicly reward virtuous merchants, as in ancient Rome where the best merchants were allowed to join the equestrian order: "Commerce influences the manners. Its spirit is that of frugality, moderation, prudence, tranquility, order. Whilst these subsist riches are harmless. Commerce has every where propagated the study of social habits. ... if these are the advantages of commerce, *the trader should not want for his reward* [19] (p. 131, *my italics*).

Neglecting to reward commercial virtues would discourage market transactions and, therefore, diminish the market as an institution; and without markets there can be no public happiness. Dragonetti treats the subjects of war and navigation in similar terms (pp. 78 ff.). Without adequate defence and naval trade there can be no safe commerce; therefore defence should not be left to mercenary troops, rewarding instead the pure military virtues which keep the state safe and, hence, free and

---

[19] The verb "want" is used in the archaic sense of "lack" or "be short of".

happy. A similar attitude emerges at the conclusion of an unpublished letter written by Dragonetti to his brother Gianbattista, who had asked him about the link between the first and the second parts of his book: "If I did not discuss agriculture, war, navigation and commerce, that are the…main human virtues, what would my…little treatise be worth?" (Dragonetti, in Bruni [2010]).[20]

The implication of this vision of commerce, which was quite common in Europe at that time (as Hirschman (1977) and others have explained[21]), is that Dragonetti regards commerce as part of the system for the reward of virtue. It is virtuous to satisfy other people's needs, and by facilitating mutually advantageous transactions the market rewards virtue. His chapter on commerce states:

> A thousand proofs convince us that man was made for society, but above all, the mutual dependence on mutual wants, that basis of all unions. …

> The barrenness of one place is to be supplied by the fertility of another, and industrious nations provide for the want of slothful ones. Without commerce trade is impossible. Commerce is the reciprocal communication of the produce and industry of various countries. …

> To make each individual participate of the benefits of the nature, and to give to the political body all the strength is capable of, ought to be the effect of the commerce.

> *Ibid., pp. 113, 122, 123*

One possible and legitimate reading of such passages on commerce, in line again with idea fundamental concept of the Civil Economy tradition, is that the market is a key mechanism for rewarding virtues.

---

[20] Shortly before the historical building of the Archive was destroyed in the April 6, 2009 earthquake, I had the chance to visit the Dragonetti–De Torres Archive at the National Archive of L'Aquila, where I fund this and another private letters of Giacinto Dragonetti to his brother (the Archive has been rebuilt, and now two letters and other material are available in the new building of the Archivio di Stato de L'Aquila, Bazzano via Galileo Galilei 1, Sez. Amministrativa, serie V, 42/1). Access to this material was made possible through the kind collaboration and support of Dr. Giovanna Lippi, who was in charge of the Dragonetti Archive and who was among the victims of the 2009 quake. To her goes my warmest remembrance.

[21] On the issue of commerce as civilization in the eighteenth century, see also Bruni and Sugden (2000).

From that perspective, market and trade are perfectly moral or virtuous, and mutual advantage, reciprocity, and morality go hand by hand. From this perspective, although the Civil Economy tradition emphasizes virtue and its reward, it follows a different cultural path than the one held by "communitarian" authors such as Anderson (1993), Walzer (1983), or McIntyre (1981). These authors, as we see later, create a contrast between true moral relationship and standard economic or market interactions. For Dragonetti (and Genovesi), however, the market and virtues are fully consistent one another (Bruni and Sugden 2011).

Only one sentence in Dragonetti's small book has achieved widespread notoriety, the one that Thomas Paine cited in *Common Sense*. Paine seemed to take particular pleasure in the political aspects of the pamphlet, and he quoted (on page 30 of *Common Sense*) the following passage by Dragonetti:

> A mode of government that contained the greatest sum of individual happiness, with the fewest wants of contribution [in terms of liberty] …. *The science of the politicians consists in fixing the true point of happiness and freedom. Those men would deserve the gratitude of ages, who should discover a mode of government that contained the greatest sum of individual happiness, with the least national expense.*
>
> Ibid., p. 155 [the sentence in italics is the one quoted by Thomas Paine][22]

Dragonetti's emphasis on civil virtues and their awards/rewards has not generated (as often happens) an illiberal or authoritarian vision of politics and democracy. In his political project of reforming the Kingdom of Naples, virtues, public happiness, and freedom go hand-in-hand, a vision that may put Dragonetti alongside liberal authors of freedom, happiness *and* virtues, like T. Paine or J.S. Mill.

5. The underground river of Civil Economy

What became of Dragonetti and the Civil Economy tradition within contemporary social sciences? It obviously did not enter mainstream thought in the nineteenth or twentieth centuries, not even in Italy, where it was submerged under a strong wave of criticism headed in particular by Francesco Ferrara, the most influential twentieth-century

---

[22] Paine quoted Dragonetti's thesis on happiness and freedom again in a later work (1792).

Italian economist. In the introduction to the third volume of his influential *Biblioteca dell'Economista* (First Series), Ferrara (recognizing Genovesi as the first among them) claims: "The merit of the foundation of economics goes to the English Smith, or to the French Turgot, not to Genovesi, Verri, or Beccaria" (1852, p. xxxvi). According to him, the proper science of economics was to be found abroad, not in the works of the classic Italian authors. A later generation of economists, including Pantaleoni and especially Pareto, maintained this outward-looking gaze rather than looking more deeply into the tradition of Civil Economy.[23]

Through the eighteenth century Dragonetti's book achieved widespread notice all over Europe, thanks also to Gravier, the publisher. Later editions were published in Venice (1767), Modena (1768), and Palermo (1787). To my knowledge, it was translated into French (printed in Naples in 1767), English (1769), German (1769), and Russian (1769). In some cases it was bound together with Beccaria's *On Crimes and Punishments*. There is a Spanish edition dated 1836 (in Spain, and in Germany as well, Genovesi's *Lezioni* were in the same years translated and influential), translated by the famous jurist Ramon Salas of the school of Salamanca, again in joint edition with Beccaria's text. Other editions may well exist. Not surprisingly, the school of Bentham also mentioned Dragonetti, but in polemical tones (he received strong criticism particularly from Dumont: see Dragonetti 1847, p. 116).

---

[23] The tradition of Civil Economy, however, never truly disappeared. Like an underground river it kept flowing in the spirit of a few economists both in Italy and elsewhere, who in various ways have continued to cultivate an idea of economics as a source of civil development, closely linked to civil virtues (not just self-interest), to public happiness (and not just to the wealth of nations), and mindful of the role of institutions (but without going so far as Hobbes did in *Leviathan*). In Italy, such economists have included Antonio Scialoja, Giandomenico Romagnosi, Carlo Cattaneo, Fedele Lampertico, Marco Minghetti, Giuseppe Toniolo, Francesco Vito, Luigi Einaudi and, among the contemporary ones, Paolo Sylos Labini, Siro Lombardini, Giorgio Fuà or Giacomo Becattini would be mentioned. The tradition of Civil Economy thinking has been fed mainly by economists who practice a non-theoretical but mostly applied approach, as well as scientists, politicians, jurists, and some exponents of the Italian tradition of social economy. In a way, however, the most genuine heirs to the economic tradition initiated by Genovesi and Dragonetti have been those who actively promoted the Italian cooperative movement, such as Ugo Rabbeno, Vito Cusumano, Luigi Luzzati, Ghino Valenti, Leone Wollemborg, and those who founded and kept going rural credit unions, and consumption and production co-operatives. They have given a truly valuable contribution to the process of civil development invoked by Genovesi and other civil economists.

In the early nineteenth century, Melchiorre Gioja was the first in Italy to take up Dragonetti's issue again openly, in *Dei meriti e delle ricompense* [*Of Merits and Rewards*]. In the Introduction he acknowledges the previous work carried out by Dragonetti on this subject. Various versions of both books (Dragonetti and Gioja) followed in the first half of the nineteenth century.[24] After the many-sided and controversial figure of Gioja linked himself to the topic of virtues and rewards, however, all such interest disappeared.

Dragonetti bound the topic of inquiry tightly to Genovesi's school of civil virtues. All of *Lezioni di economia civile* has been built around this theme.[25] The Apulian Giuseppe Palmieri, who belonged to the same Neapolitan tradition, dedicated an entire chapter of *Riflessioni sulla Felicità Pubblica relativamente al Regno di Napoli* (1788) to virtue.[26]

When Genovesi passed away in 1769, his system of economic thought was still unfolding (at the time, he was working towards the third edition of the *Lezioni*). Somehow, his death halted Dragonetti's pursuit of the very same project of research. He never carried out the project outlined in the Treatise, and nor did anyone else. The story might have been different had Genovesi had a few more years to work on his *Lessons*, which never achieved a status comparable to the

---

[24] Also in the historical archive in L'Aquila, I found an 1848 edition of *Of Virtues and Rewards* (Naples, Stamperia del Tirreno). The editor of that volume, Lelio Fanelli, included almost in its entirety the previously published biography of Alfonso Dragonetti.

[25] See, for instance, volume II, chapter X, on the subject of public trust, which contains the key idea that civil virtues ought to be promoted and cultivated, also by the State.

[26] He wrote: "It shall be said that the power and fear of Sanction in Society act as a restraint to human instinct and maintain it within the limits assigned by Law; but this one restraint operates only in those Citizens that public opinion has already found to be mean-spirited. If no other restraint is to be had, then all Citizens will become such" (ibid., p. 42). He then remarks: "Sanction renders Law perfect, but it does not suffice to ensure observance. With natural Laws its effect, even if certain and inevitable, makes a modest impression, partly because it arrives slowly and rather late, it does not immediately follow the violation. Indeed with Civil Laws the effect could be more prompt, but it isn't and, what's more, it is uncertain because it is intended at their elusion. In vain therefore we turn to sanctions hoping to achieve compliance to laws. The only sure guarantors to obtain the observance of laws are the adherence to one's own dues and the fear of shame. The first is ingenerated by the love for virtue the second from the respect for public opinion, in case this is founded on the very same virtue" (ibid., p. 46).

Wealth of Nations but it could perhaps be compared to Smith's *Lectures in Jurisprudence*, an intermediate step between moral philosophy and economics (Bruni 2006).

Some handbooks of the "History of Economic Thought" still mention the ideas of Genovesi and Filangieri, but Dragonetti disappeared altogether after Ferrara and Luigi Cossa's history (1875). Neither is he included in Franco Venturi's influential *Settecento Riformatore* (1969). The failure of a theory of virtues and rewards to develop within the mainstream tradition of Political Economy is a corollary of the interrupted Civil Economy tradition.

6. What can Dragonetti teach us today?

There is an intrinsic value in bringing to light an author who, although unknown today, had been part of the active debate that has shaped the modern history of social and economic ideas. The history of economic thought is richer for this rediscovery of a protagonist in the European Enlightenment. In the case of Dragonetti's *Delle virtù e de' i premi*, however, there is a second value associated with a reconsideration of his ideas and work – namely, the important, if yet incipient, new streams of research in economic and social sciences.

In particular the issues present in Dragonetti's theory can be fruitful and inspiring for two fields of social sciences – the new literature on rewards compared to punishments, and the debate on virtue ethics and the market economy.

The issue of rewards is gaining ground in both economic theory and in practical experiments. Concerning rewards/awards, Bruno Frey and Susanne Neckermann have focused in particular on awards, albeit in the sense of medals or academic, artistic, military prizes. This meaning of awards captures only a part of Dragonetti's idea, which is much more general than the strict symbolism that Frey and Neckermann explore. Dragonetti surely had in mind medals and symbolic prizes, but his basic sense award has to do with civil virtues. On the other hand, in the literature on experimental economics the issue of rewards is gaining prominence. In the experiments, however, rewards may be slight or costly, as they are in "strong reciprocity" phenomena.[27] Neither use of "reward" captures the idea of Dragonetti's *premi*, in the sense it has been defined in this paper. A promising line of experimental inquiry

---

[27] See for a review Andreoni et al. (2003), Delgado et al. (2005) and Sefton et al. (2007).

could develop by taking into consideration the specific idea of *premi* and comparing them to punishments.

Finally, Dragonetti has something relevant to say concerning the present debate on virtue ethics and market interactions. Some would associate virtue ethics closely with a critique of the market and economics. Most virtue ethics philosophers, including communitarians like McIntyre (1981) and Sandel (2009), criticize the ethos of the market economy. They claim that since the market depends on instrumental motivations, it must lack virtue and so undermine virtue in other domains of life. Although the philosophy itself is rarefied, many of the attitudes it supports are echoed in anti-capitalist and anti-globalization ideas that resonate in public debates. An approach to the market from Dragonetti's perspective can respond to such criticisms in the same language of virtue ethics. Dragonetti's idea of commerce and the market is perfectly coherent with ethics, without renouncing standard market mechanisms, such as the search for self-interest. He suggests an idea of economy and possibly economics perfectly reconciled with virtue ethics and yet compatible with the market, an approach that can be useful in this age of economic and ethical crisis.

10
The Ethos of Civil Economy*

> When riches were but the fruits of conquest, and were not
> acquired by the industry or exertion of the husbandman, the
> artist or the merchant, they certainly corrupted the people,
> encouraged idleness, and hastened the decline of nations.
> 1…In our days a rich people are always the most laborious
> and free people. There are, therefore, no longer the same
> reasons for the fear of riches. On the contrary, they are both
> desirable, and the acquisition of them should be the study of
> the legislature, because they are the best support of national
> happiness and the external, as well as internal liberty of a
> state.
>
> G. Filangieri, *The Science of Legislation*

1. The point so far

In this chapter we attempt to present a different idea of the market and
of its ethos (as opposed to the one offered by Smith) and in doing so we
take the civil economy as our starting point. The characterization of the
market as "civil" and friendly shall be a preliminary point of arrival in
our discussion, but we shall not stop there.

In the eighteenth century, the Neapolitan school of civil economy
signified mainly (though not exclusively)[1] the development of a civil
and Franciscan humanistic ethics, built around the concept of *philia*, but

---

* This chapter, in particular the second part, is based on Bruni and Sugden
(2008).
[1] This tradition had several modern sources, such as Newton, Locke, and
Vico.

also influenced to some extent by Christian *agape*.[2] We can also think of the Neapolitan tradition as a development of the same project that began with Aristotle and that was then taken further with the Roman republican thought of Cicero, Sallust and Seneca. The same project was later picked up and 'christianized' by Aquinas and by the Franciscan school, until the synthesis wrought by Civil Humanism in the fifteenth century. After the Renaissance and with modernity, we observe the first real break in this tradition, which we have termed "classic", when, in the passage from Luther to Hobbes, life in common was reformed on new anthropological grounds. We have already mentioned how *philia* would then evolve (or regress) into market exchange.

The Neapolitan school of civil economy, thanks to the critical role of mediation played by Vico (who transformed this tradition from classical into modern, but without subscribing to Hobbes' anthropological arguments), was the last significant attempt to graft the classic tradition into modernity, by offering a view of the market as reciprocity, as *fides*, as *philia* (still with its typical *communitas* and its typical exclusions). This tradition never became prevalent in the modern social sciences. Nonetheless, it remains alive today and (in accord with our *karst* river metaphor) it continues to flow "above-ground" through this important stretch of time.

In this chapter we consider the possibility of conceiving the market as a civil fraternity. I have championed this theoretical claim for about one decade now, together with British economist and philosopher Robert Sugden, who, while also drawing from Hume, Smith, Hayek and Buchanan, found in Genovesi as well as in civil economy thinking an important source of inspiration for a different ethos of the market.

2. The market as mutual assistance

As we considered Genovesi and his notion of "mutual assistance" in the previous chapter, we mentioned how conceiving the market in that way, and not just in terms of mutual advantage, has significant implications, which we shall now examine.

First of all, the idea of the market as mutual assistance makes the metaphor of the "invisible hand" somewhat less mysterious. Anyone who had the experience of teaching economic theory knows how

---

[2] Traces of such influences may also be found in Dragonetti's notion of virtue, which goes beyond the Stoic view (of individual perfection), specifically adding the idea of sacrificing for the sake of the common good.

surprised students typically are when they find themselves confronted, pretty much immediately, with the logic of market exchange. In people's minds a sort of mercantile fallacy seems to exist, which is more pervasive than ordinarily thought (or at least more than us economists ordinarily think). This fallacy has various manifestations that lie in the background of common-sense in the understanding of economic matters. A first and deeply-rooted fallacy consists in conceiving political economy as a sort of household management: it consists in picturing the economy of a large collectivity (State, city, ...) more or less like the economy of a family (the Greeks' *oikos-nomos*). If a family undergoes a moment of crisis, parents have to solve the crisis (by working more, saving, redistributing wealth and resources within the family, etc.); similarly, one could think, if a state undergoes an economic crisis, politics can and must solve the problems and can, for instance, find a solution to world poverty simply by redistributing wealth from the more affluent to the poor. Reasoning in these terms, one falls into this mercantile fallacy, because one carries out the same reasoning of those seventeenth-century economists who understood the national economy like they understood the domestic economy and ascribed the most critical role to politics and to the King. Those who reason this way make a mistake in economics that is similar to the mistake made by those who, even after Newton or Einstein, continue to believe that the sun revolves around the earth, or in the existence of the ether. Today, on the contrary, we know – thanks in particular to Hayek – that the government only plays a small part in the re-launch of the economy and in its orientation, since the largest role is played by millions of separate subjects who only possess fragmentary information (as showed especially by Hayek in the twentieth century).

A second "fallacy" is more directly related to our discussion of the market. This consists in thinking of the market as a "zero-sum game" (an exchange where there is a given cake and the various slices are ascribed through negotiation to the participants in the game): this was also originally a mercantile idea, according to which commerce (international commerce in particular) was thought of as enriching one part (those gaining gold and silver) and impoverishing another (which in the exchange lost gold or silver).

This second fallacy, or quite simply this second mistake, is what leads those who have little understanding of economic theory to deny the idea that when the market exists and functions properly all those involved in the exchange may have the chance of improving their initial positions (although not all in the same way, as asymmetries may exist).

As a matter of fact, if one thinks of the market as based on individual interests, what comes to mind are cases where a subject benefits in an opportunistic way to the detriment of another: once again, we tend to read the market like Genovesi's students, i.e. as a Prisoner's Dilemma (unrepeated), where even when agents trust each another, such trust is bound to be exploited by the other. By focusing on mutual assistance and collective advantage, as we have seen, Genovesi is telling his students to look at the market (and in general at civil society) as a large space where there are opportunities to trade leading to mutual advantages (the most important of which consists in creating markets capable of replacing feudal society).[3]

This view of the market makes it harder to understand the linkage between mutual interest and the common good because the actor's intention in this case is also oriented to the advantage of those with whom he or she interacts on the market. Here – unlike in Smith's theory of the "invisible hand" – a direct connection arises between the agents' *intentions* and the *effects* of their actions. The possibility of friendship, or *civil fraternity*, as the market paradigm also derives from this approach: the market has a certain moral content (and morality directly refers to intentions) and well-functioning societies require that this moral sense be fostered and made explicit. In fact, this book is also an attempt to gain a better understanding of the "moral" nature of market relations, where by "moral" I refer to that general group of principles that, in any given society and culture, govern judgment in terms of approval or disapproval, of good or bad, within human behaviour.

In civil economy thinking, a market that shows a moral and fraternal attitudes does not necessarily imply (nor does it exclude) the renunciation of one's own material gain to the benefit of our partner in the exchange. Behaviours of this kind are what Wicksteed (1933[1910]) would have called "tuistic". Genovesi tells us that it is possible to maintain a fraternal attitude towards those taking part in an exchange on the market, without necessarily having to embrace altruism. The idea of fraternity or friendship, as found in Genovesi, is not a kind of behaviour (like altruism, for instance) or a set of preferences (social or "other-regarding", as we shall see), *but rather it is a way of perceiving and reading the market as the collective action of a team.*

---

[3] Genovesi's critique of mere assistance to the poor is well-known and we find it also in the *Lezioni*: his politics was about creating opportunities so that the poor could work, hence allowing all to overcome the feudal logic of benefactors and beneficiaries.

For this reason, civil economy is different from today's prevailing understanding of market relations. Two aspects mark this distinction and show its significance. The first aspect, well visible in Smith's theory of the "butcher, the baker and the brewer", is the idea that partners in a market exchange are mutually indifferent and that the market, in the words of philosopher David Gauthier (1986, p. 84), when competitive is a "morally free zone", i.e. a zone where there are no moral constraints. In such an approach, which we have referred to as Smithian, the beneficial consequences of the markets in terms of development and wealth are non-intentional. In this sense, market relations are not substantially *social*.

As we try to express this concept in terms of our previous chapters, we must observe that it is generally acknowledged that if there is a sphere of genuinely social human relations, this exists outside the market and is characterized by relational forms that cannot be found within market interaction. In fact, economists, yesterday like today – even the ones who are more tightly inscribed within the official tradition of economics – typically believe that this sphere of "genuine" social relations may only exist in family life, in friendship, and in various forms of civil commitment; but, ordinarily, it these spheres have been thought of as having nothing, or too little, to do with the economic sphere. This is a point on which the tradition of civil economy differs from the Anglo-American tradition that has become mainstream.

3. How to analyze sociality in economic theory?

Aside from "mutual indifference", there is a second dimension that characterizes the conventional notion of the market and that is significant for the sake of our discussion about the ethos of the market. This second dimension is not so much the product of Smith's own thought, but rather of the post-Smithian developments in economic science in recent decades. I am referring to the idea that the concern, or the unconcern, of an individual towards another is a matter of *individual preferences*. To say that a certain person A has a concern for another person B basically means that according to A's preferences B shall attain a higher level of consumption or income and that, as a consequence of these preferences, A is willing to sacrifice part of his or her own consumption (or income) in order to improve B's situation.[4]

---

[4] Mutual indifference (in the Smithian sense) is represented in this game by the absence of "pro-social" or "other-regarding" preferences.

According to this perspective – which is still present today in those strands of economics that deal with behaviours that are not self-interested – being genuinely social means having "other-regarding" preferences, i.e. being willing to sacrifice part of one's own advantages to the benefit of others.

In contemporary economic theory, social (or other-regarding) preferences are normally translated by assuming a certain degree of altruism, i.e. a positive concern of a person towards the consumption or well-being of another.

Recently, more specific models have been developed, often based on experimental lab evidence. For instance, Bolton and Ockenfels (2000) have assumed that people (some people, at least) have preferences that are sensitive to differences between one's own income and the incomes of others; they assume, in other words, that people are "inequality averse". Rabin (1993) has suggested instead that preferences are informed by "reciprocity", leading them to reward those who behaved "kindly" to them in the former round of an interaction (assuming a sequential game) and to punish those who didn't.

What these theories have in common is that the element that determines whether preferences are "social" is typically revealed by the willingness to sacrifice one's own interest in order to reward or punish others – also, it should be noted, such models represent an important innovation within economic theory and they must be regarded with satisfaction by those wishing to enrich the anthropological basis of economic and social science. The basic game in these models (that are for the most part experimental or theoretical) is the so-called

---

[5] In the version of the game that is commonly employed in lab experiments analyzing reciprocity and fairness, there are normally two players, A and B, who are asked to interact within a sequential game. A has two options available: to trust B, or to not trust B, in which case the game ends straightaway (in this case, for example, the initial endowment may be divided between the two, e.g. 10 euros total yielding 5 euros each). If A decides to trust B, they then move on to the second phase of the game, where B has full control: the money sum is multiplied (e.g. by 3, giving 30) and B can decide whether to keep the money entirely (thus not reciprocating the trust previously received from A) or to give something back to A – incidentally, we should note that lab evidence basically contradicts what standard economic theory would predict. Similar games or variations of the "Trust Game" include the so-called "Investment Game" (A receives 10 euros and, if he or she does not trust B, B gets nothing and A keeps it all) and the "Gift-Exchange Game" (where A and B receive the same sum and they simultaneously have to decide whether or not they trust each other).

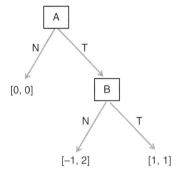

Figure 10.1 The Trust Game

"Trust Game".[5] If we reduced the game to its most basic structure, it could be illustrated as follows:

Standard theory (rational choice theory) excludes the possibility that A may rationally trust B, since it assumes that if A chooses to trust B (*t*), A knows that B will then compare 2 with 1 and eventually decide not to reciprocate A's trust, thus resulting in A receiving -1 (below 0, which represents the *status quo*).[6] Therefore the only equilibrium of the game in a non-repeated framework is (0,0): A ends the game after the first move (*n*).

The theory of social preferences, in turn, envisions the possibility that A may rationally trust B based on the assumption that if A believes B to have social preferences (and believes therefore B might reciprocate A's initial kindness at his or her own expense in the second round), then A may play "*t*" in the expectation that B, in view of his or her social preferences, may play "*r*", thus reaching the equilibrium (1,1), *where both agents are better off compared to the status quo* (0,0).

This theory certainly seems (and is) in line with Genovesi's understanding of the economy, but with an important difference. Rabin's theory (and in general all those theories gathered under the label of "strong reciprocity") allows reaching the cooperative outcome in a Trust Game (whose logic is similar to the Prisoner's Dilemma)[7] thanks

---

[6] It must be noticed that in this representation, the payoffs (0, 1 – 1, 2) are expressed in terms of monetary (or material) rewards, not in terms of utility or preference satisfaction – an assumption that is also required by the other games we have previously introduced.

[7] In fact, this kind of literature employs games that are partly different from the Prisoner's Dilemma for being sequential (and non-simultaneous), like the "Trust Game" or the "Ultimatum Game". However, the relational logic of interaction remains essentially the same.

to the inclusion in the theory (and hence in the game's payoffs)[8] of social preferences of this kind.

What difference is there compared to a theory *à la* Genovesi? Considering the theory of *social preferences* we will see that *in fact* the relation between the agents does produce a mutual benefit. But – and this is the point – the intentional content of the relation is not mutual advantage, but rather the punishment or rewarding of the other player according to my own preferences. There is in these models and games no notion of a "joint action" or of "mutual advantage"; the parts remain separate and independent individuals.

On the other hand, taking inspiration from a theory *à la Genovesi*, we may describe the Trust Game (and trust phenomena in general) in a different way. Genovesi would suggest moving from a theory based on "I" (basically like Smith's theory or standard theory, but also the theory of social preferences) to a theory based on a "we", where each person asks herself: "what shall *we* do"? Which line of action is the best for *us*? How to read a Trust Game in a "we-thinking" perspective?

Let us go back to the representation of the Trust Game: in this picture, I have highlighted two outcomes: (0,0) and (1,1).

A 'Genovesian' view of the civil economy leads to the suggestion that the players, in order to regard the game in a correct and civilly

---

[8] The game is illustrated by assuming that the objective (or utility) functions of the agents, and hence their preferences (the utility functions represent the preferences of the players), are more complex than those employed by the standard theory. For example: according to standard neoclassical theory the utility function of A is equal to $U_a = f(I)$, where I is the income or material payoff in the game, which is the *only* variable in the agent's function: there is no motivation other than I (or consumption, or in general material rewards). On the basis of this function and of the standard assumption of non-satiation (more is better than less), the game equilibrium (0,0) is eventually achieved. If, instead, we assume like Rabin and other social preferences authors that agents are also concerned about inequality in income distribution (inequality aversion) and/or about the motivations of their partners in the game (kindness), then we shall adopt a more complex utility function to calculate the game's payoffs (payoffs are simply a representation of the agents' objective functions that reflect their preferences). In addition to $U_a = f(I)$, such function will also contain other variables (thus allowing to embed these other dimensions in the agents' preferences). For instance, in its very basic form, a function that embodies psychological elements, can be indicated as $U_a = f(I + \alpha)$ where α represents these other components in the agent's preferences, i.e. the non-material aspects that nonetheless motivate the agent and affect utility (in fact in the models α represents several different parameters, covering the various aspects of each single theory: inequality aversion, reciprocity ...).

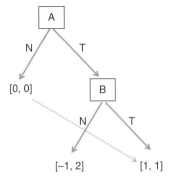

Figure 10.2   The Trust Game revisited

fruitful way (thin arrow), ought to compare (0,0) and (1,1), like we saw in the previous chapter when considering "culture as a game". It is as though the agents had to maximize a sort of 'social utility function', as if they formed a single agent, who, confronted with the choice between (0,0), (–1,2) and (1,1), would definitely choose (1,1), because it yields a higher sum result (2 > 1). Society can only function when it regards the civil game (including the market) as a passage between a certain non-cooperative *status quo* to one that entails a mutual advantage without lingering in opportunistic dynamics during the second phase of the game, because if this attitude of individualistic concern prevailed, fear would leave the agents stuck in (0,0), as in a sort of Hobbesian state of nature.

A central role in this theory, similarly to Rabin's, is played by intentions, but these are the kind of intentions we could indicate as "collective", as opposed to "individual". If we know, collectively, that it is "best for us" to choose the combination "trust" for A and "reciprocate" for B [Ta/Rb], then the game turns into a sort of joint action aimed at achieving a common outcome, under the assumption that the two think alike, that they feel like a "team". There is no sacrifice, but only a renunciation of opportunism, based on the common awareness that opportunism would leave both players stuck in the *status quo*. B is not rewarding A for his or her kindness (by choosing to reciprocate); B is only reciprocating A's intention to carry out together an operation that is mutually advantageous. Indeed it is important that each agent has good reasons to believe the other is not an opportunistic player, not a "cheeky" one (a "birbo" in the words of Genovesi), because when this happens the entire construction of a civil economy falls apart, together with its civil and economic development – as history often has showed and still shows, unfortunately, even in the land of Genovesi.

The difference between a theory à la Genovesi and the theory of *social preferences* might appear of little importance; in fact, it becomes very important as soon as we try to analyze even the most ordinary relational dynamics as they occur within the market. In these cases, each agent "objectively" benefits from taking part in the market. But according to the notion of morality and sociality entailed in Rabin's theory and in the theory of "strong reciprocity", for instance, the baker is not "social"(nor moral) for the fact of choosing to simply sell bread to anyone wishing to buy bread (as opposed to not selling it), because he makes no "sacrifice" in making this choice. In the same way, a customer is not "moral" when he or she buys bread and "that's it". In the theory of social preferences, which today is gaining increasing popularity from among theories trying to inject economics with a moral content, there is no place for genuine and moral reciprocity within "normal" market transactions unless someone makes sacrifices: "civil" bakers are not enough, bakers must also reward and punish their customers at their own expense. In this sense, we are left with market theory as a morally neutral zone, where we cannot ordinarily experience genuinely social relations. A civil economy, as we have seen, had a different vocation and considered, even considers, the economy as intrinsically civil, because meeting each other to trade with a friendly and non-opportunistic attitude is already a moral pursuit.[9]

The distinction between a Genovesian approach to market sociality and the theory of social preferences is important for the analysis of those cases where the market's ability to function depends on trust. Let us consider a context where contracts are not "enforceable", i.e. where there are no institutions (or no reputational effect) guaranteeing that the other will do his or her part even when there is an incentive to behave in an opportunistic manner. We may think of all those sequential games (even non-repeated) where one part must act before the other; imagine a situation where goods must be delivered before they have been paid for. How can we explain the frequency of these types of transactions (in spite of what the standard theory would predict)? The theory of social preferences would explain this by requiring, as

---

[9] Dragonetti's ethics of virtue, for instance, despite having been developed outside the logic of "collective rationality" and despite focusing on the individual person, still is expression of a concern with the *common good* and of a view of society whose components are bound to each other.

in a sort of Trust Game, that B rewarded the kindness showed by A in the first round by renouncing to part of his or her own gain, to the benefit of A.

Even though in this case the relation is mutually advantageous (the exchange does take place), B is asked to sacrifice part of his or her gains for A (provided that B has a high enough degree of inequality aversion, or that B is sufficiently sensitive to A's motivations, or both).[10] This theory entails a radical distinction between economic exchanges, which take place through "enforceable" contracts, and exchanges where such contracts cannot be implemented: mere self-interest operates in the first, altruism and sacrifice in the latter. To me, this seems to be an overly demanding requirement and, above all, one that forces us to confine the market's "morality" to exceedingly narrow domains, like a "fill-in" in a normality that remains substantially immoral.

Let's recap. The conventional way of conceiving market relations is characterized today within economic (and social) theory by two great contra-positions: the market vs the social and self-interest vs altruism.[11] The conceptual framework of modern and contemporary economic theory doesn't offer a way of conceiving relationships between individuals *simultaneously* as a mutually advantageous exchange where no part wishes to act altruistically or to renounce to a slice of economic benefit *and* as a genuinely social interaction whose moral value is determined by its social content. I strongly believe that the absence of such a possibility has the effect of limiting our understanding *both* of the market *and* of human relations in general.

In fact if we remain within contemporary economic theory, on one side we cannot describe market relations as a genuine form of reciprocity given the fact that they are aimed at mutual advantage – how

---

[10] B's ability to reciprocate might depend on his or her own degree of inequality aversion (which, in this case, would operate independently of A's motivations: this line of thought derives from the School of Zurich of Fehr & colleagues), as well as from the desire to "reward" the motivations that led A to take a risk by trusting B (this line of thought originates instead in Rabin 1993). Recent models combine both explanations. For a survey of the different explanations, please refer to Stanca, Bruni and Corazzini (2009), who outline the results of an experiment trying to further investigate the relation between B's behaviour and A's motivations.

[11] Such contrapositions are not perfectly overlapping. For instance, there some market analyses where the agents seem to act on the basis of social preferences, but at the same time there are some reductionist theories that explain even the most intimate relations in terms of maximization of self-interest.

many pages have been written by philosophers and economists to defend the claim that "true sociality" begins where pure market relations end, thus making the market and the world increasingly less humane. On the other hand, as a different face of the same coin (theory), economic theory (and even social theory) is unable to represent non-market relations as also mutually advantageous, like the ones shared by friends or family members; this is to say that if an exchange yields mutual advantages, this is immediately transformed into something that is essentially less noble: the relation then turns into a mere contract, a relation with a "mercenary" quality, to say it with Dragonetti (whose position we have already considered).

This chapter, but also most of this essay, is an attempt to move past this dualistic vision, which so far has not benefited the market (which, so frequently depicted as immoral, is increasingly fitting the picture); nor has it benefitted the non-market (where the habit of associating family and friendship with pure gratuitousness often masks relations dominated by power as well as pathologies of all kinds: gender issues within traditional communities are a good example of this danger).

4. Mutual assistance vs mutual advantage

In order to continue developing our discussion on the civil economy as a possible market paradigm that is relevant *today*, we must still come to terms with an objection that, if not properly addressed, may end up being fatal. We have argued that the basic idea of the message addressed by Genovesi to his interlocutors, yesterday like today, is that when agents operate on the market they must be motivated by the intention of "being helpful to each other". Within the market economy, however, individuals always tend to act in such a way as to be helpful to one another – otherwise the exchange would not take place. What, then, is the great difference and novelty of Genovesi's approach to the market? Is it ultimately just a difference in wording? Smith was certainly well aware in his writings that the market can function and expand because each person comes up with ways of being useful to others and relies on this mutual utility rather than on the "benevolence" of fellow-citizens.

The mechanism that allows for the coordination of the actions of the various agents in the market, who try to be useful to one another, is the *price system*: from this mechanism and from the signals that prices incorporate, each agent is induced to be useful to others. This "utility" is measured by the willingness to pay for the goods and services on offer.

This is an essential feature of the market system, as masterfully argued by Friedrich Hayek (1948). This feature allows the development of that "knowledge division" that is no less important or essential within the market economy than Smith's "division of labour": in large-scale economies it is impossible for each citizen to gather all the information that the price of a good "incorporates", and hence to figure out the value of one's own activities. Such information may only be transferred through the price system (in a well-functioning market). In a market economy, due to this informational problem, the only way to be truly helpful to others – as Hayek would argue, along with all contemporary economic theory – is to elaborate price signals efficiently and to act in a way as to optimize one's resources. If this is the case (and I have no good reasons to claim that it isn't), then what does it mean to act, as Genovesi says, with the intention of being helpful to each other?

Let's consider an example from the *Wealth of Nations*. Smith (1976[1776], pp. 121–122) points out that the salaries of miners are higher than the salaries of other workers who are equally skilled, but who work in other areas of the economy. Smith explains this circumstance by arguing that in jobs that entail worse working conditions, higher salaries are a form of compensation. In this case, and without appropriate incentives, it would be naïve to expect that the miners' desire to be "helpful to others" could lead workers in eighteenth century Newcastle to choose mining rather than carpentry – at least in the quantity needed to satisfy Londoners' demand for coal. Similarly, it would be naïve, today, to ask workers in the non-profit sector to accept lower salaries only for the sake of being "helpful to each other".[12]

From this point, Smith naturally draws one conclusion: in order to be consistent with the proper functioning of a free society and with a market economy, any moral or social discussion concerning the market must be consistent with the idea that individuals choose their own economic activities in response to price signals. The question thus becomes: how can we reconcile the idea of the market as mutual assistance with this basic principle of the market economy? Not answering this question would amount to saying that Genovesi's civil economy is only possible in small pre-modern communities or within some marginal parts of the modern market economy – a message we cannot subscribe to.

My suggestion (along with Sugden), which emerges from our discussion so far, is that market interactions (we could say "contracts") can be

---

[12] The factual evidence that such workers are forced today to receive lower salaries anyway is of course a different matter.

understood and represented as the things that makes the parties into a collective agent with reference to that particular joint action that is the object of the contract. From this perspective, which is a legitimate translation of the view of the market held by civil economy thinking, the contract binds each party in the contract to do his or her part in order to achieve their common objective. This objective is the joint benefit that derives from the contract, indeed within the specific limits defined by the transaction. In doing his or her part, each agent is moved by the intention to take part in a combination of actions directed to the benefit of the entire "team". Hence, when a potential customer turns to the baker, the content of his intention may be expressed and deconstructed as a proposal of this kind: "I offer that we undertake a joint action that will benefit both of us: you help me to satisfy my need for bread, and I help you to satisfy your need for money. Together we perform this joint action, we form this (temporary) team".

If the two reach an agreement, the customer will intentionally wish that the baker also benefit from the exchange, and vice versa.[13] Therefore, agents have the conscious intention to be "helpful to each other". *The mutual advantage lies inside the transaction*, whose content is thus not limited to the pre-condition of the commercial agreement.

This is one way of making Genovesi's notion of 'mutual assistance' compatible with market economy. However, it shall be noticed that in such perspective, the collective action (or mutual assistance) comes into existence *during* the execution of the contract; it does not offer beforehand the motivation *for* the contract. In choosing which contract to subscribe to in order to satisfy one's needs, each individual is free to choose a partner based on one's own preferences and on price signals. For instance, the implication that a customer might choose a certain baker for the purpose of helping him (for example because the baker is going through a moment of economic crisis) finds no place within the logic I have outlined so far.

Only when the contract is sealed does the customer's commitment to the common aim actually begin. So, for example, Genovesi (and us too) would not advise an entrepreneur this way: "Choose provider A because he's going through rough times, even though his prices are higher than B's". The entrepreneur's choice can (and must, in a way) follow price signals (in a well-functioning market), and only once he has chosen his providers freely can he behave with him as someone who belongs to the same team. This way the analysis of exchange as mutual assistance

---

[13] This approach to the market works well when looking at long-term economic interactions (think for instance of the contracts in a firm).

is compatible with the acknowledgment of the role of signals in the market.[14]

What differences are then implied by this view of the market? What added value does it carry, compared to the standard or Smithian view?

First of all we shall ask how the subjects involved *perceive* the relation and the overall human experience they go through during market transactions. Reading the contract as a collective action (and not just as *immunitas* or mutual indifference) changes the "affective tone" of the relation. Even if market relations are associated with feelings of friendship and benevolence, it is possible that Smith's *correspondence of sentiments* might arise – this is, according to Smith (1759, pp. 13–23) one of the greatest sources of well-being. On the other hand, reading and living the market as mutual indifference, or worse as opportunism, is something that in the long run makes economic life sad and scarcely habitable.

But – someone might object – is it possible for market relations to be fraternal when the parts involved stand on a plane of objective economic inequality (in terms of income, contractual power, ...)? To answer, we shall look back at Smith's example of the customer and the baker. Could their relationship be described as "fraternal" if, for instance, the baker has a small bakery in the suburbs and the customer is a rich city banker? Or, conversely, if the baker works for a large and rich chain of bakeries and the customer is a poor student?[15] The first answer is also a question in itself: Why shouldn't it be possible? There is no doubt that, on one

---

[14] A view like Genovesi's does not lead to the creation of informal economies between "friends", where commercial partners are chosen for reasons of "friendship" – in time such operations can often lead to a lack of economic sustainability. I believe that the challenge posed by experiences of social economy approaches, like the Economy of Communion, or Fair Trade, or Ethical Finance, is to combine together price signals with an authentic spirit of fraternity. If, on the contrary, these two levels are mixed up (and one chooses a provider because he is a "friend" or because it is "part of the project"), then this may be a dangerous path to choose. While this choice is not necessary in order to make of the market a civil realm, we must recognize that a certain willingness to do something more might be precious in order to fix distortions and make it even more civil.

[15] This point opens up to an interesting discussion about the logic of altruistic punishment, which is present in the theories that make use of social preferences, such as "strong reciprocity": in these models and experiments the subjects reject offers they consider unfair (in an ultimatum game, for instance) at their own expense. For example, if A offers B 2 out of 10, keeping 8 for himself, B will often refuse in order to punish A (when if B refuses, they both gain 0). My own approach would agents to discourage such refusals, because this aversion to inequality, which we all have, should not be encouraged, because it leads us to miss mutually advantageous exchange opportunities.

side, fraternity and friendship are more easily established among equals (in economic and social terms, or even in terms of age...), but it seems equally true that if civil society wishes to develop sentiments of friendship and mutual assistance it must also favour and allow its members to have a friendly disposition towards those who are different in various respects, including their economic profiles. No one can allow us to live a certain economic encounter, here and now, as fraternal, even if our judgment on a certain firm and economic system may be very critical.

Can we work to build a more fraternal economy and world and simultaneously live the single economic relation fraternally, here and now? Is it possible, for instance, to work in Fair Trade and at the same time to live positively the relation with the airline flying us to Brazil (better if with lower emissions)?

We could also ask a different question: how far does the commitment to act fraternally towards the other party in the contract *extend?* Especially in those (very frequent) cases of incomplete contracts, which are *non-enforceable* or *one-shot* (where there is no reputational effect in play)? Let us imagine, for instance, that Francesca goes to a tire dealer to buy a pair of winter tires. Francesca asks for a specific brand (that perhaps she saw on TV) and Giulio, the vendor, knows (due to asymmetric information) that there is another brand offering the same quality at a cheaper price. In an approach *à la* Smith, Giulio the vendor ought to simply sell Francesca the tires she asked for on the basis of mutual indifference (and of the anti-paternalistic approach entailed by individualistic theory). What would civil economy thinking prescribe in this case? According to Genovesi, would Giulio have an obligation as a vendor? And what obligation would that be? An analysis of the market as mutual assistance offers us a framework to assess these issues, whereas they would make no sense within the framework of economics as we know it today – a fact that by itself has a certain significance, given that choices of Francesca and Giulio are the ones that basically take up most of our time at the market. You can even imagine Francesca as someone who has entrusted her savings to Giulio as her financial adviser.

According to this view of the market, a market contract between Francesca and Giulio makes them part of a collective agent whose intention is to achieve a common benefit in a certain domain. Therefore, in this perspective, the idea that Giulio might deliberately take advantage of Francesca's ignorance is questionable, to say the least. But how far can we go? The answer depends on how we conceive "mutual assistance" and common intention. We move between two extremes. The more frugal would lead us to consider that the collective intention consists in reaching a mutual benefit *given the preferences, the information and beliefs of each agent at the time of the contract:* such restrictive interpretation of reciprocal assistance, at a closer look, does not bring us much further than the old mercantile ethics of *caveat emptor* (buyer beware). At the opposite extreme someone might argue, instead, that the two parties must define the common benefit in terms of a common notion of well-being. Then, for instance, a barman may have doubts as to whether he should offer a tenth shot of grappa to a customer who is already high, or to the youngster who is about to go home driving after a night at the discotheque. If, in fact, market relations are intended as mutual assistance, the parties may incur moral responsibilities towards each other, responsibilities that go beyond what the contract would prescribe.

A similar point, and even more strict, may be raised with regard to economic relations that take place *over time.*

As another example, we may imagine that Alba is a homeowner and that she asks Franco, a contractor, to carry out some works in her home for the purpose of building her an attic. After the beginning of the works, Alba realizes that she would very much like to make a small variation to the agreed project, which would create no extra cost for Franco. At this point, Franco finds himself in a situation of monopoly. He can take advantage of the situation and refuse to modify the original plan they had agreed upon unless Alba pays extra. But if the contract had been sealed from a "team"-like perspective, or from the perspective of mutual assistance, it seems natural that Franco's opportunism is not coherent with such perspective.

5. The redistributive effects of exchange

We shall introduce one further question: what can we say, from within our perspective, about the negotiation process that *precedes* the contract? What is the role of the division of the "gains from trade" of the added value generated by the exchange? Is it possible that an excessive emphasis on the "slice" of surplus ascribed to each individual might compromise the "affective tone" and the sentiments of friendship that are typical of a market intended as mutual assistance?

These are difficult questions, but in this case too it is possible to attempt an answer. First of all we must note that the attempt to maximize self-interest in the division of the gains that are generated by an exchange is not a necessary condition for the smooth running of a market economy. What is required, instead, is the creation of added value, regardless of how that will later be divided among the parties – an aspect that is often forgotten by those who theorize the maximization of profit as the aim of the firm. What is truly necessary is that the subjects who exchange and operate on the market create wealth together: from this point of view, Genovesi's phrase "try to be helpful to each other" is certainly valid. But we can go further. If we address all those taking part in an exchange (or a group of students of economics, for instance), collectively, we could say to them: *"when you see an opportunity to generate added value through an economic operation, do not put too much effort into defining how to split the earnings. Try the most obvious and straightforward division, establish it in rough terms, and concentrate on the creation of the common benefit"*. It shall be noted, however, that such a recommendation shall be directed at any potential partners, *collectively* considered.

These subjects cannot be advised to ignore the division of profits unilaterally when they deal with others (in this case, in fact, there would be a risk of exploitation and of opportunistic behaviours). Such a recommendation, then, entails a form of reciprocity, which says: "only behave this way with people who share your own market culture". This said, we could thus sum up Genovesi's phrase about the division of gains: "If you wish to make a deal together (especially a long-lasting one), don't worry too much about defining 'the slices of the cake' you will create: rather, worry about the cake, about creating many, because later in time, unless you are opportunistic and dishonest, you will converge towards a fair distribution rule".[16] Such advice, for instance, is truly effective when a group of people, especially if young, come together to create a firm: in these cases, advice *à la* Genovesi is by far the wisest and most effective because it greatly reduces the costs related to transactions and contracts and because it reinforces the feelings of mutual trust. It is also worth remembering that the entrepreneur is ultimately a "creator of cakes", with the ability to innovate.

Another effect is also in play. The perception that future gains will be divided according to a fair criterion (without letting too much time go by before defining all details of the division) can make it psychologically simpler for the partners to build something collectively. A fair division of future gains can help reduce opportunism in the future stages of the relationship. This hypothetical advice may also be extended to

---

[16] Indeed, throughout Genovesi's civil discourse there is one underlying assumption which shapes his entire vision of the market: i.e. that mutual advantage and mutual benefit ought to be sought in the respect of laws and oriented towards good. Without this implicit assumption even a deal of the mafia or camorra might appear as "fraternal" (those familiar with the deep bonds of friendship and honor that tie people to each other know this well).

potential partners: "Find a simple and basically fair division of future gains when you act together with people who share your own market culture". But, we shall ask, is this also good advice for a single person? A person who follows this advice will end up, in some cases, with a lower share of the gains compared to the share she would have gained by sticking to a stricter and more careful approach to the division of gains. In turn, she will spend less time and effort and will have a lower probability of raising disputes against colleagues, which often paralyze contracts, businesses and firms. In the long run she will probably live life more peacefully, and even in economic terms she might not do badly. Finally, here too there is a role for institutions: the way they are shaped can create incentives for the pursuit of mutual advantage, or it can create individual opportunism, as we shall discuss.

At this point we can perhaps better understand the "humanism of the civil economy", of mutual fraternal assistance even within the market, which Genovesi tried to communicate to his students, to the people of Naples, and to the Italians of his time. His students were completing a course on the mechanisms of a market economy (that Genovesi hoped to establish in the Kingdom, which still had a substantially feudalistic character). The fundamental lesson to learn, according to Genovesi, was to make everyone's best in order to "come up with ways of being helpful to each other". I have tried to show that the meaning of his sentence may thus be summarized: "a civil economy is a network of relations of mutual advantage". This was the first insight: read the market not as a matter of shrewd people, not as a Prisoner's Dilemma kind of game, or as a zero-sum game, but as a "collective action", which, although risky, can bring advantages to all involved, without having to worry too much about the redistributive aspects of gains – an attitude that often kills many firms before they are even born.

Those taking part in this network generate advantages for themselves and their partners. Creating a tight network and many markets means to link people in collective actions, where each person grows thanks to others. This is a civil economy.

Today we know, thanks especially to the work of sociologists studying "social capital", that one of the main factors of cultural backwardness is represented by the mental mindset we use to read the market as well as civil life (Gambetta, 1993; Putnam, 1993): societies grow, even though they may start out in an unbalanced way (in terms of income distribution) when they read economic and civil relations as mutually advantageous. They remain trapped in poverty when they regard others as someone to exploit or from whom they should protect themselves.

I believe that Genovesi's insight has lost none of its currency or of its civil and economic significance.

6. An application: the "market of care"

In this final part of the chapter, we focus on one application of our discussion, which so far has been carried out in abstract terms and presented with ad hoc examples. Now we are going to test the significance of this discussion, imagining reading from the perspective of civil economy a certain socio-economic realm that is becoming increasingly important both for civil life and for the economy: i.e. care services. In fact, questions about "morality", "affective tone" and non-opportunism become especially relevant when one enters territories where the economic dimension impacts domains that have a strong affective value, such as the care of our parents, of our children, of our own health and of the health of our dear ones.

There exists, in fact, a general preoccupation for the penetration of market mechanisms into domains that are highly questionable from the ethical, relational and motivational points of view. It is my opinion that reading the economy and the market in the perspective of a civil economy may offer new elements of hope when we think of how to combine the needs of a market in constant expansion, and constantly weaving through our lives, with needs that are typical of relational goods and of care.

From this point of view the current situation is not that different from the one in place while Smith and Genovesi were writing their theories.

Even in eighteenth-century Europe people used to live with the concern that the development of commerce might compromise the ethics of virtues as well as Christian morality from their very roots: the old debate about luxury contains many of the challenges that can still be encountered when thinking about how the market replaces the family and the communities in terms of the supply of relations of care and proximity. And yesterday, like today, such "replacements" also have a great positive potential: the transformation of the unequal society into one that is more free and equal, yesterday; the liberation of many, women especially, from a duty of care that is not entirely chosen, today.

It is a matter of fact that today many of the services that were once guaranteed by the family, the community, or by churches, are gradually being provided by paid workers. At the same time, workers in these domains (education and health) were associated in traditional societies with some form of "vocation" (in the case of women, especially); they were expected to be animated by incentives and motives beside the monetary ones. Today, on the contrary, doctors and call-centre workers, university professors and miners alike, all are treated in the same way: all rational individuals who respond to incentives. At the same time, when we turn to people in occupations that are "relationally sensitive", we continue to expect that certain "something more"; we believe, or wish to believe, that among their objectives there might be some other elements beside the mere salary (even though we are indeed more disillusioned and cynical than just a few years ago).

Recently, an attempt was made in economic theory to explain how it may be possible to keep these two dimensions, the market and "vocations", together – a theoretical attempt that also operates within the social preferences movement and that, we will see, is not entirely convincing, but still well worth discussing and examining.

This economic literature assumes that the firm supposes that a candidate with a "vocation" is not exclusively interested in his salary or in material incentives (as instead assumed by standard theory), but that he or she will also ascribe an intrinsic value to the activity he or she is asking to take on, an intrinsic value that starts from the satisfaction (or utility) that candidate derives from the job.[17]

In other words, vocation is translated in an intrinsic *non-monetary* or non-material reward that the subject derives from carrying out that certain job. It is thought, therefore, that the worker has *both* intrinsic motivations (vocation) *and instrumental* motivations (salary), to which he or she ascribes different weights: a worker with a vocation would be, therefore, someone who ascribes a certain positive value (>0) to the intrinsic component. When there is a vocation, the amount of the salary is not the only determining factor for candidates.

For Heyes (2005, p. 564), "vocation" is the desire of a worker to do an activity to which she attributes an intrinsic value and reward. If, therefore, the salary offered by the employer (W^*) is lower than the

---

[17] In more formal terms, we might say that the candidate's preferences can be represented by the following utility function: $L = \alpha W + (1-\alpha)M$, where W is the salary, M is the intrinsic reward that the person derives from the activity, α is the weight ascribed to salary, and $1 - \alpha$ is the weight ascribed by the worker to intrinsic motivations, which here we assume as inversely correlated to the weight ascribed to salary. In such models, saying that a worker has no vocation corresponds to ascribing α the value of 1. On these, see Bruni and Smerilli (2011).

salary offered by the market (W), when a worker accepts the lower level of salary, his mere behaviour (acceptance) already indicates in itself that this worker has a positive level of vocational or intrinsic rewards, since the difference in well-being between the salary he or she could get anywhere on the market and the salary he or she is accepting (with $W^* < W$) is compensated by the intrinsic satisfaction that he or she derives from that job; the "remuneration gap" is filled by the happiness of being "in a desired vocation". If, for example, the worker was willing to work without a salary (as a volunteer, for instance), this would reveal that the well-being the worker derives from that given job comes from the intrinsic reward of his or her "vocation".

These conclusions come from models that basically share the slogan: "getting more by paying less", such as Katz and Handy (1998), a study about the selection of managers in the non-profit sector, or Heyes (2005), about the remuneration policy in the health sector in the UK (noticing, in particular, how the best nurses are paid less).[18]

The key assumption of these theoretical models concerns the existence of a *direct proportionality between the genuine quality of motivations and the willingness to sacrifice one's material benefits* (salary). But, we might ask, are we sure that acceptance of a low salary is truly the right way of testing a person's intrinsic motivation or vocation? The first objection to this theory is offered by standard theory of "adverse selection": no one can guarantee that a salary lower than the market salary will not single out poorly skilled workers (with little or no motivation), who only accept a lower salary simply because they cannot find higher salaries. It would be possible to counter this radical objection by assuming that the candidates are selected through a skills test and that only those who pass this first stage will be offered the lower salary as a way to select "vocationally oriented" candidates. But this second solution does not sound convincing, either.

---

[18] The Australian economist Brennan (1996) offers a model that is partly different. He is not recommending paying less, but rather composing the salary in such was as to make it relatively more appealing for those with vocation. In the example of university scholars (who are the subject of his study), he notices how in order to induce the candidates' self-selection it is necessary to lower a lower salary than the market salary, but at the same time to fill the gap with forms of *fringe benefits* (e.g. research funds) that are appreciated in a selective way, i.e. only by those who have an academic vocation. Handy and Katz (1998) themselves, beside "paying less", suggest this self-selection mechanism (p. 258), in particular in the academic field, where, they suggest, research-oriented professors evaluate research funds as being more important than other colleagues with a lesser sense of 'vocation'.

Before suggesting a reading of this matter in the spirit of Genovesi, I shall briefly recall the critique that a group of female economists make of such theories (Nelson 2005, Folbre and Nelson 2000). These scholars claim that for a long time the supposed equivalence between genuine motivations and sacrifice has served to conceal the prevarication and exploitation of women inside the family. By tracing a clear-cut distinction between the domains of work and economy, on one side, and the home, on the other, and by idealizing the role of the woman inside the house as wives, mothers, sisters and loving daughters, economic theory has rendered acceptable something that, objectively considered, are in fact relations of exploitation towards women and has portrayed the acceptance of women's inequality as a female virtue (leaving women a primacy in love in order to compensate an asymmetry in terms of opportunities and freedom).

Julie Nelson claims that the models we have seen of personnel selection within the care sector have the effect of turning the old chauvinist view into a theoretical discussion, leading to the application of lower salaries in those occupations that deal with care services – occupations that still today largely remain a female prerogative. According to this critique, lower salaries in the non-profit sector and in home care would enable the cultivation of a vocation only in those women who have a certain economic independence or rich husbands, whereas women with greater economic difficulties would be forced to accept other non-vocational jobs. The mistake, according to the feminist critique, consists in thinking that a certain activity may be carried out either "for love" or "for money", and not for both reasons at the same time.

This feminist line of thought seems to move in the same direction as civil economy thinking. And this is certainly true, but only in part. Let's see why.

Nelson introduces a third form of motivation (compared to the two standard Smithian forms): intrinsic motivations, that don't concern the opposition between self-interested vs altruistic, but that, here again, must be "protected" from market relations. What does it mean for Nelson (and Folbre) to work for love and for money *at the same time*? These authors interpret the "genuine" and authentic quality of the relation with others as the presence of an intrinsic motivation towards one's own job.

Following the work of Bruno Frey (1997, pp. 88–102), Folbre and Nelson interpret "intrinsic motivations" as a matter of individual identity and authenticity: a person has intrinsic motivations for a given activity if this is carried out 'for its own sake, rather than as a means to reach a result that is external to the action itself. Frey, in turn, is deeply influenced by the psychological theory of Edward Deci and Richard Ryan (1985).

Ryan and Deci (2000, p. 56) offer the following definition of intrinsic motivation: "satisfactions rather than for some separable consequence. When intrinsically motivated a person is moved to act for the fun or challenge entailed rather than because of external prods, pressures, or rewards".

Therefore, in contrast with the idea of 'getting more by paying less', Folbre and Nelson (and Frey) observe that monetary gains can reinforce intrinsic motivation if these are perceived as the *acknowledgment* of a worker's commitment rather than as a means of *controlling* one's job.

The implication of this argument seems to be that the authentic relation of care (*caring*) is compromised when the relation between care-giver and the care-taker is perceived "purely" as a market relation, when "work", in the words of H. Arendt, becomes mere "labour" (Folbre and Nelson 2000, p.133).

If, therefore, care is offered against payment, the relation of care becomes exactly like the one between a vendor and a buyer of any other good (like potatoes or fridges).

This distinction between relations of exchange (in the form of 'paying for specific services') and relational goods ('building relational networks') that are only seen as compatible with intrinsic motivations, then, ultimately results in a way, even if less attractive and interesting, of reconsidering Smith's distinction between market and genuine sociality.[19] In particular, it is not recognized as authentic and genuine the motivation of workers (in any sector, from mining to care services) to earn a living and support their family with dignity: why shouldn't it be considered "authentic" and fully humane from the moral point of view to act only out of these motivations? If we deny that even these "economic" motivations can be authentic, we end up excluding an enormous range of actions that, together, make up the existence of a large proportion of women and men within our society.[20]

---

[19] A more detailed discussion comparing our approach with the approach of Nelson may be found in Bruni and Sugden (2008, the last section in particular), along with the responses of Nelson (2009) and Gui (2009) and to the counter-response (Bruni and Sugden 2009).

[20] A very recent phenomenon is that of women who emigrate to richer countries than their countries of origin in order to look after the elderly or the sick ones, or to carry out domestic work: why shouldn't it be moral or genuine to think that these people carry out such jobs "for money", to support, with that

Nelson and Folbre's approach avoids the dichotomy interest/altruism, but eventually gives rise to another one: intrinsic/extrinsic motivations – a distinction that, as the reader will remember, Dragonetti (and myself alongside him) had already overcome by claiming that to reward virtues (even in material ways) does not make them "mercenary", and that even "external" or extrinsic rewards must go together with virtue.

If actions with intrinsic motivations are opposed to instrumental actions, how can it be possible to imagine a market interaction that can be virtuous, if a certain essential amount of instrumentality is inherent in the market? In fact, prices operate as signals that allow each agent to choose those action in which a person can be most helpful to others, but only if agents on the market act (also) according to the motivation of how much they receive by exchanging with them. This is exactly what Deci and Ryan refer to as "separable consequences", which they do not regard as possible for intrinsically motivated activities.

If, then, authentic care and moral society are compatible only with intrinsic motivations, we continue to place the market and these "vocational" worlds in radical opposition – unless we choose to entertain, as a large part of the Communitarian literature does, an abandonment of the market in favour of more informal economies of gift-exchange: but can this really be a concrete proposal in our time?

In these theories on the subject of care we also find the idea that the market relation cannot be *in itself* authentically and genuinely social and moral, not even when it is intended and represented in the correct terms (as we are also trying to do): in the civil economy tradition, the market remains as such, but it *can* also be expression of fraternity! Dragonetti reminded us that commerce and the market, when correctly intended as mutual assistance, are "virtues". It may be wise than to start from here.

How could we represent the market of care-giving in the perspective of the civil economy?

Suppose Alberto is old and a widower, partly invalid and with a good pension; he can live by himself in his home, with regular visits by a nurse (or "caregiver"). Barbara is unmarried, she has a daughter and she earns her living by being a home nurse. She is good at her job, she's nice and very lovable, but she has no particular "intrinsic motivation" to work without an economic reward.

---

money, their own families? We want that even a care-giver from Lettonia has a "vocation" that drives her to look after our own elderly?

Alberto can, therefore, "be helpful" to Barbara by rewarding her work and Barbara can be helpful to Alberto by looking after him – all perfectly in accord with Genovesi's moral. Barbara feels satisfied both because she can earn and live well and because she can be helpful to Alberto. Vice versa, Alberto is happy because he is being looked after and because he knows that this way he is helping Barbara to support her family: why shouldn't this relationship be authentically social? What is it missing in order for it to be genuinely moral?

Let's imagine, now, a different Alberto, who instead complains that he is not receiving "genuine" care because he is not happy that Barbara carries out her work *also* for money; he wishes she did it *exclusively* for reasons of intrinsic satisfaction. This new Alberto desires not only someone who looks after him: he wants someone who takes care of him *only as a vocation*. And we may imagine a different Barbara, who complains that, having to work for a living, she cannot realize her own identity in other activities that would be more congenial to her personality (like painting, for instance), but that cannot earn her a living. From the perspective of the market as mutual assistance, these kinds of "complaints" are ultimately childish refusals to accept living in a free society on a level of dignity and equality with others.

Today Genovesi and Dragonetti would perhaps reply to such protests: *"you cannot expect to satisfy your needs through someone else's vocation. You are not authorized to ask for the sacrifice of others in order to satisfy your sense of authenticity. You must learn to live in this world, which is a place where water flows towards the sea, and civil life is structured according to norms of reciprocity"*.

7. One more step?

The discussion carried out in this chapter must not lead us to argue that in market relations, in care-giving in particular (both inside and outside the market) there is no need for sacrifices and intrinsic motivations. Rather, I strongly believe the opposite is true and I have argued this many times in this essay as well as in other writings. Vocational workers are important and in some cases even essential, and everyone, inside or outside the market, benefits from dealing with them. To work with intrinsic motivations and to sacrifice oneself for the sake of others goes well beyond the contract; these involve more fascinating human experiences that often give rise to working environments that are more humane and livable for those who have that vocation and for all.

The argument I have tried to advocate in this chapter is another: despite wishing that there can be as many people as possible living market relations as a place of authentic vocation and sacrifice, I believe that the market can, nonetheless, be thought of as civil and civilizing, as a fully moral and authentic place, even when these dimensions (which can be present in certain moments and in certain people), are not present or go through a moment of crisis or, anyway, they do not prevail; we are certainly happier when we find in our market partners a certain "something more" in terms of motivations, but it is equally possible to make an experience that Genovesi would call one of "fraternity", when we operate with others within a joint action, where we are correct and non-opportunistic and we develop a mutual sense of friendship.

There is not, then, a natural opposition between "market" and "society", like John Stuart Mill used to think (1988[1869]), an author whom I implicitly consider very close to the tradition of civil economy thinking, in his beautiful essay *The Subjection of Women*, where he argued that the only truly civil society is the one that practicing in "the family the same moral rule which is adapted to the normal constitution of human society" (pp. 45–47).

Between conceiving working life as sacrifice and vocation and understanding work and the market as mutual indifference, there is then one third possibility: it is the one suggested by the civil economy tradition, for which the issue is not so much to "import" elements of sociality into the market, but to read and experience the market as a moment in civil life, just like other places of life: for Genovesi the market is a piece of life in common, whether civil or uncivil, depending on how we imagine and live, according to our intentions, feelings and actions. Reciprocity, in its various forms, is the law of the market, simply because the market is civil society.

11
Evolution, Virtues, Rewards, *Philia* and Beyond

The greatest of these is love.

Paul, *Corinthians* 1, 13

1. Naples and Glasgow compared

By way of a conclusion we shall propose an interpretation of the analytical elements that have characterized our journey and, at the same time, we shall compare the system of Civil Economy with Smith's system of Political Economy. We have seen that Smith and the Scottish Enlightenment thinkers entertained their own anti-feudal polemic; but Smith also thought that the market mechanism would introduce a structure of incentives enabling the market to consolidate through evolution. The view held by Genovesi and Dragonetti was similar in that they did not perceive a conflict between virtue and self-interest. However, whereas Smith regarded the individual pursuit of self-interest as *directly* virtuous and capable of giving rise to the common good, even if unintentionally, for the authors of Civil Economy it's the very search for common good that is virtuous – though no contradiction is assumed between private interest and the common good.

Therefore according to Dragonetti and Genovesi, one further element was needed to trigger the positive civil effects of commerce: an element that neither Smith nor later thinkers in the tradition of Political Economy had envisioned, but one more in line with the classic Christian tradition, i.e. civil virtue, and its rewards.

The ethos of Civil Economy suggests a notion of the *rewarding of virtue*, which combines two elements:

a) first an *"award"* (as specified in Dragonetti's theory), a component directly linked to virtue: it is the external but also the intrinsic reward for virtuous actions when deliberately carried out as acts of common good. We shall indicate this component by δ and add it to the utility function of cooperative agents.[1]

b) a civil, or *institutional*, component that civil society sets aside for virtuous citizens who intentionally operate for the common good. We have seen that this dimension plays an essential role within Dragonetti's framework, because without it punishment alone wouldn't be enough to drag Neapolitan society out of its feudalistic structure and culture. This component is expressed by the standard pay-offs of the game, and specifically by parameter *a*.

In previous chapters we have examined the contractualist solution to the cooperation dilemma traditionally proposed after Hobbes and Locke, as well as the solution proposed in the spirit of the essentially evolutionary approach of Smith and Hume.

The reader might remember that, given the initial pay-off values (4,3,2,0), for cooperation[2] to emerge over a Stag Hunt type of game, the Smith–Hume solution required a relatively high threshold value ($p_c > \frac{2}{3}$). A world *à la* Smith evolutionarily produces cooperation (i.e. cooperation emerges through evolution) in those cases when society is characterized from the beginning by a high rate of cooperation. To prevail, cooperation requires a civil culture that can count from the start on a high number of cooperators (this also applies to games, such as the Stag Hunt, that are less demanding than the Prisoner's Dilemma[3]).

We may now pick up where we left off and turn to "translating" the matrix of numerical pay-offs into letters:[4]

---

[1] From an analytical point of view, a further distinction may be made between two components of δ: δ' and δ", to indicate respectively the intrinsic and the standard awards. Here we shall omit this distinction to avoid overcomplicating the analysis.

[2] In the perspective prevailing across Northern and Southern Europe during the Enlightenment, the market was almost considered as an extensive cooperative enterprise.

[3] In a Prisoner's Dilemma type of game, on the contrary, the critical threshold value is 1: all players must cooperate from the start – at least in a game with only two polar strategies, i.e. cooperation and non-cooperation.

[4] In this version, we assume there is no difference in the pay-offs of noncooperators, regardless of whether only one or both players should choose to not cooperate (the non-cooperation pay-off is always *b*, unlike the matrix in the previous chapter where it was 3 in the first case and 2 in the second). Note that to have a Stag Hunt type of game, we must have: a>b>0.

	Stag	Hare
Stag	a,a	0,b
Hare	b,0	b,b

Figure 11.1   Stag Hunt in a world *à la* Smith

	Stag	Hare
Stag	a+δ; a+δ	+δ; b
Hare	b; +δ	b;b

Figure 11.2   Stag Hunt in a world *à la* Dragonetti

In a world à la Smith, characterized by this set of pay-offs, the threshold value for the number of cooperators (i.e. the number above which cooperation is sure to prevail over time) is b/a.[5]

How would this result translate to a world inspired by the ideals of Dragonetti and Genovesi (i.e. of Civil Economy thinking)?

One of the possible ways to represent the kind of humanism expressed by the Civil Economy approach is to add the component δ to the material or objective pay-offs of the game ($a,b,0$). This equates to claiming, in line with the core principles of Civil Economy, that the choice to cooperate (e.g. to risk a reciprocal behaviour and trust the other player in a Stag Hunt) is not exclusively dictated by the material pay-offs, but also by the symbolic rewards associated with the action itself – a remuneration that is not just a material or strategic (i.e. depending on the choice of others) outcome. We may call this variation of the game a *Stag Hunt à la Dragonetti*.

Like Dragonetti, we reject that material and intrinsic incentives may be incompatible with each other (i.e. we rule out the possibility of *crowding out* between standard and intrinsic payoffs); we're assuming therefore that their values may simply be summed. This way, when the player chooses to cooperate, she receives, on top of the material pay-offs, also an intrinsic reward (measured in this game by the parameter δ whose

---

[5] As proof, re-calculate the expected utilities by applying the new pay-offs: $U_c = p_c a + (1\ p_c)0$, and $U_n = p_c b + (1\ p_c)b$, which entails $p_c > b/a$.

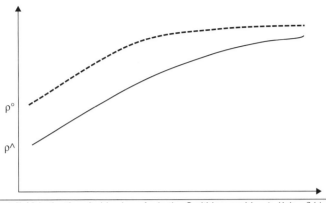

ρ° (*b/a*) is the threshold value of ρ in the Smithian world. $\rho^\wedge$ (*b/c* − δ/*a*) is the threshold value in a Civil Economy context. Notice that to insert δ makes easier the emergence of cooperation.

Figure 11.3   Dragonetti case

value is set between 0 and *b*).[6] On the other hand, when the player chooses not to cooperate (Hare), he or she always obtains *b*, regardless of the other player's behaviour.

We can thus calculate the players' expected utilities. These functions provide a measure of one strategy's success over the other and take roughly the shape of a parable (as previously observed). With this we turn from a Hume–Smith (or Scottish) world into a Genovesi–Dragonetti (or Neapolitan) world. In the latter world (or Humanism) the threshold value p_c becomes: $\frac{b}{a}+\frac{\delta}{a}$.[7]

Compared to the Smithian case (in which $p_c > b/a$),[8] in this new setting *à la* Dragonetti, cooperation requires fewer cooperators due to the intrinsic remuneration whose effect is to "discount" or reduce the critical threshold of cooperation. The presence of the intrinsic component makes cooperation easier to achieve. This effect of δ is well illustrated by the following graph:

Let's take a look at the parameters that affect the threshold value of p_c (*a,b,*δ, 0).

---

[6] It shall be noted that for the game to remain a stag hunt it must be: δ<b.

[7] A proof of the theorem is outlined below: $U_c = p_c(a+\delta) + (1-p_c)\delta$; $Un = p_c b + (1-p_c)$ b. Then $U_c > U_n \Longleftrightarrow b/a - \delta/a$.

[8] If we rewrite the threshold value with numerical pay-offs, we will find that $p_c > 1/2$ is exactly equal to b/a.

First, the new threshold value reveals a direct relation between p_c and b, the latter also representing the pay-off that expresses a sort of "non-cooperation premium": in the game b is always the pay-off received by non-cooperators (the choice to play Stag never returns b).

The interpretation of the pay-off b is then fairly straightforward: when in the game of civil life uncivil behaviours are incentivized and civil virtue discouraged, it corresponds in our model to an increase in the value of b.

a) An inverse relation exists between p_c and a: an increase in a reduces the threshold value for the emergence of cooperation. What does it mean? The parameter a may be described as "the civil prize for cooperation": only cooperators obtain the pay-off a in the game. Therefore the interpretation of a is also straightforward: it measures the level of social recognition of cooperative behaviours, i.e. the civil, institutional and public, reward of virtue.

In other words, if society encourages cooperation also through laws and institutions, if virtues are acknowledged, then that society will require a lower initial "critical mass" of cooperators in order to trigger civil development.

b) Finally, *an inverse relation exists also between p_c and δ*: if cooperators are given a prize for cooperation, in that population we will need a lower initial number of cooperators because the beginning of the virtuous cycle requires less demanding conditions. At the same time, for high values of p_c, the intrinsic reward may be lower.

c) If $\delta = 0$ the model imitates a Smithian setting. This means that a Smithian world may be seen as a special case of the Dragonettian world.

Further elements may be added to the analysis by isolating δ in the equation that expresses the critical threshold of cooperation. By isolating δ instead of p_c, we can see that cooperation emerges over time if $\delta > b - p_c\, a$.

This expression of the threshold value is also very interesting and insightful. It highlights other aspects in the relations between the value of the intrinsic remuneration and the *objective elements* of rewards (a, b):

– If b is high, rewards must be higher in order to activate cooperation: in other terms, where opportunism and non-cooperation receive high pay-offs, rewards must be more effective (or at least they must weigh relatively more within the individual utility function).

– If the value of *a* is relatively high, then δ may be lower: there is a relation of substitutability between δ and *a*.[9] If a society tends to *objectively* favour behaviours moved by civil virtue (with laws, right institutions, rules of justice, etc.), then the rewards (prizes) of virtue don't need be very high for cooperation to emerge in time – and vice versa, as just discussed. Once more we find that there's a nexus between the various rewards of civil virtue: both kinds work in the same way by making easier (or at least less difficult) the introduction and long-term consolidation of a logic of cooperation, of an actual *civil economy.*

In summary, the kind of Humanism that inspired the Neapolitan reformers entailed a synergy between several elements:

– Fair laws, fair institutions, and opposition to feudal privileges (the role of parameters *a* and *b*);
– The presence of awards δ,[10] which in order to be effective and sustainable must be accompanied by civil and institutional support.[11]

This is all very well illustrated in a beautiful letter written by Genovesi in which he comments on Beccaria's *On Crimes and Punishment*:

I have read briefly the disquisition about punishments and crimes; but I couldn't read it entirely: in the little I have read, it seemed to

---

[9] An assumption that is implicit in the choice of writing the utility function as an additive function, which is typical of goods that are perfect substitutes.

[10] Somebody may ask why these symbolic forms should be among the parameters that justify the emergence over time of one behaviour (cooperation, for example) over another. In previous works (Bruni 2008; Bruni and Smerilli 2011) I have critically discussed this point and reasoned based on the assumption that cultural evolution should be exclusively the result of choices made in response to the material pay-offs (*a* and *b*). Today I am less certain of this methodological choice (which, however, yields the advantage of being economical and cautious), and I reckon that given the central role of imitation mechanisms within cultural evolution, it is impossible to exclude *ex ante* the symbolic effect of imitative phenomena. If we imitate the happier individuals in the game of civil life, then it may not be as arbitrary to imagine a cultural evolution in which symbolic and premium components play a role. In the final part of this essay we shall further articulate this consideration.

[11] We cannot simply ask those trying to resist 'pizzo' (extortion) or 'camorra' to be virtuous: civil society, and the State, ought to work on awards and punishments that must be proportionate and credible.

me to see a thinking man, frank, keen on the good of man, and nonetheless desirous to promote it in a way that I don't consider the safest ... nor do I believe that excessive severity might benefit greatly; and I would rather therefore lean onto a sound education. But in a country that has been corrupt and dissolute for a long season, how and how long will it take to introduce a good education?

Genovesi 1962[1765], pp. 179–180

There is one more question to consider: can we trust that the considerations and analysis presented thus far are a fair representation of the considerations about rewards/awards and virtues?

From a certain point of view the results we have arrived at bear at least some relevance for our own contemporary society, although it is also apparent that one passage in particular is still missing in our argument. If on one side the representation of the institutional aspects (expressed by the relative values of the pay-offs a and b) shows a certain consistency, the rendering of the concept of rewarding virtue in terms of the payoff δ that we have added to the regular pay-offs of the game is less robust.

A superficial understanding of economic theory is enough to reveal that such a reward is basically no different than a conventional sanction (or punishment): we could have come to the same analytical results simply by adding to the function a pay-off with a negative sign for non-cooperators, a technique which closely resembles the classical solution of any theory based on "crimes and punishments". In fact, some differences may be retrieved in terms of the educational and "promotional" value of law (like Norberto Bobbio used to say). The punishing of crimes and the rewarding of virtues are not just two opposite versions of the same operation: the civil impact of the two tools is remarkably different, as highlighted by several ancient authors, as well as Dragonetti (or Frey today).[12]

As already pointed out by Hume (1739), laws and constitutions were conceived in response to the assumption that crooked citizens will produce more crooks. Law, punishment and rewards are also symbolic signals, not just instruments of social control.

---

[12] The use of rewards and punishments to promote cooperation has great relevance. The human community clearly needs both, although admittedly the costs associated with rewards are typically lower as opposed to the costs of punishing (at least while cooperators are relatively few) and also over time the symbolic effect of rewards tends to produce more civil virtues within the population.

In recent years the theme of rewards has been relaunched in economic literature by Susanne Nackermann, Bruno Frey and others, who have combined this theme with the theories on *crowding out* involving incentives and performances in activities with intrinsic motivation which he first developed in the late 1990s. With his studies Frey has shown how the introduction of rewards and the intensification of their use to encourage civil virtues may lead to positive effects in civil life. In particular, Bruno Frey and Susanne Neckermann demonstrate the social advantages of rewards, especially if compared to monetary incentives.

These researchers show that

> [...] the material costs of awards, consisting of a certificate for the wall or a small trophy, are typically low for the donors, but the value to the recipients may be very high.... Due to their vague nature and ex post performance evaluation, awards are more adequate incentive instruments than monetary payments when the recipient's performance can only be vaguely determined ex ante and/or measured ex post.
>
> Nechermann and Frey 2009, p. 4

All this suggests that a successful implementation of cooperative behaviours over time may be supported by rewards, and not just by sanctions. This result is relevant and holds in a variety of civil settings. Consider for instance the theme of Corporate Social Responsibility (CSR).[13] Given its essentially voluntary nature and considering also that limited recourse can be made in this context to the punishment of uncivil behaviour, CSR grows at a pace which is necessarily proportional to the reward of good practices (both at the institutional and at the "micro" levels).

2. Virtuous citizens, but also civil institutions

In this chapter we have seen that the social reformation project, as well as the humanistic approach of Neapolitan civil economy, were articulated over two levels: one (twofold) micro-level and one more institutional level.

The first level, a micro-subjective, ethical and individual one can be further divided into two sub-levels (1a and 1b);

1a: The first dimension of the individual micro-level is purely educational and cultural: the "reformer", i.e. the civil economist, must show

---

[13] On a Civil economy approach to CSR and on the differences between such an approach and the standard or Anglo-Saxon one, see Bruni (2012).

to her or his interlocutors (students as well as policy makers) that the market is not the place where the "cheeky" ones are rewarded. In terms of our discussion, Genovesi would perhaps argue that the market is not a Prisoner's Dilemma, but a Stag Hunt.

1b: The second micro dimension is linked to the premium attached to civil virtue, which we have indicated with δ.

There is, moreover, one macro-institutional level. The micro-individual and cultural level, in fact, is not enough to overcome the dry-spells of the feudal world and of underdevelopment: civil economy and civil society need institutions that reward civil virtues (while discouraging opportunistic behaviour, rather than encouraging them). As we have seen in the previous chapter, where we ventured to a reading of the current market in the spirit of Genovesi, a society animated entirely or prevalently by intrinsic behaviours is not desirable. First of all, the approach of civil economy sees people as bound by relations of reciprocity and it sees virtue as an invitation to be "helpful to each other". If, instead, we aimed only at intrinsic rewards, we might end up in a community where the agents are all moved by intrinsic rewards (each cultivating their own vocation), but where perhaps each runs an activity that others regard as useless. Civil society is a net of relations where people satisfy each others' needs. Intrinsic motivation is not sufficient in order for an action to be good and to produce the common good.[14]

Civil humanism as we have encountered it in these chapters has therefore *many dimensions*: it ascribes critical importance, and even a certain priority, to "ethical faith" (to say it with Genovesi), to the individual dimension, to horizontal relations between citizens inside civil society; but it does not neglect or forget the co-extensive role of institutions, of the state, of jurisprudence and laws.[15] This view of civil life is, therefore, in line with the ethics of Aristotle and Cicero, but cannot be purely reduced to the ethics of virtues. Moreover, public happiness, individual utility and interests are also present, but we cannot identify the philosophy of civil economy with utilitarianism (which, instead, is key to the thought of Beccaria). Civil economy acknowledges the role of civil pacts and of the State, but it is not a contractualist, nor a Hobbesian, theory of civil society.

---

[14] I have explored this theme in Bruni (2008).
[15] Elsewhere we have remarked how the humanistic view of civil economy thinking may be seen as having three dimensions: market, civil society, state (see Bruni and Zamagni 2007).

The civil economy of Naples and the civil tradition it embodies (from the Romans to civil humanists) thus contains its own vision and theory of life in common, that cannot be simply viewed in terms of other theories circulating in the eighteenth century or today.[16]

3. Beyond *philia*

This essay could have ended with the previous section. Instead, I decided to offer up this large part, where I shall try to extend our discussion to territories that remain largely unexplored by economic and social theory (yesterday just as today).

For Aristotle and for the Roman republican thought, as for civil humanism, *philia* is the foundation of the entire dynamics of the *polis*. The characteristics of *philia* have dominated the highest moments of European history: in classical Greece, in the Christian Middle Ages, in civil humanism or in the Naples of the Enlightenment, *philia* represented the underlying social bond: less powerful than *eros*, but more capable of generating those loose, yet essential links that are at the heart of the community's and the city's life and development.

Over the first chapters of this book, which now perhaps feel quite distant, we laid the foundations of the discussion that was then developed in the second part of the essay, highlighting the radical ambivalence of life in common as well as the main solutions, or attempts, that have been proposed to control or even eliminate it. In particular we have met the sacred community, *philia*, law and jurisprudence, and,

---

[16] For instance, to consider Dragonetti's philosophy of the "reward of virtues" seriously would mean, among other things, to not only value or reward civil entrepreneurs, as we've seen briefly, but also those who build a family and who responsibly have children: it is not only a matter of birth "incentives", nor is it a matter of "punishing" other forms of cohabitation; instead, it's about recognizing that those who freely choose to sacrifice certain dimensions of their own personal interest (like some dimension of their professional career, for instance) for the sake of the common good (allowing other citizens to grow up well) carry out some virtuous forms of behaviour that ought to be also institutionally rewarded – and this is the opposite of what happens in Italy, where not only is the family not rewarded, but it is even discouraged and penalized in many ways, and not only in economic terms. Having children is not part of the "social contract" (as Dragonetti would argue) and therefore it cannot be imposed by society; nevertheless those who voluntarily do these virtuous deeds ought to encounter a reward that might consist, today, in a more family-rewarding fiscal system, as well as in suitable nurseries and in more flexible working contracts for people who have children.

most of all, the great "erotic" solution of the modern economy in the tradition of Smith. We then showed how the civil economy approach was essentially a continuation of the tradition of *philia* and civil virtues, a tradition that never died out and that is still alive today in many forms of social and civil economy. *Eros* is moved by desire and need, not by gratuitousness. *Phlia* is exclusive and elective, more open to gratuitousness. Yet, *phlia* is a type of love that cannot last in time without reciprocity, because the intrinsic reward of virtue (which we have indicated with the parameter δ) cannot transform cooperative action ("stag" in our game) into a dominant or unconditional choice, i.e. into *philia*, as Aristotle has taught us. We love the friend as long as he or she remains of a friendly disposition and shows it in some ways (through a certain behaviour, for instance; see Sugden 2004, Bruni 2008). In *philia* a certain willingness to forgive is present, but this is not unlimited. In other words, *philia* is a form of *conditional reciprocity*, even though its "being conditional" is different and less radical than in the contract or in *erotic love* (Marion 2006).[17]

For the most part, civil and economic life may be explained as an entanglement of *eros* and *philia*, i.e. the passions that move entrepreneurs, the mutuality inside cooperatives, the dynamics that go on inside organizations, needs and consumption.

But if the Greeks' *philia* and *eros* were enough to express all the shades of human relations, humanity would not have "invented" *agape*. And if the latter has been invented, then it must have always existed, and therefore we cannot afford to ignore it – not even the economy can, for it is life. There is in the human person a need and desire for something that goes beyond, something larger than the already broad *eros* and *philia*, something that goes beyond the limits of the ego, of the couple, of friendship, of the community. It is a desire that arises suddenly, as we ask more from ourselves and from others. When we perceive this desire deep inside and we try to answer it, the season of *agape* begins inside ourselves.

There is in human beings a dimension of action that is as powerful as it is fragile and that we encounter every time we are capable of acting unconditionally, that is, every time we act without our behaviour or choice being motivated by our reckoning about *ourselves* or about *those* other agents who will reciprocate our action. In fact, there are some people, who, due to their strong intrinsic and ethical motivations, do not reason strategically in certain choices, but are willing to enact a

---

[17] In Bruni (2008) I have outlined the features of these two forms of reciprocity, their similarities and differences.

certain behaviour or a given culture even in the absence of the others' responses.[18] This is also what happens, for instance, in the fields of environment, of law, of human rights, and continuously in art, in science and in large parts of the social and civil economy, and more generally in all those choices that can be characterized as "ethically sensitive", where human beings may be capable of consistency and perseverance – even in solitude, even in the absence of reciprocity.

In all these unconditional actions, at the same time, actors also have a strong desire of reciprocity, for without reciprocity the experience of gratuitousness cannot be long-lasting and cannot fully flourish. Many founders of ideal or value-based organizations (Bruni and Smerilli 2011), of movements that have produced social as well as civil innovations, people who have opened up new opportunities for the "human" dimension in history, often these are people who are willing to go on even by themselves, but who nevertheless – and this is the point, as well as a key to reading this kind of action – are hurt by the lack of response from their fellow-travelers, even though the wound of non-response is not deep enough to make them refrain from their unconditional action. Such experiences constantly inhabit the ford of this vital paradox, nurturing authentic human development and, ultimately, life itself.

Art, science, the struggle for human and environmental rights may not be truly understood without considering this dimension of action that makes us capable of moving forward, capable of idealistic, symbolic or, more exactly, vocational gestures, even in the absence of support from others, of their esteem and response. Always when dealing with 'vocation', *eros* and *philia* cannot suffice (although they may be necessary) to explain the life of people and of communities.

This is why, in order to express this dimension of action, we use a different word from *eros* and *philia* (although in synergy with these two): *agape*.[19] We have briefly touched on this in Chapter III, when we introduced it as a sort of oxymoron or paradox: *unconditional reciprocity*, that is a form of reciprocity unconditional with respect to the choice,

---

[18] A word that arises today even in social sciences and that closely recalls these dimensions of *agape* is "gratuitousness" (Bruni 2012). We deal with gratuitousness each time a certain behaviour is performed out of intrinsic motivations and not primarily in view of an objective that is external to behaviour itself.

[19] I also wish to point out that the description of the traits here ascribed to *agape* (in particular, unconditional reciprocity) are not intended as a theory of *agape*, but only as an attempt to highlight some dimensions of *agape*, without exhausting them.

but conditioned by the choices of the other as far as the outcomes are concerned.[20]

Finally, the agapic action might take many forms: an act of listening, of cooperation, but also a refusal or a punishment, because *agape* is most of all a *dimension* of actions rather than the content of any action.[21] In particular, *agape* describes the 'excess', beyond needs and interests, and for this reason it lies, yesterday and still today, at the heart of one of the greatest human, social and economic innovations.[22]

In the next paragraph I shall try, if daringly, to capture some of the dynamics of this logic of action inside the theoretical framework we have developed so far, opening to new horizons, posing new questions, suggesting new answers.

4. Agapic Games

At our point of departure we shall consider a world *à la* Genovesi which, as we have seen, would be built on *philia*. Its ethos will then be

---

[20] This does not mean that intrinsic reward belongs exclusively to *agape*: *philia*, for instance, knows intrinsic motivation too, but here, unlike in the case of *agape*, the role of intrinsic motivation and reward might not play a critical role (we have seen this in Dragonetti). Such dynamics have been discussed in other works (Bruni 2008), where I have shown that the difference between *agape* and *philia* may even be regarded as a difference in the "intensity" of the intrinsic reward: *philia* might have it, but not in such a "strong" version as to push the friend to continue loving even when reciprocity has been absent for a long time. For this reason, the intrinsic motivation of *agape* (ε) shall be distinguished from that of *philia* (δ).

[21] It might be more correct to imagine *agape* as a distinct form of human relation, going alongside the other two (*eros* and *philia*). This is the classic theory of Nygren (1990), who sees *agape* as a form of human relationship different from *eros* and *philia* that only together with the other two gives a full idea of what human love is. In fact, it suffices to consider that the Bible employs the same verb (*agapao*) to describe both the extent of God's love for the world (Gv, 3.16) and to exhort husbands to love their wives (*Ef.*, 5.22). *Agape* is more properly 'transcendental' (in the Medieval sense, not in the Kantian), a way or modality of living potentially every form of human relation.

[22] The logic of *agape*, and we must stress this, is unconditional, but not "non-tuistic", because although the response of the other is extremely important, one still goes on, perhaps while suffering, even when this is missing. Although in this respect the ethics of *agape* is different form Kantian ethics, they resemble each other closely (because they both share this idea of unconditionality). My version of *agape* is therefore different from the theory of the French sociologist Luc Boltanski (2012) who does not associate *agape* with any form of reciprocity: I claim that *agape* renounces the calculus of the equivalence but does not renounce reciprocity (although it is unconditional).

informed by the assumption that the two agents feel part of a team, that they have joint intentions and that both feel "reassured" that the person they have in front is also a "we-agent", rather than an "I-agent" (Sugden 1993). This is, we might say, the basic element of all relational debates taking *philia* as their paradigm: the agents' choices are conditional to the behaviour (or to the expectations about the behaviour) of the other/s. Even when there is (or can be) an intrinsic reward associated with cooperative behaviour, *this is not enough* to make cooperation continue in the absence of the "reassurance" that the other agent will cooperate or that the other agent is also a "we-agent" (Smerilli 2012). In other words and in the more standard language of theoretical economics, we may say that the logic of *philia* can be represented in a repeated game through a strategy that starts out with a risky act of cooperation, later interrupting cooperation if this is not met with reciprocity.[23]

In what follows, we shall ask what happens in human interactions when that intrinsic payoff (δ) becomes significant and higher than a certain threshold that turns the cooperation strategy into an unconditional strategy because cooperation becomes then preferable even when material payoffs are low due to the other's non-cooperation, or in other words, because cooperation is preferred to non-cooperation even when we realize that we are alone in doing our part.[24] In order to distinguish this logic that we associate with *agape* the logic that we previously associated with *philia*, we shall now call the intrinsic payoff ε. Let's start again from the Stag Hunt, with reference to Figure 11.4 below.

A / B	Agape	Non-Agape
Agape	$\varepsilon+4,\varepsilon+4$	$\varepsilon,2$
Non-Agape	$2,\varepsilon$	$2,2$

Figure 11.4   The Agapic Game

---

[23] This strategy is also known as "Brave Tit for Tat" (Bruni 2008).

[24] Thinking of a family, for example, this is the case of a person who prefers to be "exploited" by other members by taking on himself or herself all the cleaning and cooking, compared to a situation where no one cooperates, thus leaving the house in a state of neglect: in these cases the logic becomes "better myself alone than no-one". On this, see Bacharach (2006).

In this case, if ε is higher than a certain threshold value (here equal to 2),[25] the choice of "agape" might be unconditional (i.e. it might be followed regardless of the other's behaviour).[26]

Here again there are two possible outcomes:

a) the game of reciprocal *agape*;
b) the game of unilateral *agape* (or the game of *agape-without-reciprocity*).

The first case applies when both (or all) players are in a "state of *agape*" (Boltanski 2012): here, they can reach the highest equilibrium,[27] in which, on top of the optimal material pay-off, the players also receive an ideal reward (E).[28]

Is it possible to move away from this optimum? As long as e is high for all players (>2 in our case), no one has interest or good reasons to move from the equilibrium of mutual *agape*. If, on the other hand, there is no ideal reward in a player, or if there is but at some point it starts to decrease until it reaches a level below the threshold value, we can go back to a classic Stag Hunt game where we cannot predict which equilibrium will be selected (whether the "high" or "low" one).

When there is a decrease in e, there can be two cases:

2*a*) both players experience the same deterioration in e, and we therefore return to a standard "Stag Hunt" game for both players;

---

[25] This threshold value depends on the value of the matrix of the game's pay-offs and hence on the players' utility functions. In this version of the Stag Hunt the pay-off for non-cooperation is always 2 (without distinguishing, as in the first part of this book, between unilateral [3] and mutual non-cooperation [2]).

[26] *Agape* becomes an "unconditional" action but not "unconditioned", because – in the logic of what I have called "unconditional reciprocity" that applies perfectly to agapic actions – the other's behaviour does affect the *outcomes* obtained, although it does not determine nor condition the *choice*. In the game of *agape*, the expression "cooperate" may be misleading because, as said, living *agape* does not simply amount to "cooperation" in a game.

[27] An outcome, the latter, which is technically both a 'Pareto optimum' and a 'Hicks optimum'.

[28] We may add that in the case of reciprocal *agape*, ε is not the same as in unilateral *agape*: happiness that arises from reciprocity, intended as an encounter of gratuitousness, has by nature a different intensity compared to the case when one carries on alone. I cannot tell which one might be "higher", but in real life the two ε's are certainly different (even though in our analytic discussion, *ope parsimoniae*, we shall omit this distinction).

2b) only one of the players experiences a decrease in motivations, while the other continues to have a high e and hence to opt for the unconditional action.[29]

This second case is especially interesting, because it anticipates a second game, which we may call the "game of unilateral *agape*". Here too we have two possible situations. First of all, (2a): it is possible that even without e (or when this is too low) in one of the players, the higher equilibrium may continue to be selected, because even in terms of material payoffs alone, reciprocity is for *both* players preferable to non-cooperation.

A new interesting perspective opens up here. If, for instance, player B has lost his or her intrinsic motivations, but trusts that A's intrinsic motivations might still be high (and that A will then continue to "play" *agape* unconditionally), then in individual terms it will still remain strictly convenient for B to continue pursuing the strategy of reciprocity. Revealing A's own agapic culture makes the other player capable of selecting the cooperative equilibrium, thus overcoming the risk/payoff dilemma.

(2a) Unilateral *agape* with cooperation (see Figure 11.5):

A / B	Agape	Non-Agape
Agape	4+ε;4	
Non-Agape		

Figure 11.5 Unilateral *agape* with cooperation

But there can also be a second scenario, i.e. (2b): B might change strategy and choose non-reciprocity, hence determining the worst possible outcome for A (and 2 for B instead of 4).

A possible case that often occurs in real life is when B begins to feel disutility, or discomfort, from the relationship of cooperation with A.

---

[29] Since e is a subjective value, each player has his or her own level of ε, which is distinct from the one of the other (in our discourse, in order to avoid complicating things, we have assumed one ε for all players).

We indicate such disutility with a parameter {, which has a negative value (being an "evil"). If, in fact, this parameter becomes greater than the threshold value (4-ε < 2), then B will start to prefer non-reciprocity, and will thus push the game towards the worst outcome for both (ε,2):

(2b) Unilateral *agape* without cooperation (see Figure 11.6).

A/B	Agape	Non agape
Agape		ε, 4
Non-Agape		

Figure 11.6

This is, for example, the situation that might arise within an "agapic community" (i.e. value based organizations, or in a religious community, in NGOs, charities, etc.), when someone starts to lose their intrinsic motivation and continues to stay in the same community. Initially, although he or she may no longer ascribe to cooperation with the same "agapic" significance as other members in the community, this agent may continue to behave in a cooperative manner simply because cooperation yields better results and a better life. It is possible, however, to reach a moment where the *cultural dissonance* with others might begin to produce a sense of uneasiness, which leads this person to prefer isolation and non-cooperation (and eventually, in some cases, an exit from the community, from the "game") with damage for himself or herself (who may no longer benefit from the advantages of cooperation), but also for the community (which loses a cooperative subject and the material advantages of cooperation).[30]

In other cases, instead, where the social or organizational dynamic is best described by a Prisoner's Dilemma, a non-cooperative and opportunistic subject, who is confident about the other's agapic behaviour,

---

[30] It is, therefore, important for communities or relationships built on *agape* to have an understanding of how to coexist positively with the diversities and crises of certain subjects, so as to make it possible to experience cooperation and reciprocity also among others, including those who may have lost (if temporarily) their intrinsic motivations. Otherwise, cultural intolerance produces a loss of well-being in all those involved.

may have an incentive to take advantage of the other's cooperation.[31] By way of an example, we may think of an entrepreneur whose ethical culture leads him to pay taxes, while being surrounded by others who take advantage of his cooperation; or of a family member who serves and looks after the others, perhaps even deriving an intrinsic reward from it, with the others who are "being served" indulging in this situation, taking advantage of the intrinsic rewards of another.

It is interesting to notice that even unilateral *agape* constitutes an equilibrium (showed in scenario 2b): the choice of *agape* for A and of *non-agape* for B, with the objective datum that A's material resources (health, time, income...) decrease, while B's prosper.

It is always necessary to bear in mind that the unconditional action motivated by a strong intrinsic reward is radically ambiguous: it is an extraordinary factor of innovation and human development but, as we have often remarked, it can also be at the heart of serious individual and collective pathologies. When the ideal reward compensates for low or non-existent material rewards, and when therefore little importance is ascribed (in making one's own choices) to results and feedback from others and from history, then there is the risk of persevering in choices that lead firms to go bankrupt and people to fall ill. This is why it is necessary to carefully dose unconditionality, a dimension with an extremely high potential and risk for oneself and for others.[32]

This ambivalence and this paradox associated with *agape* can explain why history shows *agape* as evolving, or at times decaying, into other forms that are the classical ones we encountered in the first part of this essay:

a) *elective philia* and communitarianism: in these cases opportunists, not the trustworthy ones, are expelled from the community: in the

---

[31] The reader will remember that the Prisoner's Dilemma is a game where, unlike the Stag Hunt, the higher payoff is ascribed to the player who chooses to non-cooperation when the other chooses cooperation (4,1), i.e. to the free-rider.

[32] Once again I wish to emphasize that unconditionality and intrinsic reward form one of *agape's* dimensions. For this reason it seems sensible to assume, as I have done in previous works (Bruni 2008), that inside the same person several repertoires or strategies of action may coexist, differing only in their degree of unconditionality and that each person who is interested in the affirmation of cooperation must decide whether and how much conditionality he or she wishes to apply to a certain game.

language of our game, what happens is that the share of those living *agape* (which now, having lost its universalistic and inclusive nature, has changed into something else) in the community is made equal to 100%, in order to safeguard the equilibrium of "agapic" reciprocity. The election, in *philia*, must be perfect (with zero tolerance), because especially in contexts such as of the Prisoner's Dilemma kind, the defection or the change in culture of a single member is enough to make non-reciprocity prevail over reciprocity.

b) *hierarchy-Leviathan*: confronted with the difficulties and the wounds of *agape* there is a risk of receding to the hierarchical community, so sanctions and restrictions upon freedom are introduced. It is possible to be together, but without the freedom that is typical of *agape*, and communitarian and social life thus become a network of contracts and rules "without gratuitousness" aimed at enabling life in common, now no longer agapic (nor, at this stage, of *philia*). There have been many historical examples of communities that, after an initial phase of unconditionality and fraternity, later took a step back and eventually turned into totally hierarchical and formal realities.

But is there a sense or meaning for *agape* through the various historical unfoldings, considering that history shows us experiences of agapic *communitas* that are transitory and basically unstable phenomena? I shall dedicate the conclusion of this chapter entirely to this question.

5. A fundamental law of human development

Agapic actions, precisely because they constitute a non-solution to the "wound" of the other, often have generally a transitory nature, that in history looks much like one hour of a day that will not get to midday.

However, I believe that even if *agape* truly was an experience destined to evolve over time into other less tragic logics, nonetheless it has played, plays, and will continue to play a fundamental role in human matters. Every time, in fact, that *agape* crosses the path of history, it fecundates, leavens and transcends human experiences, never leaving history the way it found it. Such a crossing, even when it only lasts a few decades, or years or days, leaves its mark in history, since after every encounter with *agape*, both *philia* and hierarchy are never left unchanged. Thus, after the early apostolic period, the hierarchical community of the church is no longer the ancient sacred community: they still share several characteristics, but the experience of *agape* has now contaminated and transformed it forever. After experiencing the Franciscan agapic fraternity, the market is no longer the same as in the late Roman Empire or in the

Athenian agora of Aristotle and Pericles. The care of the ill, of youth, of immigrants is no longer the same after the encounter with the experience of gratuitousness of Vincenzo de' Paoli, Don Bosco, Francesca Cabrini. India is no longer the same after Gandhi, neither is South Africa after Nelson Mandela; even our cities change forever once they have been touched by the founders of cooperatives for the excluded, by real artists, by unconditional-truth lovers. When *agape* encounters history it opens up new possibilities, it enhances the degrees of freedom, changing it forever.

The history of what is human proceeds thanks especially to a passage of a baton of agapic experiences: without Christianity we would not have had Francis, without Francis we would not have had the many charismata of the "care of poverty" in the modern age;[33] without credit unions and savings banks today we would not have ethical banking and without the cooperative movement we would not have known social cooperation; and we could continue. Any experience that has its origin in *agape* will absorb its seed and, even though it might transform itself for any reasons, that seed has now made the earth fecund and its DNA will move down to others who will modify it in this vital run-up that is the sap of history. For this very reason, even in the experience of the most anonymous of markets we can still sense the echoes of the Fransciscan fraternity and, in the latter, of the *agape* that gave rise to it, and we can redeem experiences like these as authentically human as we come across their foundational and original roots.

Woe to those who would stop the process of creation of prophetic and idealistic experiences, such as the ones that arise out of gratuitousness–*agape*, only for fear that they may not be sustainable over time or that they may be destined to last for a little time only with the same initial radical force: this would mean blocking civil progress, which is the real human innovation, and hence blocking history, which proceeds as a continuous process of agapic experiences soon evolving into other things, but that, through their death, will eventually let the human emerge. Each person who starts working on his or her land, who

---

[33] The great charisms, such as the Franciscan one, for instance, which is capable of renewing itself, of rediscovering one's own prophetic roots; it has continued to inspire wonderful agapic experiences yesterday and today, and shall continue tomorrow. At the same time, Francis' "state of *agape*" was considered incautious from the very start by his own followers and by the institution of the Church, thus perhaps leaving many of Francis' prophetic and charismatic dimensions unable to develop with their entire force. On this point, see also Boltanski (2012).

undertakes something animated by gratuitousness, in doing so pushes forward the "pickets of what is human", adding a new bolt in the rock. And those who will start climbing up again tomorrow, with new experiences of gratuitousness, will be able to start a few meters, or centimetres, higher. In *agape* there is real civil and human innovation, because it is this "excess" that truly innovates and creates something new.

In any part of the world and in any situation, every time a person experiences *agape* in or outside the markets, she does not give up when confronted with sorrow or exploitation; instead she risks her life to escape the logics of death and blackmail and dares to introduce an economy of gratuitousness even in contexts dominated by egoism and consumerism; then, the *agapic ethos of the market* and civil society becomes history.

Conclusion

Nothing pleases us more than to observe in other men a fellow-feeling with all the emotions of our own breast; nor are we ever so much shocked as by the appearance of the contrary.

Adam Smith

The market society is the most radical solution to the painful ambivalence of life in common. A growing part of civil society looks to the day when it will be possible to create a network of contracts that, thanks to the culture of immunity, will regulate all human relationships, from health to education, from politics to family. In this way we'll have eradicated the interpersonal vulnerability.

The reasoning we have developed in this book has been mainly a journey through the potentialities and the ambiguities of human relationality, seen from the standpoint of economics. Social life is the only place where the social animal can flourish, but the hand that the other gives in search of company is a hand that can hurt me. This ambivalence of human relations has been probably the key category of the issues we met along this journey, because it is also the main message coming from the great authors who have explored social life, including the economy. This book has attempted to offer a critical analysis of some of the major attempts to resolve this radical ambivalence, but, at the same time, it has dared to propose some experiments for complicating the economic and social discourse.

The various solutions we have seen to the ambivalence of communal life have the aim of managing, controlling, and reducing the suffering of interpersonal relationships. From this perspective, the solution represented by the market and its ethos has been the most radical: it has tried the final resolution, that is the replacement of the other person through the artificial creation of a social system in which to live together without personalized encounters, with all being mediated by the market. With Modernity, and the economy within it as its primary expression, the narrative of the 'wound of the other' is merely glimpsed without being welcomed or loved. Also for this reason, the ethos of the market is also, and perhaps principally, the promise of a new humanism without the need to encounter the other in flesh and blood. It is concerning, for instance, to observe the eclipses of the body in our societies, because only the body says true diversity. Similarly worrying is the growing culture of immunity, immunization from the poor, the migrants, and the mentally ill.

This humanism, however, is now revealing all its fragile quality, and for this reason the night in which we are living is much more profound than its economic and financial dimensions. If we don't accept in our individual and communitarian life the small vulnerabilities of our day-by-day encounters with others, we are very fragile in front of the great vulnerabilities, when huge crises come, as today Western capitalism tragically shows.

In this essay we have discussed the nature and genesis of this ethos of the market, which goes much beyond the economic sphere, becoming an ethos of social life *tout court*. Therefore, although our discourse was meant to be a reflection about economic life, as the chapters went by it became a reasoning about the nature of life in common in contemporary post-modern market societies.

At the same time, we have shown that there are many ethoses of the market: the Smithian one, still dominant today; the one of Civil Economy based on *philia*; and I have ended this book by suggesting the ethos of *agape*, always possible, fragile and painful, and always standing in front of us.

I am convinced that the market works properly as a means and place of civilization when society makes it possible for several market ethoses to coexist, without any imperialism of domination of one over the others. Civil life is always nurtured by biodiversity and promiscuity. And as democracy is guaranteed by the plurality of parties, the market is an ally of democracy and of the common good where alimented by many ethoses, included the ethos of *agape*. And any reductionism that leads from many to one is a great impoverishment of the quality of our democracies and freedom.

The defence of this pluralism of the forms and ethoses of the market, where cooperatives, family businesses, value-based organizations, charities and corporations see each other as allies, is the task of those people, like myself, who most appreciate the conquests of civilizations made possible by market economy. In fact, although we have highlighted some problematic aspects of the ethos of the capitalistic market, nevertheless the tune and the spirit of the analysis embodied in this book is very far from that of communitarian philosophy, which considers the ordinary economic transactions on which we all depend for our survival to be somehow inauthentic. Such an attitude toward the market is just a romantic yearning for a lost Rousseauian age of economic innocence or a disturbing alienation from real life (Bruni and Sugden 2011).

The thesis of this book has been that although this opposition between truly moral behaviour and ordinary market relations can find support in some sectors of public opinion, particularly in times of economic and financial crisis, such a cultural attitude is nevertheless childish and dangerous, because any economic system and civil society depends on exchange to satisfy mutual needs. I have claimed that there is another way of looking at the market as a domain of interactions, i.e. the Civil Economy approach, that considers economic interactions to be *at the same time* moral and mutually advantageous, where sociality and morality do not deal with particular kinds of motivation but with joint intentions and actions.

What this approach calls for is a way to provide a mature way of thinking about markets. Normal economic dealings do not require greed, competition or self-interest, but mutual advantage and civil fraternity.

Fraternity is in fact the forgotten principle of Modernity in Western society. When the founders of Modernity announced the new principles of the new world, *liberté egalité fraternité*, they said something crucial: individual freedom and social equality are not enough for building the new post-*ancient régime* society, because neither liberty nor equality say "bond", relationships *among* persons. Market society has tried to invent a new bond of society, the cash nexus, but the paradoxes of happiness on the one hand, and the structural economic crisis of the last years, on the other, are eloquently saying that the nexus is too frayed and must be reinforced by a new form of civil fraternity – but not the fraternity that refers to shared bloodlines in family and clan ties and neither the fraternity often used by closed and discriminating communities. Rather, it is civil fraternity combined with freedom and equality. This fraternity or civil friendship on the part of the members of a community means feeling part of a common destiny, of being united by a link less exclusive and elective than intimate friendship, but which is capable of generating feelings of reciprocal sympathy, and which can and should even be expressed in ordinary market transactions.

Today the market is more and more inhabiting our lives, penetrating even in the most intimate dimensions of our relations (health, care, children). We may try to defend ourselves, and live this transition as a necessary evil. Or, we can try to make care-givers, nurses, teachers into allies in a new social pact, where we interpret and experience even the market as cooperation, mutual assistance, as a passage of life, as civil economy. Personally I have no doubts on the path to take.

References

AA.VV. (Various Authors) (1852), *Raccolta di costituzioni italiane*, Biblioteca dei comuni italiani, Tipografia Economia, Turin.

Actis-Perinetti, L. (1960), *Gli illuministi italiani,* edited by Loescher, Turin.

Aldridge, T. (1984), *Thomas Paine's American ideology*, TUP, Toronto.

Anderson, E. (1993), *Value in ethics and in economics*, Harvard University Press, Cambridge Mass.

Andreoni J., W. Harbaugh, and L. Vesterlund. (2003), "The Carrot or the Stick: Rewards, Punishments, and Cooperation", *American Economic Review*, 93, pp. 882–893.

Anscombe, G.E.M. (1958), "Modern Moral Philosophy", *Philosophy*, 33, pp. 1–19.

Argyle, M. (2001), *The Psychology of Happiness*, New York: Taylor & Francis.

Aristotle. (1988), *Politics*, Edited by Stephen Everson, Cambridge University Press, Cambridge.

Aristotle. (2009), *The Nicomachean Ethics*, Oxford World's Classics, Oxford.

Aristotle. (2011), *The Eudemian Ethics*, Oxford World's Classics, Oxford.

Bacharach, M. (2006), *Beyond Individual Choice: Teams and Frames in Game Theory*, Princeton University Press, Princeton.

Baggio, A.M. (2007), *Il principio dimenticato*, a cura di, Città Nuova, Roma.

Banfield, E. C. (1958), *The Moral Basis of a Backward Society*, The Free Press, Glencoe IL.

Bargellini, P. (1980)[1930], *San Bernardino da Siena*, Morcelliana, Brescia.

Beccaria, C. (1995)[1764], *On crimes and punishments, and other writings*, Cambridge University Press 1995. First Italian edition, *De I delitti e delle pene*, Livorno.

Becker, G. (1996), *"Accounting for tastes"*, Harvard University Press, Cambridge, Mass.

Bellamy, R. (1987), "'Da metafico a mercatante': Antonio Genovesi and the development of a new language of commerce in eighteenth-century Naples." In Pagden (1987).

Bentham, J.(1998) [1789], *Introduzione ai principi della morale e della legislazione*, Utet, Milano.

Benveniste, E. (1971), *Problems in general linguistics*, University of Miami Press, Miami.

Benveniste, E. (1976), *Il vocabolario delle istituzioni indoeuropee*, 2 vols, Einaudi, Turin.

Bianchini, L. (1855), Principi della *scienza del ben viveresociale, e dell'economia pubblica e degli stati*, Stamperia Reale, Naples.

Binmore, K. (1994), *Playing Fair. Volume 1 di Game Theory and Social Contract*, 2 vols, Cambridge Mass, MIT Press.

Binmore, K. (2005), *Natural Justice*, OUP, Oxford.

Bobbio, N. (1993), *Thomas Hobbes and the natural law tradition*, University of Chicago Press, Chicago.

Boltanski, L. (2012), *Love and justice as competences*, Wiley and Sons, San Francisco.

Bolton G., and A. Ockenfels (2000), "ERC: A theory of equity, reciprocity, and competition", *American Economic Review*, 90, pp. 66–93.

Brennan, G. (1996), "Selection and the currency of reward", in Robert Goodin (ed.) *The Theory of Institutional Design*, Cambridge University Press, Cambridge, pp. 256–275.

Bruni, L. (2002), *Vilfredo Pareto and the birth of the modern microeconomics*, Elgar, Cheltenham.

Bruni, L. (2006), *Civil Happiness*, Routledge, London.

Bruni, L. (2008), *Reciprocity, altruism and civil society*, Routledge, London.

Bruni, L. (2010), "Su Delle virtù e de' Premi di Giacinto Dragonetti (e una polemica di Benedetto Croce)", *Il pensiero economico italiano*, 1–2010, pp. 33–49.

Bruni, L. (2011), "On Virtues and awards. Giacinto Dragonetti's interrupted path of Civil Economy", *Journal of History of Economic Thought*, in press.

Bruni, L. (2012), *The wound and the blessing*, New City, New York.

Bruni, L., F. Comim, and M. Pugno (2008), *Capabilities and Happiness*, edited by OUP, Oxford.

Bruni, L., and P.L. Porta. (2003), "*Economia civile* and *Pubblica felicità* in the Italian Enlightenment", *History of Political Economy*, Supplement n. 35 pp. 361–385.

Bruni, L., and P.L. Porta. (2005), *Economics and Happiness: Framings of Analysis*, edited by Oxford University Press, Oxford.

Bruni, L., and R. Sugden. (2000), Trust and Social Capital in the Work of Smith, Hume and Genovesi", *Economics and Philosophy*, 16, pp. 21–45.

Bruni, L., and R.Sugden. (2008), "Fraternity. Why the market need not to be a morally free zone", *Economics and Philosophy*, 24, pp. 35–64.

Bruni, L., and R. Sugden. (2009), "Fraternity, intrinsic motivation and sacrifice: a reply to Gui and Nelson", *Economics and Philosophy*, 25, pp. 195–198.

Bruni, L., and R. Sugden. (2011), "Why should the devil have all the best tunes? Reclaiming virtue ethics for economics," paper presented at the conference "Market and Happiness", Milan, 8–9 June 2011.

Bruni, L., and L. Stanca. (2008), "Watching alone: relational goods, television and happiness", *Journal of economic behavior and organization*, 65, pp. 506–528.

Bruni, L., and A. Smerilli. (2010), "The value of vocation. The Crucial Role of Intrinsically Motivated People in Values-based Organizations," *Review of Social Economy*, 67, pp. 271–288.

Bruni, L., and A. Smerilli. (2011), "The emergence of the cooperation in a heterogeneous world", *Homo Oeconomicus*, in press.

Bruni, L., and S. Zamagni. (2007), *Civil Economy*, Peter Lang, Oxford.

Bruni, L., and S. Zamagni. (2009), *Dizionario di Economia Civile*, edited by Città Nuova, Rome.

Carlyle, T. (1898)[1850], *Letter-Day Pamphlets*, London: Chapman and Hall.

Cassani, A. (2002), *Diritto, antropologia e storia. Studi su Henry Summer Maine*, Clueb Bologna.

Cavalli, Sforza L., and M. Feldman. (1981), *Cultural Transmission and Evolution: A Quantitative Approach*, Princeton University Press, Princeton.

Chiodi, G. (2006), "La rivalità tra fratelli come paradigma della conflittualità politica", in *Politiche di Caino. Il paradigma conflittuale del potere*, edited by D. Mazzù, Transeuropa, Ancona-Massa, pp. 3–50.

Coda, P. (1994), *"L'agape come grazie e libertà. Alla radice della teologia e prassi dei cristiani"*, Città Nuova, Rome.

Corning, P. (2005), *The new evolutionary synthesis*, Oxford University Press, Oxford.

Cossa, L. (1875), *Introduzione allo studio dell'economia politica*, Hoepli, Milan.

Cotta, G. (2002), *La nascita dell'individualismo moderno. Lutero e la politica della modernità*, Il Mulino, Bologna.

Croce, B. (1959)[1947], "Il libro 'Delle virtù e dei premi' del Dragonetti", in *Nuove pagine sparse*, vol. 2, Ricciardi, Naples, pp. 235–237.

De Tiberiis, G. (2010), "L'illuminista oscurato. Oltre le pene per una normative premiale delle virtù e de' premi di Giacinto Dragonetti", *Frontiera d'Europa*, XVI, n. 1, pp. 183–270.

Deci, R. M., and E.L. Ryan. (2001), "On Happiness And Human Potentials: A Review of Research on Hedonic and Eudaimonic Well-Being", *Annu. Rev. Psychol.*, 52, pp. 141–66.

Delgado, M. R., R.H. Frank, and E.A. Phelps. (2005), "Perceptions of moral character modulate the moral system of rewards during the trust game," *Nature neuroscience*, 8/11, 1611–1618.

Dionigi, Areopagita. (1981). *Tutte le opere. Gerarchia celeste – Gerarchia ecclesiastica – Nomi divini – Teologia mistica – Lettere*, edited by P. Scazzoso, introduzione e apparati di Enzo Bellini, Rusconi, Milan.

Doria, M. P. (1710), *Della Vita Civile, s.l.*, Napoli.

Dragonetti, A. (1847), *Le vite degli aquilani illustri*, Perchiazzi, L'Aquila.

Dragonetti, G. (1769) [1766], *A treatise on virtues and rewards*, Johnson and Payne, London. First Italian edition [*Delle virtù e de' Premi*], Naples.

Dragonetti, G. (1788), *Dell'origine dei feudi ne' regni di Napoli e di Sicilia*, Stamperia Reale, Naples.

Dumont, L. (1980), "Homo Hierarchicus. The Caste System and Its Implications", Chicago, Chicago University Press.

Edgeworth, F.Y. (1881), *Mathematical Psychics*, Kegan & Co, London.

Eliade, M. (1961), *The Sacred and the Profane: The Nature of Religion* (trans. Willard R. Trask), Harper Torchbooks, New York.

Esposito, R. (2002), *Immunitas. Protezione e negazione della vita*, Einaudi, Turin.

Esposito, R. (2007), *Terza persona*, Einaudi, Turin.

Esposito, R. (2009), *Communitas: the origin and destiny of community*, Stanford University Press, Stanford. Italian edition 1998.

Fehr, E., and S. Gachter. (2000), "Fairness and retaliation: The economics of reciprocity", *JEP*, 14, pp. 159–181.

Ferrara, F. (1852), *Biblioteca dell'economista*, vol. 3, a cura di, prima seria, F.lli Pomba, Turin.

Filangieri, G. (1806)[1780], *The Science of Legislation, Vols. 1, 2* (trans. Sir Robert Clayton), Emery and Adams, Bristol.

Folbre, N., and J. A. Nelson. (2000), 'For love or money – or both?', *Journal of Economic Perspectives* 14, pp. 123–140.

Fontaine, L. (2008), *L'économie morale. Pauvreté, crédit et confiance dans l'Europe préindustrielle*, Gallimard, Paris.

Foot, P. (1978), *Virtues and vices*, OUP (2002 ed.).

Foscesato, M. (2009), Francesco da Empoli e Pietro Strozzi: un dibattito su usura e speculazione nella Firenze del Trecento, Tesi di Laurea Magistrale in Scienze Economiche, Università di Siena.

Frey, B. (1997), *Not just for the money*, Edward Elgar, Cheltenham.

Freud, S. (1913), *Totem and Taboo. Resemblances Between the Mental Lives of Savages and Neurotics*, Moffat, Yard and Co, New York (first English edition 1918).

Gambetta, D. (1993), *The Sicilian Mafia: The Business of Private Protection*, Cambridge, Mass., Harvard University Press.

Gauthier, D. (1986), *"Morals by agreement"*, Clarendon press, Oxford.

Genovesi, A. (1765–67), *Lezioni di commercio o sia di Economia civile*, critical edition edited by M.L. Perna, Istituto Italiano per gli studi filosofici, Naples, 2005.

Genovesi, A. (1777), *Spirito delle leggi del Signore di Montesquieu, con le note dell'Abbate Antonio Genovesi*, Tomo Secondo, Domenico Terres Libraio, Naples.

Genovesi, A. (1962), *Autobiografia e lettere*, Feltrinelli, Milan.

Gioja, M. (1848)[1818], *Del merito e delle ricompense*, Tipografia della Svizzera italiana, Lugano.

Girard, R. (1977), *The violence and the sacred*, John Hopkins University Press, Baltimore.

Greif, A. (2006), *Institutions and the path to the modern economy. Lesson from medieval trade*, CUP, Cambridge.

Grotius, H. (1957)[1625], *Prolegomena to the Law of war and peace*, Bobbs-Merrill, New York.

Gui, B. (2009), "On mutual benefit and sacrifice: A comment on Bruni and Sugden's "Fraternity"", *Economics and Philosophy*, 25, pp. 179–85.

Gui, B., and R. Sugden. (2005), *Economics and Social interactions*, edited by Cambridge University Press, Cambridge.

Gurevich, A. (1995), *The Origins of European Individualism* (Making of Europe), Wiley Blackwell.

Hayek, F. (1948), *Individualism and Economic Order*, University of Chicago Press, Chicago.

Herreros, F. (2008), "The State and the Creation of an Environment for the Growing of Trust", *Rationality and Society*, 20, pp. 497–521.

Heyes, A. (2005), "The economics of vocation, or 'Why is a badly-paid nurse a good nurse?'", *Journal of Health Economics*, 24, pp. 561–569.

Hirschman, A.O. (1977), *The Passions and The Interests. Political Arguments for Capitalism before Its Triumph*, Princeton University Press.

Hobbes, T. (1994)[1651], *Leviathan*, Hackett Classics, Indianapolis.

Hobbes, T. (1998)[1642], *On the citizen*, Cambridge University Press, Cambridge.

Hollis, M. (1998), *Trust within reason*, CUP.

Hume, D. (1978)[1740], *A Treatise of Human Nature*, Oxford University Press.

Hutcheson, F.(1998)[1725], *Inquiry into the Originals of our Ideas of Beauty and Virtue*, London.

Katz, E., and F. Handy. (1998), "The wage differential between non-profit institutions and corporations: Getting more by paying lesse?", *Journal of Comparative Economics*, 26, pp. 246–261.

Locke, J. (1988)[1690], *Two Treatises of Government*, Cambridge University Press, Cambridge.

Luhmann, N. (1990), *I sistemi sociali. Fondamenti di una teoria generale*, Il Mulino, Bologna.

Luther, Martin. (1962), *Selections from his writings*, edited by John Dillenberg, Quadrangle Books, Chicago.

Luther, Martin. (2008), *The Essential Martin Luther*, Wilder Publications.
MacIntyre, A. (1981), *After Virtue*, Notre Dame University Press, Notre Dame, IN.
Mancini, I. (1990), *L'ethos dell'Occidente*, Marietti, Genova.
Marion, J.L. (2006), *The erotic phenomenon*, Chicago University Press, Chicago.
Mauss, M. (1950)[1923–24], *Essai sur le don*, Presses Universitaires de France, Paris.
McCloskey, D. (2006), *The Bourgeois Virtues: Ethics for an age of commerce*, Chicago University Press, Chicago.
McIntyre, A. (1981), *After virtue*, Notre Dame University Press, Notre Dame.
Mill, J.S. (1988)[1869], *The Subjection of Women*, Hackett, Indianapolis.
Mill, J.S. (1920)[1848], *Principles of political economy*, Macmillan, London.
Morineau, J. (2010), *L'esprit de la médiation*, Erés, Toulouse.
Natoli, S. (2003), *La felicità. Saggio di teoria degli affetti*, Feltrinelli, Milan.
Neckermann, S., and B. Frey. (2008), "Awards as Incentives." Working Paper Series ISSN 1424–0459, University of Zurich.
Neckermann, S., R. Cueni, and B. Frey. (2009), "What is an award worth? An Econometric Assessment of the Impact of Awards on Employee Performance", CESifo Working Paper No. 2657.
Nelson, J.A. (2005), 'Interpersonal relations and economics: comments from a feminist perspective', in Benedetto Gui and Robert Sugden (eds), *Economics and Social Interaction: Accounting for Interpersonal Relations*, Cambridge University Press, pp. 250–261.
Nelson, J. A. (2009), "A response to Bruni and Sugden", *Economics and Philosophy*, 25, pp. 187–93.
Nussbaum, M. (1996)[1986], "The fragility of goodness: Luck and Ethics in Greek tragedy and Philosophy", Cambridge, CUP.
Nussbaum, M. (2005), "Mill between Aristotle and Bentham", in Bruni and Porta (2005), pp. 170–183.
Nygren, A. (1990), *Eros e agape. La nozione cristiana dell'amore e le sue trasformazioni*, EDB, Bologna.
Pagden, A. (1987), *The Language of Political Theory in Early Modern Europe*, edited by A. Padgen, Cambridge: Cambridge University Press.
Paine, T. (1792), *Letter addressed to the addressers to the late proclamation*, Symonds, London.
Paine, T. (1797), "Agrarian reform," in *Rights of Man, Common Sense, and Other Political Writings*, edited by Mark Philip, Oxford, UK: Oxford University Press, 1995.
Paine, T. (1923)[1776], "Common Sense", in *Selection of the works of Thomas Paine*, Harcourt, New York.
Palmieri, G. (1788), *Riflessioni sulla pubblica felicità relativamente al Regno di Napoli*, Pirotta e Maspero, Milan.
Pantaleoni, M. (1898), "Esame critico dei principi teorici della cooperazione", ripubblicato in Pantaleoni M., *Erotemi di economia*, Laterza, Bari, 1925.
Pareto, V. (1906), *Manuale di Economia Politica*, Critical Edition, edited by Montesano A., Zanni A., and Bruni L., EGEA, Milan. The English edition is forthcoming in 2012 (Oxford University Press).
Pelligra, V. (2007), *I paradossi della fiducia*, Il Mulino, Bologna.
Penna, R. (2007), *Il DNA del cristianesimo*, San Paolo, Cinisello Balsamo.

Penna, R. (1998), *Paul the Apostle: a Theological and Exegetical Study in Two Volumes,* (trans. Thomas P. Wahl), Collegville, MN.

Peretti, A. (2009), voce "Eudaimonia", in *Dizionario di Economia Civile,* a cura di L. Bruni e S. Zamagni, Città Nuova, Roma.

Polanyi, K. (1957), "Aristotle Discovers the Economy", in *Primitive, Archaic and Modern Economies: Essays of Karl Polanyi,* edited by G. Dalton, Boston, 1971, pp. 78–115.

Polanyi, K. (1977), *The Livelihood of man,* Academic Press, New York.

Pseudo-Dionysus. (1981), *De coelesti hierarchia, in* (1981) *Tutte le opere. Gerarchia celeste – Gerarchia ecclesiastica – Nomi divini – Teologia mistica – Lettere,* edited by P. Scazzoso, Rusconi, Milan.

Rabin, M. (1993), "Incorporating fairness into game theory and economics", *American Economic Review,* 83, pp. 1281–1302.

Ravasi, G. (1999), *Genesis. The words of creation,* edited by Allemandi, London.

Rawls, J. (1971), *A theory of justice,* Harvard University Press, Harvard.

Reinert, S.A. (2005), "Republican mercantilism out of the context: on the Italian reception of John Cary's essay on the State of England". Paper presented at the Conference for the 250th anniversary of the "Cattedra of Commercio e Meccanica, Istituto per gli studi filosofici", Naples, 6 May 2005.

Ries, J. (1982), *Il sacro nella storia religiosa dell'umanità,* Jaca Book, Milan.

Robbins, L. (1932), *"The nature and the significance of economic science",* Macmillan, London.

Robertson, J. (2005), *The Case for the Enlightenment: Scotland and Naples, 1680–1760,* Cambridge University Press, Cambridge.

Rousseau, J.J. (2009)[1755], *Discourse on the origin of inequality,* Oxford University Press, Oxford.

Sahlins, M. D. (1972), *Stone Age Economics,* Aldine, Chicago.

Saint Thomas Aquinas. (2000), *An Aquinas reader,* Mary T. Clark, Fordham University Press, New York.

Saint Thomas Aquinas. (2002), *Political Writings,* edited by R. W. Dyson, Cambridge University Press, Cambridge.

Sandel, M. (2009), *Justice: What's the right thing to do?* Penguin.

Schiavone, A. (2012), *The invention of law in the West,* Harvard University Press, Cambridge, Mass.

Sefton, M., R. Shupp, and J. M. Walker. (2007), "The Effect of Rewards and Sanctions in Provision of Public Goods," *Economic Enquires,* 45/4, pp. 671–690.

Sen, A. (1999), *Development as Freedom,* New York, OUP.

Sidgwick, H. (1901[1874]), *The methods of ethics,* Macmillan, London.

Silver, A. (1990), *Friendship in commercial society. Eighteenth century social theory and modern sociology,* «American journal of sociology», 95, pp. 1474–1504.

Skinner, Q. (1978), *The Foundation of Modern Political Thought,* Cambridge University Press, Cambridge.

Skyrms, B. (2004), *The Stag Hunt and the Evolution of Social Structure,* Cambridge University Press, Cambridge.

Smerilli, A. (2012), "We thinking and Vacillation between frames", *Theory and Decision,* (in press).

Smith, A. (1976)[1776], *"The wealth of nations",* edited by R.H. Campbell and A.S. Skinner, Oxford University Press, Oxford.

Smith, A. (1978)[1763], *Lectures on Jurisprudence*, edited by R.L. Meek, D.D. Raphael, P.G. Stein, Oxford University Press, Oxford.

Smith, A. (1984)[1759], *The Theory of Moral Sentiments*, edited by D.D. Raphael and A.L. Macfie, Oxford University Press, Oxford.

Smith, M.J. (1995), *Games, memes and Minds*, Review of Books, vol 42, New York.

Spencer, H. (1893), *Principles of sociology*, 2 vols, Williams and Norgate, London.

Stanca, L., L. Bruni, and L. Corazzini. (2009), "Testing theory of reciprocity", *Journal of economic behavior and organization*, 71, pp. 233–245.

Sugden, R. (1993), "Thinking as a team: toward an explanation of nonselfish behavior", *Social Philosophy and Policy*, vol. 10, pp. 69–89.

Sugden, R. (2001), *The evolutionary turn in game theory*, JEM, 8, pp. 113–130.

Sugden, R. (2004), *The Economics of Rights, Co-Operation and Welfare*, Palgrave Macmillan, London. First edition 1986.

Sugden, R. (2005), "Fellow-feeling", in *Economics and Social Interaction: Accounting for Interpersonal Relations*, edited by B. Gui and R. Sugden, Cambridge University Press, Cambridge, pp. 52–75.

Summer, Maine H. (1875)[1861], *Ancient Law its connection with the early history of society, and its relation to modern ideas*, Henry Holt & Co., New York.

Supiot, A. (2007), *Homo Juridicus: On the Anthropological Function of the Law*, Verso Books, London.

Strauss, L. (1967), *Jerusalem and Athens: some preliminary reflections*, New York City College, New York.

Taylor, Ch. (1985), *Philosophical papers*, Cambridge University Press, Cambridge.

Taylor, Ch. (1988), *Sources of the self: the making of the modern identity*, Cambridge University Press, Cambridge.

Todeschini, G. (2007), *Visibilmente crudeli. Malviventi, persone sospette e gente qualunque dal Medioevo all'età moderna*, Il Mulino, Bologna.

Todeschini, G. (2009), *Franciscan Wealth, From voluntary poverty to market society*, Franciscan Institute, Saint Bonaventure University.

Todorov, T. (2001)[1995], *Life in common: an essay in general anthropology*, University of Nebraska Press.

Tönnies, F. (1887), *Gemeinschaft und Gesellschaft*, English translation *Community and Society*, East Lansing, Michigan State University Press, 1957.

Truni, F. (2008), *La pace di Tommaso d'Aquino*, Città Nuova, Rome.

Tuomela, R. (1995), *The Importance of Us*, Stanford University Press, Stanford.

Venturi, F. (1969), *Settecento riformatore*. Volume primo, "Dal Muratori al Beccaria", Einaudi, Turin.

Venturi, F. (1972), *Italy and the Enlightenment*, Longman, London.

Vico, G. (1984)[1744], *The New Science of Giambattista Vico: Unabridged Translation of the Third Edition*, Revised translation of the third edition by Thomas Goddard Bergin and Max Harold Fisch, Cornell University Press, Ithaca NY.

Walzer, M. (1983), *Spheres of justice. A defence of pluralism and equality*, Basic Books.

Weber, M. (1978)[1922], *Economy and Society*, University of California Press.

Wenham, J. G. (1998), *New Biblical Commentary. Chapters 1–15*, Word Books, Waco (Texas).

Wicksteed, P.H. (1933)[1910], *The Common Sense of Political Economy* (edited by Lionel Robbins), London, Macmillan.

Wootton, D. (1994), *Republicanism, liberty, and commercial society, 1649–1776*, Stanford University Press.

Wootton, D. (2000), "Helvetius: From Radical Enlightenment to Revolution", *Political Theory*, Vol. 28, pp. 307–336.

Zanghi, G. M. (2008), *Gesù abbandonato maestro di pensiero*, Città Nuova, Rome.

Index

220   *Index*